Philosophy and the
Study of Religions

Wiley Blackwell Manifestos

In this series major critics make timely interventions to address important concepts and subjects, including topics as diverse as, for example: Culture, Race, Religion, History, Society, Geography, Literature, Literary Theory, Shakespeare, Cinema, and Modernism. Written accessibly and with verve and spirit, these books follow no uniform presciption but set out to engage and challenge the broadest range of readers, from undergraduates to postgraduates, university teachers and general readers – all those, in short, interested in ongoing debates and controversies in the humanities and social sciences.

Already Published

Philosophy and the Study of Religions

A Manifesto

Kevin Schilbrack

WILEY Blackwell

This edition first published 2014
© 2014 Kevin Schilbrack

Registered Office
John Wiley & Sons, Ltd, The Atrium, Southern Gate, Chichester, West Sussex, PO19 8SQ, UK

Editorial Offices
350 Main Street, Malden, MA 02148-5020, USA
9600 Garsington Road, Oxford, OX4 2DQ, UK
The Atrium, Southern Gate, Chichester, West Sussex, PO19 8SQ, UK

For details of our global editorial offices, for customer services, and for information about how to apply for permission to reuse the copyright material in this book please see our website at www.wiley.com/wiley-blackwell.

The right of Kevin Schilbrack to be identified as the author of this work has been asserted in accordance with the UK Copyright, Designs and Patents Act 1988.

Library of Congress Cataloging-in-Publication Data applied for.

Hardback ISBN: 978-1-4443-3052-6
Paperback ISBN: 978-1-4443-3053-3

A catalogue record for this book is available from the British Library.

Cover image: Religious procession, Belarus. Photo © Vasily Fedosenko / Reuters
Cover design by Nicki Averill Design & Illustration

Set in 10.5/12.5pt Bembo by Aptara Inc., New Delhi, India
Printed in Malaysia by Ho Printing (M) Sdn Bhd

1   2014

For Sasha, whom I could not love more.

Contents

Preface

This book was written to expand our understanding of the role of philosophy in the study of religions. It is in the first place a critique of the way that the discipline of philosophy of religion is practiced at present, though it is also addressed to those in the study of religions outside philosophy who look to philosophy for tools that can help them with their work.

Concisely put, this book proposes a transition from an old way of doing things, what I call "traditional philosophy of religion," to a new way that I sketch over the next seven chapters. In one sentence, what I am recommending is this: philosophy of religion ought to evolve from its primary present focus on the rationality of traditional theism to become a fully global form of critical reflection on religions in all their variety and dimensions, in conversation with other branches of philosophy and other disciplines in the academic study of religions.

The traditional view, in brief, has been that philosophy of religion pursues a set of interconnected questions concerning the evidence, logic, justifiability, or warrant for belief or lack of belief that God exists. (I describe the full range of work in traditional philosophy of religion in the first section of Chapter 1.) Although I was trained in the questions that constitute traditional philosophy of religion, and I consider them to be legitimate, live questions, my critique of the traditional view of the task of philosophy of religion is threefold. First, the traditional view is *narrow* in the sense that it does not engage more than a few of the actual religions of the world. It does not engage the religious teachings outside a classical conception of God; in fact, it often defines God in such a narrow way that it regularly excludes the theistic views of many who do believe in God. Second, it is *intellectualist* in that it engages only the doctrinal dimensions of the religions it does cover.

It is rare to find any treatment by philosophers of the ethical, political, and ritual practices in which the majority of religious people seek to learn and perfect their piety. And third, it is *insular* in the sense that traditional philosophy of religion does not play well with others: with the exception of Christian theology, and sometimes Biblical studies, traditional philosophy of religion draws very little from and contributes very little to the other disciplines in the study of religions.

Each chapter in the book addresses a distinct issue and for that reason one can read the chapters independently of each other. Nevertheless, I wrote them to trace a particular path toward a broader understanding of the roles of philosophy in the study of religions. Here is that path.

In the first chapter, I argue that the task of philosophy of religion should grow and that—to address the three problems of narrowness, intellectualism, and insularity—it should grow in three specific ways. First, the task of philosophy of religion ought to grow so that it excludes no religious traditions. At present, it is rare to find a course or a textbook in philosophy of religion that includes forms of theism other than classical theism; even rarer will such courses or textbooks include pantheistic, panentheistic, or nontheistic religious traditions; and even rarer still—almost never—will one find a philosophical treatment of polytheistic religious traditions. But all religious traditions include reason giving in some form, and so the task of philosophy of religion should grow to include the study of the philosophical aspects of all religious traditions. Developing the discipline in this direction would bring philosophy of religion into conversation with scholars of the religious traditions of east and south Asia, North and South America, Africa, Australia, and elsewhere. Second, the task of philosophy of religion ought to grow so that it takes full account of religious practices. At present, philosophers of religion focus primarily on religious teachings as they are found in the texts of religious thinkers. But not all religious communities have a class of text-writing thinkers, and even when such a class of religious thinkers exists, the concern to state and defend one's religious beliefs is a relatively small part of the lives of religious people. The discipline of philosophy of religion therefore ought to develop the tools to provide philosophical accounts of the aspects of religion other than explicit, written arguments. It ought to include the philosophical study of worship practices, sacrifices, spiritual disciplines, liturgies, rites of passage, contemplative exercises, and ceremonies. Developing the discipline in this direction would bring philosophy of religion into conversation with scholars of performance, ritual, and embodiment. And third, philosophy of religion ought to grow to be reflexive. At present, philosophers of religion too often take the concepts operating in the study of religion unreflectively, as if "religion" and "belief" and "God" are stable concepts whose meanings have not varied from one time period or culture to another. Philosophers ought to see the study of religions as itself a practice that deserves philosophical reflection. They therefore ought to develop what one might call the philosophical study of the study of religions. Developing the discipline in this direction would bring philosophy of religion into conversation with its own institutional and conceptual history, and with poststructuralist, deconstructive, and genealogical approaches to the study of religion. My hope is that my readers will agree not only that one *could* include these three broader sets of questions in philosophy of religion but also that philosophy of religion is their proper home.

The second chapter develops the proposal that philosophy of religion should pay appropriate attention to religious practice. In this chapter, I join those who have argued that philosophers of religion should include in their purview not only the textual versions of the doctrines asserted and defended by religious intellectuals but also the performed dimensions of how ordinary people live their religious commitments. Paying greater attention to how people live religiously will lead philosophers of religion to join with anthropologists, historians, and other scholars who focus on religious practices. I don't think that religious practices will attract wide interest among philosophers, however, unless the practices can be seen not merely as *expressing* religious thoughts (as if what a religious community "really" teaches is articulated only in the texts written by their intellectuals) but also as themselves examples of thinking. The aim of this chapter therefore is to explore how religious practices themselves—prayers and pilgrimages and circumcisions, for example—can be seen as opportunities for inquiry in which religious practitioners investigate and make judgments about the nature of their environment. Toward this end, I argue first that philosophers of religion should adopt an embodiment paradigm in the sense that they see a religious body not only as a passive object on which culture operates but also as the seat of subjectivity and of religious being-in-the-world. I then recommend two theoretical tools. The first is the theory of conceptual metaphor that lets us see ways in which abstract religious thought draws on embodied knowledge learned in the physical exploration of the world. The second is the theory of extended mind that lets us approach the material aspects of religious practices as cognitive prosthetics that help the practitioners remember and process information. The two theories complement each other in that the theory of conceptual metaphor focuses on embodied knowledge that is largely prelinguistic and to that extent common across cultures, whereas the theory of extended mind focuses on aspects of religious practices that are culturally particular. Together, they provide tools for those interested in seeing religious practices as thoughtful.

The third chapter reflects on the concept of religious belief. Given the diversity of ways of being religious around the world, coupled with the turn to practice that I recommend, one might ask whether the concept of belief should continue to have a central role in the future of philosophy of religion. Indeed, the central role given to belief in the study of religions has been increasingly criticized as misleading or distorting, if not completely illegitimate. Some argue not only that scholars of religion should give more attention to the material aspects of religion, but also, more radically, that one can and should completely explain religious behavior without the concept of beliefs. In this chapter, I consider two objections from the critics of belief. The first is that since one can observe others' religious discourse and practice, but not their beliefs, the assumption that all religious people have beliefs saddles the academic study of religions with a problem of access. The second is that in its pursuit of orthodoxy, Christianity has made the category of belief central, but other religions have not and therefore the assumption that all religious people have beliefs saddles the academic study of religions with a problem of cultural bias. I argue, however, that the critics who raise the problem of access largely assume a dualistic or Cartesian account of belief, and I draw on more recent dispositionalist and interpretationist accounts of belief in order to highlight the ways in which beliefs are embodied and social and, to that extent, public. And I argue that the critics that raise the problem of cultural bias are right to do so, although the solution is not to drop the concept of belief but to distinguish between creedal belief as an interest that only some religions share and intentional belief as an aspect of human action that is presupposed whenever we attribute agency.

In the first three chapters, then, I call on philosophers of religion to re-conceive their discipline as global, practice-centered, and reflexive; I make a proposal about how philosophers might include the study of religious practices as modes of inquiry; and I clarify the senses in which beliefs are and are not essential to religions. A serious obstacle arises for a cross-cultural philosophy of religion, however, from those who point out that the very concept of religion is not a concept that one finds throughout history or around the world. "Religion" is instead a relatively recent creation of the modern west. How can philosophers study religion globally if religion is merely a local concept? In the fourth chapter, I examine the arguments that "religion" is a rhetorical term invented as part of an ideology that privileges modern western political arrangements and that therefore one should not assume that the concept corresponds to realities outside the western scholar's imagination. Against that view, I describe the ways in which the world in which we live is composed not only of physical facts (like molecules, gravity, and mountains) but also social facts (like politics, economics, and religion). I then make the case for a critical realist view in which one can see religion as a certain cultural pattern that exists "out there" in the world, even independently of the modern western label.

The fourth chapter's argument that one *can* speak of religion as a cross-cultural phenomenon leads naturally to the fifth chapter's argument about how one should do so. What practices, beliefs, stories, people, and institutions should be classified as the religious ones? In this chapter, I examine the two primary and often-contentious strategies for defining religion—the functional and the substantive—and I then propose that the definition that is most useful for the study of religions (and, happily, the one that also best captures how people today speak of religions) is the one where the two strategies intersect. That is, I recommend that religion is best understood *both* functionally as making promises about how participation functions to solve problems in one's life *and* substantively as putting participants in touch with what I call superempirical realities. A "mixed" definition of religion like this one is especially useful, I hold, because of what it excludes. Specifically, this definition does not count as religious (i) beliefs or feelings about superempirical realities that are not tied to participation in social practices, and so it would not include as religious a purely inner, private state. And it also excludes (ii) ultimate concerns or orientations to life and that are not tied to superempirical realities, and so it would not include secular humanism, Marxism, or fans of sports teams.

The definition of religion I recommend in the fifth chapter centers on the claim that religious practices appeal to superempirical realities, realities whose existence is said to depend on no empirical thing. To take a ready example, prayer often involves an appeal to God. For philosophers, however, to interpret religions in this way as making claims about the nature of reality raises questions about whether such religious claims could be true. And answering such questions becomes even more difficult if one holds, as I do, that some religious claims are not empirical at all but rather seek to describe metaphysical realities that cannot be known through the tools of science. Such metaphysical claims are today often seen as hopeless or discredited. And many twentieth-century philosophers have taken "overcoming

metaphysics" as their goal. In the sixth chapter, however, I seek to rehabilitate metaphysical claims by arguing, first, that philosophical opposition to
metaphysics is generally based on a certain (modernist, subjectivist) picture
of a gap between mind and world that must be "mediated," and therefore,
second, that contemporary philosophers interested in pursuing metaphysical questions should shift to a picture of experience without that gap. I
take as allies in this project Donald Davidson's Wittgenstein-inspired version of pragmatism, the critical realist movement in philosophy of science,
and accounts of intelligent behavior from the emerging field of embodied
cognitive science. In brief, I argue that if all experience of the world is fil-
tered by one's concepts, and those filters differ from one religion, culture,
or language—or even one individual—to another, then there is no way to
adjudicate rival claims about the world and metaphysical claims become suspect. But if one's experience of the world is unmediated or direct, then it
is possible to speak both of a shared world and of the possibility of rational
claims about the character of that world in general.

The overarching goal of this book is to articulate and begin to develop
a vision for philosophy of religion as global, practice-centered, and reflexive. The final question that I address is: how would such a vision for the
discipline relate to the other parts of the academic study of religions? The
last chapter of the book therefore argues for a certain map of how the
evaluative questions that characterize most philosophy of religion relate to
the descriptive and explanatory questions pursued in other disciplines. I see
the academic study of religions as a multidisciplinary field in which there
are distinct kinds of inquiry pursued, and I seek to show that the evaluative
questions that philosophers of religion ask are a legitimate and, ultimately,
an inevitable aspect of descriptive and explanatory approaches. The different
kinds of work done in the field are not autonomous but are connected by
"bridges" that I seek to identify. According to my map, the academic study
of religions is constituted by three kinds of work, namely, the descriptive
work presupposed by all the other questions in the field, and then the two
kinds of critical work: explanatory questions about the causes of religious
phenomena and evaluative questions about the reasons that can be given
for them.

In the spirit of a manifesto, I have streamlined the chapters by moving
most of the references to the bibliographic essay at the end of each chapter.
Those looking for my sources or for additional reading on the subjects I
discuss can find them there.

Preface

The goal of an academic work is often to enter into an established debate, to explain the two sides to its audience, and then to argue that one side is more persuasive than the other. That is not the kind of goal I pursue in this book. My goal in this manifesto is to move away from established debates, to go to the edge of the field of the academic study of religions where there is little or no consensus about the future of the field, and to make suggestions about how the discipline of philosophy can contribute. Although in each chapter I do argue for a position on each of the questions I raise, my primary hope is not that the book settles some debates but rather that the book illuminates new and productive ways in which philosophy can contribute to the study of religions.

Acknowledgments

Although I wrote my dissertation at the University of Chicago with Chris Gamwell, Paul Griffiths, and Phil Devenish 20 years ago, and this book does not overlap with that project at all, I want to thank them nevertheless for their friendship and for the guidance that they have had on my work as a scholar. My views that philosophy of religion ought to develop the tools to take a global perspective, that human agents are not separated from their environments by language, and that clarity in metaphysics supports the rest of one's theoretical work are indebted to their examples.

Several friends read or discussed parts of the book with me. I would especially like to thank Kevin Carnahan, Paul Griffiths, David Henderson, Christopher Hoyt, Craig Martin, J. Aaron Simmons, Bryan Rennie, Tyler Roberts, John Whitmire, and the students in the WCU philosophy club for helpful discussions of this project. Thanks too to Amy McKenzie for her meticulous help with the book.

I am also grateful to the faculty of the department of religion at Wake Forest University, especially Jay Ford, for the opportunity to present a version of Chapter 1 there; to the faculty of the department of religion at Amherst College, especially Andrew Dole, for the opportunity to present a version of Chapter 2 there; to the faculty of the department of Philosophy and Religion at Drake University, especially Timothy Knepper, for the opportunity to present a version of Chapter 6 there; and to the UGA graduate department of religion, and especially Will Power, for the opportunity to present and discuss an earlier version of Chapter 7 as the 2011 George E. Howard Lecture at the University of Georgia. The book was also improved by the critical responses of the anonymous reviewers arranged by Wiley-Blackwell. I am grateful for the careful attention these colleagues gave my work and for the extended scholarly community they help to create.

Lastly, I want to thank Rebecca Harkin for her encouragement and patience on this project.

Chapter 1

The Full Task of Philosophy of Religion

i. What is "Traditional Philosophy of Religion"?

In this book, I am arguing that philosophy of religion should expand the traditional understanding of its task and take a broader view. Here at the beginning, however, I want to put on the table what my alternative is an alternative *to*. "Traditional philosophy of religion" defines its task in terms of the rationality of theism and this is the primary focus found in most philosophy of religion journals, textbooks, and courses.[1] As I mentioned in the preface, my critique of traditional philosophy of religion is that it is it narrow, intellectualist, and insular. Despite that critique, I am not arguing that traditional philosophy of religion is not a rich and multifaceted discipline. Here is one way that one can organize the variety of the central debates in the traditional approach. (I use a flowchart to map these debates, and it may help to follow that chart in Figure 1.1)

First, the most basic division in the field comes between those theists who argue that there exists a being worthy of worship and those who argue that there does not (or that, if there does, we cannot know it). Some of the atheist or naturalist philosophers in this latter camp hold that belief in a God of perfect power and benevolence cannot be reconciled with experiences of gratuitous evil. They argue either that, given those painful and demoralizing experiences, the claim that a benevolent God is decisively disproven

Philosophy and the Study of Religions: A Manifesto, First Edition. Kevin Schilbrack.
© 2014 Kevin Schilbrack. Published 2014 by John Wiley & Sons, Ltd.

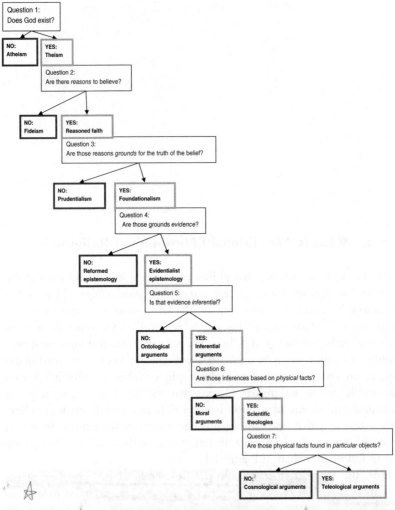

Figure 1.1   Traditional Philosophy of Religion: A Flow Chart.

or at least that, given the amount of suffering in the world, the truth of the claim is unlikely. Other naturalists argue that we cannot make sense of the unusual idea of a being who knows the future or that is all-powerful or that exists necessarily. Others in this camp argue that the lack of a clear revelation or experience of God—what is sometimes called "divine hiddenness"— justifies skepticism about God's existence. Such views have been popularized

4

in bestselling books by the so-called New Atheists, and some atheist or naturalist philosophers of religion have developed their positions with great sophistication.

By contrast, the philosophers of religion who are theists hold that there does exist a being worthy of worship. I divide the theistic philosophers into two camps. The first maintains that the faith that God exists is the kind of commitment that can be supported by reasons, reasons intelligible to those who do not yet share that commitment. Let's call this commitment: reasoned faith. I will come back to this group. The other group of theists holds that faith in God, properly understood, is not the kind of commitment that can be supported by such reasons. These theists are persuaded, for example, by Søren Kierkegaard's account of faith as a passionate and subjective commitment, or by Richard Braithwaite's account of faith as an attitude about one's values and not about facts, or by Ludwig Wittgenstein's account of faith as drawing its sense from a set of ungrounded practices or form of life. Philosophers of religion in this camp hold that there are no criteria by which faith can be justified that are not internal to that commitment or way of looking at the world. Call these theists: fideists. As an illustration of fideism, consider the philosophers of religion who are inspired by Wittgenstein's observations about religion when he says, "The point [of belief in God] is that if there were evidence, this would in fact destroy the whole business. Anything that I would normally call evidence wouldn't in the slightest influence me."[2] From this perspective, what religious communities teach is not a set of opinions or hypotheses or truth claims that can be compared to facts about the world, but rather ways of living and speaking. To agree with the fideists that theistic beliefs are not held on the basis of reasons is not necessarily to consider religion *un*reasonable. As Wittgenstein says, those who believe in God "don't treat this as a matter of reasonability." Fideists therefore argue that one misinterprets theistic beliefs if one thinks that they are either warranted or unwarranted, and the task of philosophy of religion for those in this camp is not to assess the warrant or justification for belief in God. The task, instead, is to clarify what it means to live and speak as a believer.

Let me now return to those theists who do seek to marshal a reasoned faith. I also subdivide these philosophers of religion into two camps: on the one hand, there are those who argue that it is reasonable to believe in God because, they argue, one can provide some grounds that belief in God is true. Call these theists: foundationalists. I will come back to this group of philosophers in a moment. The other group of theists argues that although the belief that God exists, properly understood, is not the kind of belief that one can prove true, or even probable, theism can nevertheless be reasonable. They make a prudential case that it is good to believe or that one ought to believe that God exists. Theism might be reasonable simply because, as Blaise Pascal famously argues, given the eternal stakes at play, it is in one's interest to believe. (As a billboard near my house similarly suggests: "If you are living as if God does not exist, you had better be right," and the bottom of the billboard is covered with flames.) William James also proposes a way of believing reasonably without grounds. In a trenchant analogy, he says: if a mountain climber becomes stuck on a precipice and, to get back home, she needs to make a jump that she has never made before and cannot prove that she can make, it is still reasonable for her to believe that she can (and must!) make the jump, and it is still reasonable for her to attempt the jump, rather than staying stuck on the mountain.[3] Such arguments don't offer grounds that theism is true, though they do offer reasons to believe it.

The foundationalists who argue that there are grounds for the belief that God exists I divide based on whether they hold that the grounds are direct or indirect. One example of direct grounds for belief is perception. To take an example, in a case when I am having a face to face talk with my brother, I would believe the proposition *this is my brother*, and I would be warranted in doing so, but we would not say that I believe because I have evidence or clues from which I was able to infer that this is my brother. If someone asked me afterwards, "How did you know that it was your brother you were talking to?," I could answer, "Because he was right there." My reason for belief is not indirect or via any other belief. Analogously, these theistic philosophers argue that those who believe in God do not do so because they have evidence or clues from which they are able to infer that God exists. Rather, they believe that God exists, and they do so justifiably, because they simply perceive God's presence. They point out that, in fact, we hold many beliefs in this direct way: the belief that *the world is more than five minutes old* and the belief that *other people are not robots* are not beliefs that we base on careful examination of the evidence. These philosophers argue that the theistic belief in God, like the memory belief that I had a grapefruit for breakfast or the perceptual belief that there is a cup in front of me right now, is grounded directly. It is a belief on which other beliefs can then come to be based. In this way, theism can structure the practices and values that make up one's life, but it is based in a foundational way on direct experience and not on other beliefs that are more basic.

Other theistic philosophers hold that apart from these claims of perceiving God directly, there is indirect evidence that God exists. Call this latter group:

6

evidentialists. When we speak of "evidence," we typically mean something that points to a reality that is not present. For example, a fingerprint can be evidence left by the perpetrator or smoke from a window can be evidence that there is a fire inside. One infers from the evidence a cause that could have brought it about, and so evidence like this can be called inferential evidence. But some evidentialists argue that God is such a distinctive reality that God's existence can be demonstrated with evidence that is not inferential. They argue that if God is properly understood as a reality that is worthy of worship, a reality that is perfect, then God's mode of existence by definition cannot be limited or weak or contingent or dependent. If it is God about whom we are speaking, then we cannot be speaking about a reality that was brought into existence or a reality that might conceivably cease to exist. God therefore must exist not only in some places or some times, but always and everywhere, neither brought into existence by something else nor capable of not existing. If God by definition has every good quality, then God by definition has the quality of necessary, non-contingent existence. And if God's existence is necessary, contingent on nothing, then God exists under all conditions. And so God must exist. Though this argument is often dismissed on the grounds that one cannot simply define a reality so carefully that—poof—that reality must exist, there is no confusion in saying that a being worthy of worship would be one that exists under all conditions.

The theistic philosophers who argue for the existence of God based on inferential evidence claim that, just as smoke serves as a sign that there is a fire, there are realities in the world of human experience that point to the existence of a divine being. Some philosophers in this camp point at physical evidence that is external to the subject. More on them in a moment. Others, however, argue that the clues for God's existence are internal and non-physical. Some argue that the best evidence from which one can infer a divine reality is morality. C. S. Lewis is a philosopher who argues in this way, holding that when people look inside themselves, they find a moral law that is not a product of human imagination or social practices, "a real law which we did not invent and know that we ought to obey."[4] If the universe is the source of that law—the mailman who put that letter in our mental mailbox, to use Lewis's metaphor—then it must be or include something like a mind, at least in the sense that it gives instructions and cares about how human beings act. Immanuel Kant also uses the experience of a moral law as evidence for theism. Kant does not infer that God must be the source of the law that one finds in one's conscience. He argues, instead, that if the moral law is not incoherent, then the happiness one earns in one's life must be proportioned to the virtue one develops. It seems painfully clear that such proportioning does not happen in this life, however, and therefore one must take as a practical hypothesis or "postulate" that God as a moral judge of the world and immortality are real.

Now consider those philosophers of religion who are theists, who hold that one can give reasons for one's faith, that these reasons serve as grounds that their beliefs are true, that the grounds are evidence, that the evidence is inferential, and that the inferences are based on facts about the physical world. These philosophers of religion argue that there are facts about the natural world from which one can infer a supernatural creator. Such arguments can be usefully distinguished into two general kinds: some of these arguments are based on *particular* objects or facts about the natural world, and others are based on facts about the *general* character of natural things. The classic example of the first strategy is William Paley's early nineteenth century argument that there are objects in the natural world whose purposeful functions can only be explained by an intelligent designer. The anatomy of the eye, for instance—including the cornea, the iris, the lens, the pupil, the chambers with their aqueous and vitreous humors, the retina, and so on, all working together to give sight to the creature—requires an explanation that the natural world alone cannot supply. Michael Behe has recently updated and strengthened this kind of argument for a supernatural designer. As complex as the anatomy of the eye is, Behe points out, it is nothing to the staggering complexity of the biochemistry of vision, the mechanisms of protein chains that respond to light by creating electrical nerve impulses. Such operations at the molecular level within the cells used to be a mystery, a "black box" to science. But now that the black box has been opened by biochemists, one can see that the mechanisms are irreducibly complex—in the crucial sense that if one part of the system were removed, the system would not function. Because they are irreducibly complex, the emergence of some parts of the natural world is inexplicable through blind chance and the gradual stages of natural selection; they therefore point to the existence of an intelligent designer.[5]

Those philosophers of religion who take up the second strategy base their arguments for God's existence not on the character of some particularly remarkable objects or states of affairs in the world, such as the eye or the apparently perfect adjustment of natural laws for intelligent life—but rather on facts about physical things in general. These are cosmological theistic arguments. One cosmological argument states that if every single physical thing is contingent, in the sense that it might not have existed, then it seems

8

that the same contingency equally applies to the set of all physical things. If we call this set of all physical things "the universe," then we can say that the universe as a whole is contingent and might not have existed. One might therefore legitimately wonder why anything exists at all. Why is there something rather than nothing? The only answer for that question would be some reality whose existence is not contingent—that is, a being that is different from the universe and everything in it because its existence is necessary. In another cosmological argument, theistic philosophers of religion argue that if every physical thing requires a cause, and the chain of causes stretches back through history of the cosmos, then at the beginning of time then there must be a first cause. They argue that the existence of God answers the question about the origin of the universe as a whole. For example, some theists hold that the scientific evidence that the world began roughly fifteen billion years ago in a Big Bang gives people reason to believe that the natural world must have a creator. The idea that the world has not always existed but rather began to exist a finite amount of time ago is a recent development in physics and, as William Lane Craig has pointed out, this remarkable, new scientific evidence lends support to those theists who believe that the world was created. Drawing on what is sometimes called the Kalam argument, after the Islamic philosophical theologians who first employed it, Craig argues that if everything that begins to exist is caused, and the universe began to exist (as the Big Bang theory holds), then these two truths together point to the need for a cause for the physical universe, a supernatural first cause of everything.

As one can see, the questions pursued in traditional philosophy of religion cover a very wide set of questions. Traditional philosophy of religion draws on debates in physics, biology, ethical theory, and modal logic. It also contributes to Christian theology and to Biblical studies. This fruitfulness notwithstanding, one can see that traditional philosophy of religion has focused on a relatively narrow topic: the rationality of belief in God. Even the philosophers of religion who are skeptics or atheists fit that description of the discipline.

There are some forms of philosophy of religion that do not focus on the kind of theistic and atheistic arguments that I have listed. For example, when we turn to philosophy of religion as it is practiced in non-Anglophone, Continental Europe, we find an approach quite different from the topics just listed. In Continental philosophy of religion, one does not find a focus on the characteristics that God must have or proofs for the existence of God. Instead, one finds a focus on religious experience, on the phenomenology of overflow experiences, and on overcoming ontotheology. Continental philosophy of religion primarily reflects on the limits of reason and on faith as a response to revelation. It is primarily concerned with the nature and limits of God-talk rather than with warrant for truth claims. Nevertheless, as one sees in John Caputo's definition of religion simply as "the love of God," Continental philosophers of religion predominantly share with analytic philosophers of religion the narrow focus on theism. In fact, as Christina Gschwandtner points out, almost all the Continental philosophers of religion from France—including Paul Ricoeur, Jean-Luc Marion, Michel Henry, Jean-Louis Chrétien, Jean-Yves Lacoste, and Emmanuel Falque—are apologists for the coherence of thought about God and for the viability of religious experience.[6] Another approach that does not pursue the theistic and atheistic arguments I listed is found in feminist philosophy of religion. Whether feminist philosophers of religion use the analytic approach or (more commonly) the Continental approach, they typically focus on the biases and distortions woven into traditional, masculine accounts of God and how these might be avoided. But the questions of theism are still usually central. Continental philosophy of religion and feminist philosophy of religion thus share a view of their task that is limited in the ways described in this chapter and to that extent they too should develop along the three axes I recommend in the rest of this chapter.

I begin this book with this enumeration of the variety of topics one finds in traditional philosophy of religion because I do not want to give the sense that traditional philosophy of religion is not already a complex and evolving discipline. As I mentioned, in one sense, the discipline is flourishing. Nevertheless, I think that the majority of Analytic, Continental, and feminist philosophers of religion operate with a narrow, intellectualist, and insular view of the task of the discipline and that therefore, as an understanding of what philosophy of religion can and should be, the traditional approach is incomplete.

ii. The First Task of Philosophy of Religion

My critique of traditional philosophy of religion is that, despite its achievements, it operates with an inadequate understanding of the task of the discipline. To avoid narrowness, intellectualism, and insularity, philosophers of religion should understand their task as having three parts: it should exclude no religions, it should give proper recognition to the centrality of religious practice to religious communities, and it should expand its conversations with the other branches of philosophy and the other disciplines in religious studies. The task of philosophy of religion would then be composed of three sets of questions. Using a geometrical metaphor, one might think of each set of questions as an "axis." The first set of questions—the first "axis"—is intended to address the criticism of narrowness, and it is generated when philosophy of religion broadens its view to include the doctrines and arguments from religions globally and throughout history.

When one takes a global view of philosophy of religion, one uncovers a host of religious philosophies outside of theism. For example, the Hindu teacher Adi Śaṅkara (788–820 CE) developed what he called Non-dualist or Advaita Vedanta which taught that since the supreme reality (which he called Brahman) is infinite, it is misguided to think that Brahman is distinct from the world and is not present here, in our midst, in our minds and bodies. It is misguided to think that Brahman is not present everywhere. Śaṅkara holds that if the supreme reality cannot be distinguished from the world, then it is a mistake to imagine that Brahman is a person who has thoughts and plans and emotions. On this view, to use Śaṅkara's analogy, the supreme reality is more like an ocean of which we are but drops. Central questions for philosophers of religion to raise then are: what reasons does Śaṅkara give that this non-dualist view of the nature of things is correct? What reasons could one give? And what arguments against non-dualism were given by Śaṅkara's Hindu, Buddhist, and Jain opponents? What arguments could one give?

A second example of non-theistic religious philosophies can be drawn from Buddhism. The Japanese Soto Zen teacher Dōgen Kigen (1200–1253 CE) was responsible for the training of monks, and he taught them the classical Buddhist doctrine of dependent co-arising or origination: everything that exists is transient and impermanent. As a Mahayana Buddhist, however, Dōgen developed this doctrine in terms of emptiness, the claim that nothing that exists can exist without dependence on other realities. If Dōgen is right about emptiness, then he provides an alternative to most versions of theism. So the philosopher of religion should ask: what reasons does Dōgen give that this view of the nature of things is correct? What reasons could one give? What arguments against emptiness were given by his Buddhist, Confucian, and Shinto opponents? What arguments could one give?

These are Hindu and Buddhist examples, and there are several philosophers of religion who are working on religious philosophies from India and Japan. There are fewer, but still some, philosophers of religion working on

11

Daoist and neo-Confucian religious philosophies of China and East Asia. There are almost no philosophers of religion working on African religions (despite the fact that, as described by Stephen Prothero, there may be 50 million people who practice Yoruba religion, which is to say that there are more Yoruba adherents than Jews, Sikhs, Jains, or Zoroastrians). There are next to zero philosophers of religion working on indigenous wisdom traditions of Australia, or North America, or South America. And there are next to zero working on the intellectual aspects of New Religious Movements.

What I am calling the first axis of philosophy of religion is the set of questions that are generated when one engages philosophically with the wisdom traditions that one finds all around the world that offer practices based on superempirical realities.[7] As the world shrinks, and global communication and immigration increase, philosophy of religion can play an important role in the interpretation and critical assessment of those teachings. I agree with Richard King: "engagement with the intellectual traditions of the non-western world has become the single most important task for the philosopher in an age of globalization."[8]

I have a friend who is a traditional philosopher of religion who agrees with this proposal in principle. He points out rightly, however, that no single philosopher of religion can master the philosophical intricacies of one religious tradition, let alone all of them. Scholarly expertise requires specialization. And so he asks: is there anything wrong from the perspective advocated in this book with specializing, as he does, solely in Christian philosophy of religion?

I have two answers. First, the proposal is not for a change in the work of any individual philosopher of religion, but rather in our understanding of the task of the discipline as a whole to which that work is meant to contribute. Insofar as philosophers of religion come to see the scope of their work as global, it may have an impact on their teaching and scholarship. But it would certainly have an impact on our understanding of what one should find in philosophy of religion journals, courses, and textbooks. It also means that my friend's department—which at present includes several philosophers of religion, all of whom specialize exclusively in Christian philosophy of religion—would see their present coverage in the discipline as one-sided and incomplete.

The second response is more critical. Many traditional philosophers of religion see their work as a defense of the truths that they find in their own religious traditions. From the perspective of this proposal, this is a legitimate goal. The flaw in their understanding of their task, however, is that they often assume a limited grasp of who their rivals are. Traditional philosophers of religion who are struck by the secular transformation of western states in modernity take it as their task to rebut philosophical naturalism. But to make the case for theism today requires engagement not only with late modern European challenges but also with the post-colonial return of religion. The flaw is the assumption that theism and naturalism are the only two "live" options. (Note that this choice is the first step on the flowchart of the positions in traditional philosophy of religion). Given that there are multiple religious traditions that offer philosophical defenses of their worldviews, to show the weaknesses of philosophical naturalism does not suffice to establish traditional theism, and those philosophers of religion who do want to demonstrate the superiority of their faith need to engage with rival religious philosophies. Simply put, one cannot make comparative claims about the superiority of one's position unless one actually compares. Consequently, those who want to defend their faith cannot succeed at their task if they do not take into account the full range of religious options, which is to say that they ought to agree to the proposal of this book.[9]

What should one call this alternative, more inclusive philosophy of religion? There are several proposals in the air. Some call it *comparative* philosophy of religion. This label, modeled on the comparative study of religion, gets at the idea that the object of philosophy of religion is multiple. And comparative philosophy of religion is cousin to the emerging disciplines of comparative religious ethics and comparative theology. But although comparison is an apt part of what alternative philosophy of religion involves, it is not a required part. Philosophers compare religions in order to identify what truths they teach; they do not try to identify truths in religions in order to compare them. This issue is avoided by the label *cross-cultural* philosophy of religion. That label might nevertheless also be misleading in that it may describe the western philosopher of religion who works on non-western philosophies, but it does not fit the non-western thinker who crosses cultures to operate on western religious thought.

To call it *global* philosophy of religion emphasizes the non-exclusivity of the project, though it may also suggest "globalization," the imposition of North Atlantic categories and values on the rest of the world. Others suggest *post-colonial* philosophy of religion, a label that foregrounds the resurgence of formerly colonized nations and their ability to speak as subjects. Similarly, to call it *post-secular* philosophy of religion gets at the failure of the secularization hypothesis and the resulting recognition that religious ways of living and thinking cannot be assumed to be irrational. Perhaps my favorite of the alternative labels is the relatively subtle: philosophy of *religions*. Adding the "s" indicates the inclusion of diverse religions. And since the word "of" can be either objective genitive or subjective genitive, this label can refer to an understanding both that religious thinkers are the object of philosophy—that is, they are what is studied philosophically—and that religious thinkers are the subjects of philosophy—that they themselves practice philosophy.

These different labels capture different emphases of this approach and one can use any of them or all of them to identify a philosophy of religion that does not exclude most of the religions of the world. Thus, one can call the view for which I am arguing in this book a post-secular, post-colonial, cross-cultural, comparative, global philosophy of religions. That said, none of the above terms is the label I prefer. The truth is that if philosophy of religion means the philosophical study of religion, then traditional philosophy of religion has simply not lived up to its name. It has become fixated on a fraction of its proper object; a more fitting name for the bulk of what one finds in philosophy of religion textbooks courses and journals would be "philosophical theology" or "philosophy of theism." To be sure, the philosophical study of theistic claims is a legitimate part of philosophy of religion. But it is a relatively narrow part and to identify the two is to confuse part with whole. Philosophy of religion properly means the philosophical study of religions in all their diversity, in all their aspects, and as a contributing part of a family of approaches in the study of religions. Thus the best name for the approach to the discipline proposed in this book is simply to reclaim the name, philosophy of religion.

iii.   The Second Task of Philosophy of Religion

In the previous section, I argued that although philosophy of religion has traditionally assumed that the subject matter of the discipline is God, the discipline should overcome that narrowness and come to understand its central task as philosophical engagement with all religious traditions, whether theistic or not. As limiting as the focus on theism has been, however, there is another assumption in traditional philosophy of religion, even less recognized, that has limited the discipline in a different way. This is the assumption that the proper objects of study by philosophers of religion are the products of religious intellectuals. Expanding the discipline to include not only the philosophies of Aquinas, Maimonides, and Averroes but also Śaṅkara and Dōgen would not change this. I therefore want to develop a view of the

14

proper task of philosophy of religion in a second direction, along an axis that is, so to speak, perpendicular to the first. Here the question is: on what *aspects* of religions should philosophy of religion focus?

If the central task of philosophy of religion is philosophical engagement with all religious traditions, it is important to see that religious communities pursue and are organized around different kinds of interests. Some religious communities not only teach their path but also seek to regulate the ways in which their teachings are explicitly understood, confessed, and described by their members. They therefore produce explicit creeds, doctrines, and theologies and they use these devices to foster orthodoxy within their community, seeking unity within their own ranks. Some religious communities also seek to persuade those outside their ranks that the community's teachings are superior. In these cases, religious communities often develop a division of labor that permits the emergence of representative intellectuals or schools who then produce statements of faith, handbooks that articulate the coherence of the teachings, arguments that provide support for them, criticisms of rival views, and so on. Following Ninian Smart, we might call this aspect of religions—the creeds, doctrines, and theologies—the doctrinal dimension of religions.[10]

The doctrinal dimension of religions has received the lion's share of the attention from philosophers of religion. But the task of developing and defending religious doctrines tends to be the work of literate elites, typically from a leisured class and typically male. When traditional philosophers of religion take the task of their discipline to be the study of these writings, they limit the subject matter of philosophy of religion to a small subset of religious phenomena. As philosophers of religion enlarge the scope of their discipline along the first axis and include the teachings of traditions around the world, they will quickly see that not all religious communities give a central role to doctrines and arguments. Moreover, the interest in religious doctrines and arguments is a relatively small fraction of the lives of religious people, even in those communities that do make such issues central. Philosophers of religions should therefore move away from an exclusive focus on the intellectual work of literate elites to develop the tools necessary to study the full range of religious teachings. What do religious communities teach their members other than doctrines?

Some religious communities are not especially interested in developing and defending doctrines. What they primarily offer to their members are not arguments but rather certain feelings, emotions, and experiences that confirm the path. A nice example of how everyday religious experiences

15

can be specific to a given religious community, tied to their teachings and practices and yet distinct from an interest in demonstrating the rationality of one's beliefs comes from Dennis Covington's account of the practices of a snake-handling church in Alabama. Covington describes a man whose wife had "gotten the Holy Ghost" at a service and who wanted to get it, finally, for himself. This desire for this experience is completely understood by the others in the congregation. So, a half dozen men pray over him and lay hands on him, and the man is "up and running from one end of the sanctuary to the other, now twirling, now swooning, now collapsing once again on the floor, his eyes like the eyes of a horse that smells smoke, the unknown tongue spewing from his mouth." After the service, however, as the man brushes sandwich crumbs from his lap, he admits to Covington that he had not had the experience that he had sought, that "it was a good service all right, but it sure would have been better if he'd only gotten the Holy Ghost." The goal was not reached.[11]

Philosophers of religion have not overlooked this experiential and affective dimension of religion. They have typically focused on accounts of extraordinary religious experiences, on numinous and mystical experiences, and on *mysterium tremendum* events. For most religious people, however, religious experiences are everyday events: the religious community promises, for example, a sense of release or forgiveness or equanimity, and the practices of the community provide a path to exactly that. To be sure, being able to have and properly identify the experience that a religious community offers typically depends on other teachings that they offer. For that reason, religious communities often teach that having the desired experience requires a process of training in discernment and regulation of desires. The pursuit of certain religious experiences is therefore inseparable from doctrines and practices. And religious experiences will therefore vary from one community to another: the racial pride felt by a Klansman at a cross-burning will differ from the enjoyment felt by an Eckist experiencing soul travel, and both will differ from the grief felt by a Shiite Muslim re-enacting the martyrdom of Hussein ibn Ali.

Other religious communities are not especially invested either in developing and defending doctrines or in cultivating certain experiences. What they primarily offer and seek to foster in their members is what they consider a morally proper life. They hold that, whether or not one is an intellectual who can articulate the religious philosophy and whether or not one experiences certain feelings, one can and ought to live rightly. They therefore take an interest in shaping behavior to be ethical. Some religious communities identify ethical behavior according to a holy law and they stress obedience to specific precepts, regulations, rules, or commandments. Others identify ethical behavior according to a specific role model and they emphasize the imitation of holy people. As with religious experiences, there is no reason to speak of religious ethics as a single type: some communities seek to develop martial virtues; others, peaceful ones. Some insist that tranquility is the highest virtue; others, passion.

Here is a fourth interest that we see in religious communities: some religious communities are interested in organizing society rightly. Their primary interest is in political practice. Take as a paradigmatic example a religious community that includes an elaborate ceremony like the Babylonian Akitu festival for installing the leader that they consider legitimate and then confirming his position by re-installing him every New Year. Many religious communities seek to organize society according to their vision of propriety. Some do this by separating men and women, some regulate the loaning of money or the payment of damages, some build monasteries, some issue definitions of marriage, and some train legal scholars who can make sure that people live according to God's revealed word. In all these ways, religious communities seek the proper ordering of society.

Fifth and finally, there are religious communities that are primarily interested in ritual practice. Take as paradigmatic examples the religious practices of circumcision, pilgrimage, or devotional worship. Some religious rituals like these are practiced explicitly for some instrumental benefit such as healing, divining the future, and protection from disease, bad luck, or enemies. Other rituals are said to be done because they are intrinsically good in themselves: "because God requires it" or "because it is right to do." Now, one cannot separate the religious practices that shape an individual's moral behavior from those political practices that organize society, and one cannot separate those interests from rituals of healing or worship. "Ethics" and "politics" and "ritual" are categories imposed on religious actions in this chapter in order better to see the diversity of religious interests. Nevertheless, it does seem that some or most religious practices—including the cultivation of virtue, the installation of a ruler, or circumcision—do not typically aim either at teaching doctrine or at having a certain experience. If this is right, then religious practices should not be seen as merely the expressions of doctrines or experiences. They embody religious interests of their own.

Any attempt to provide an "anatomy" of religion like this one will be somewhat artificial, but this particular way of dissecting the avowed interests of religious communities—in terms of doctrines, experiences, ethical practices, political practices, and ritual practices—is useful for philosophers of religion in at least two ways.

A first benefit of enumerating these multiple religious interests is that it lets us place the doctrines that serve as the object of study for traditional philosophy of religion into a richer, more multifaceted context. The five religious interests that I have listed support each other. The first interest in teaching certain truths and the second interest in teaching certain experiences—the cognitive and the affective—are distinguishable and yet intertwined, as distinguishable and intertwined as head and heart often are. But the three interests in teaching certain practices—ethics, politics, and ritual—are all ways in which religious people pursue the conative interest in shaping behavior. On my account, then, religious communities have cognitive, affective, and conative interests, and the conative interests include ethical, political, and ritual practices. This account makes the interest in developing doctrines only one of many. It thereby gives philosophers of religion a way to imagine a more inclusive task of their discipline. That is, if we conceive of these different religious interests as lying along another axis, perpendicular to the axis of different religious traditions, then we can imagine these two set of questions as forming a graph. That is, if we imagine the multiple religions as a list along the bottom (the X-axis) and the multiple interests of religious communities vertically (the Y-axis), then we create multiple boxes: Christian, Buddhist, Yoruba, and other doctrines lie along the bottom. The higher boxes would represent the Daoist rituals, Jewish ethics, Islamic politics, Navajo religious experience, and so on.

If one were to take the essays collected in philosophy of religion textbooks and put a check mark in the corresponding boxes on this graph that represent the different possible topics, almost all of the check marks would be in the box dealing with Christian doctrines. Very few checks would be found in the other boxes. The other aspects of religion—which is to say, the other interests that religious communities care about—have received very little philosophical attention. For those topics, philosophers of religion will need to develop new tools. Nevertheless, if the first axis is easy to state—the proper object of philosophy of religion is all religions—then the second axis is just as easy to state: the proper object of philosophy of religion is all aspects of those religions. On this understanding, it is the task of philosophy of religion to investigate all religious phenomena from a philosophical perspective, and not to investigate solely the work of religious philosophers.

A second benefit of this anatomy of religions is that it highlights how deeply and broadly religious communities are invested in aspects of their traditions other than the products of their representative intellectuals. To the extent that this map of religious interests is apt, religion is *largely* a set of practices in which people engage in order to make their lives better: participating in the three kinds of religious practices provides the participants with rituals that heal, with disciplines that train their children in morality, and with structures for their communal lives that reflect a higher law. On this view, religious communities take people who see their lives (or are taught to see their lives) as lost or broken or disordered and they promise their members a therapy that leads to wholeness, harmony, and human flourishing. Although religious communities have sometimes developed the most elaborate philosophies, such communities seem pre-eminently interested in practical concerns, not speculative concerns.

As noted, philosophers of religion traditionally focus on religious doctrines and arguments. Some have also focused on religious experiences, usually to answer the question whether religious experiences can justify the doctrines. Philosophers of religion have given relatively less attention to religious ethics, and much less to political and ritual practices. In the next chapter of this book, I will argue that religious practices can be seen as occasions for religious inquiry. To the extent that the affective and conative aspects of religion are not simply vehicles for the cognitive but also contribute to it, philosophers of religion should expand this object of study along this second axis.

iv. The Third Task of Philosophy of Religion

I now turn to the third and last set of questions that in my judgment should constitute the discipline of philosophy of religion, the third and last "axis." One can imagine this set of questions as the Z-axis, in the sense that the questions in this third set are not of the same kind as those in the other two. They run, so to speak, perpendicular to *both* the previous two lists of questions. Here is their focus.

Precisely because traditional philosophers of religion have shown little interest in religions other than traditional theism, ignoring the range of religions on my first "axis," and precisely because traditional philosophers of religion have shown little interest in aspects of religions other than doctrines, ignoring the range of concerns that religious communities actually

19

have on my second "axis," philosophy of religion has become a relatively *insular* discipline. By this I mean that, intellectually speaking, traditional philosophers of religion keep to themselves. When it comes to the other disciplines in the academic study of religions, philosophers do not "play well with others."

I have a funny anecdote that illustrates this insularity: I have a friend who shares with me the view that philosophy of religion ought to evolve from its predominantly theistic focus to become a cross-cultural discipline that engages religions in all their variety and dimensions. He presented a paper at a conference in which he argued that unless philosophy of religion makes this shift, the discipline would continue to be of little use to the academic study of religions. In the audience was a well-known philosopher of religion who works in the traditional style, and that philosopher raised his hand immediately to ask the first question. He stood and objected: "You claim that traditional philosophy of religion should change because it is not of use to religious studies. But I can disprove your view very simply. Traditional philosophy of religion is of use to itself. Traditional philosophy of religion is in religious studies. Therefore, traditional philosophy of religion is of use to religious studies." And then he sat back down. To define one's scholarship in such a way that it is only of use to oneself is a good illustration of what I mean by "insular"!

The absence of philosophers who contribute to this set of questions is not unrelated to their absence on the other axes. Philosophers of religion do not generally read or write about pilgrimage, dietary rules, raising children, offering sacrifices, celebrating marriage, or speaking in tongues. They leave religious practice or lived religion for the anthropologists, historians, comparativists and other disciplines in the field of religious studies. It is also true that this is a two-way street: the anthropologists and other scholars of religion almost never read philosophy of religion texts about, for example, how to reconcile belief in omnipotence with the experiences of gratuitous evil or how modal logic makes the ontological proof for the existence of God a live option. But the problem is that, if the professors and students in anthropology and the other fields in religious studies *did* work their way through a book in philosophy of religion, it would not help their work. That is, traditional philosophy of religion defines its scholarly task so narrowly that it makes much of the contribution it offers irrelevant to the other ways of studying religion. My third axis is intended to address this problem by building bridges from philosophy to other disciplines involved in the study of religions.

I identify this third axis of questions in the following way. Philosophy classically seeks to provide critical reflection on the presuppositions at work in our practices. Philosophy of law involves critical reflection on the presuppositions of legal practices; for example, it asks about the nature of justice. Philosophy of art asks about the nature of beauty. Philosophy of science asks about the nature of causality. To generalize, philosophers inquire into what people presuppose as true and real and good when they engage in different practices. To use the ten-dollar words, philosophy asks epistemological, metaphysical, and axiological questions.

Now, in addition to law and art and science, there is another practice whose presuppositions philosophers might consider, namely, the practice of the academic study of religions. What discipline provides critical reflection on the metaphysical, epistemological, and axiological issues at work in that practice? At present, the answer is: none. But philosophy of religion could provide a home for such questions, in which case philosophy of religion would include reflection not only on the philosophies of the religions around the world (the first axis) and the aspects of those religions as they are lived (the second axis) but also on the philosophical questions involved in the study of religions. This would be the third axis of philosophy of religion. One could call this set of questions: philosophy of religious studies.

What questions make up this third axis?

Philosophical reflection on the study of religion should interrogate scholarly approaches by looking at the concepts that inform their work. For example, when scholars study ascetic disciplines, marriage, sacrifice, or other religious practices, philosophers of religion might engage this work by critical reflection on the concept of *practice*. Such an engagement might clarify what it means to say that a person is an agent, that an action is or is not rational, or that an action is performed by a collectivity. It might clarify the relationship between actors' intentions and other causes of their behavior. In these ways, philosophers connect the study of religion to philosophy of action. Similarly, when scholars study teachings about ecstatic states of consciousness, communication with invisible beings, life after death, or other instances of religious beliefs, then philosophers of religion can engage this work by critical reflection on the concept of *belief*. Such an engagement might clarify the ways in which knowledge depends on embodied habits, the relation of perception and introspection, or the dependence of thought on sociality. It might clarify the relationship between religious language and religious knowledge. In these ways, philosophers connect the study of

21

religion to philosophy of mind. And similarly, when scholars debate whether or not Theravada Buddhism and early Confucianism are properly categorized as religions or whether, given the emergence of the word "religion" in modern Europe, it is appropriate to speak of religion outside the modern west, philosophers of religion might engage this work by critical reflection on the concept of *religion*. Such an engagement might clarify the concept of "tradition," the difference between emic and etic labels, or the relation between social construction and reality. In these ways, philosophers connect the study of religion to philosophy of language. Answers to questions like these are presupposed by empirical studies of religions, but I would suggest that they are properly philosophical questions.

The three kinds of examples above have to do with the ways in which philosophers of religion might critically reflect on presuppositions regarding the subject matter (i.e., the content) of religious studies. But philosophers of religion might also critically reflect on presuppositions regarding the disciplinary methods (i.e., the form) of religious studies. First, what does it mean to *understand* religious texts, discourse, or behavior? Does understanding depend in some way on the perspective of the practitioners themselves? What is the relation between the practitioners' self-understanding and the interpretation or redescription accomplished by the scholar? Second, what does it mean to *explain* religious beliefs and practices? Does explanation replace understanding? Is explanation reductive? Does explanation assume that the beliefs in question are not true? And third, what does it mean to assess, critique, or evaluate religious beliefs and practices? From what sources, if any, do the criteria of assessment come? Must critique of religion be secular? These are live questions pursued in the study of religion, but at present they are largely pursued by historians, anthropologists, and others who are reflective about their own practices. It is rare that philosophers of religion contribute to these discussions.

Of course, when one is critically reflecting on the form and the content of religious studies, there are participants to the discussion who should be included other than the philosophical ones. There can be not only a philosophy of the study of religion but also a history of the study of religion, or a politics of the study of religion, and so on. Nevertheless, I suggest that philosophy brings a distinct set of questions to these topics, namely, the axiological questions about what is valuable, epistemological about what is knowable, and ontological questions about what is real. Developing this set of questions is especially important for the health of philosophy of religion itself, because traditional philosophy of religion has been, I judge, the least reflexive discipline in religious studies. Philosophers of religion usually write not only as if the religious doctrines in which they are interested float in the air, deracinated from their particular histories and cultures, but also as if their own conceptual tools—their definition of what religion is and what philosophy is—have no history. The third axis addresses this by introducing reflexivity into philosophy of religion. It is common for philosophy to reflect on the nature of philosophy, but, strangely, this reflexivity is less common in philosophy of religion.

Traditional philosophy of religion asks metaphysical questions about reality, epistemological questions about knowledge, and axiological questions about value—in relation to traditional theism. Philosophers of religion who agree with the thesis of this book that the discipline should not exclude any religions (i.e., the first axis) would also ask those questions about conceptions of reality, knowledge, and value in Hindu, Daoist, Yoruba, or other traditions. But if *all* human practices involve presuppositions about what is real, what is true, and what is good, then it follows that the educational and scholarly practices that we do in the university—including the study of religions— also involve presuppositions about what is real, what is true, and what is good. What discipline gives us the tools to talk about these things? Many academics like to present their work as scientific or objective. But since our academic work involves presuppositions that what we teach is true and real and valuable, even the most scientific or objective scholarship is nevertheless philosophy-laden, in the sense that it presupposes answers to metaphysical, epistemological, and axiological questions. Scholars of religion therefore do not misspeak when we say that we are "devoting" our time and our energy to our academic subjects. What I described above as the first task of philosophy of religion asks: in what religions teach, what is good or real or true? But on this, the third task, the question is more personal. It is to ask: what is good or real or true in our own practices? Why do we do what we do? I want to suggest that this is a legitimate academic question, and it is a question that scholars should debate. The academic study of religion presupposes an answer to the question of what the academic study of religion is *for*. Critically reflecting on this question is a part of being a self-critical scholar, and I am proposing that this third axis is properly part of philosophy of religion.

To summarize the three axes in this proposal, then, philosophy of religion should take as its philosophical object not only the rationality of theism but also (i) the reason-giving found in all religious traditions, (ii) the full range of religious phenomena, and (iii) the study of religions itself.

v. What is the Big Idea?

This book is meant as a way to identify a way to frame the different questions in the discipline, a way that is intended to be productive for future philosophical studies of religious phenomena. The book is in this sense programmatic. But it is not the only program on the table.

Among professional philosophers, a division has developed between two "cultures" in philosophy of religion. If one can generalize or speak in terms of ideal types, the "philosophy department" philosophers of religion tend to work with the goals and the tools of analytic philosophy, and the "religion department" philosophers of religion tend to work with the goals and the tools of hermeneutic or phenomenological philosophy. The former tend to foreground the philosophical aspects of theism, and they are more likely to argue about whether religious claims about God are true. The latter are more likely to see such arguments as Christian apologetics and they are more likely to approach religious beliefs in their historical and cultural context, or even to embrace a religious pluralism or a cultural relativism. In short, there are two styles of philosophy of religion. People outside academic circles may think that philosophy tends to undermine religious belief and that religion departments "teach religion," but the truth is that one is much more likely to hear an argument that God exists in the philosophy department philosophy of religion courses than in those from the religious studies department. But the emergence of these two styles is not surprising when one keeps in mind that the philosophers who work in philosophy departments have colleagues who take questions about the nature of knowledge and reality and value seriously, and the philosophers who work in religious studies department have colleagues who are historians and social scientists and comparativists who are, in their professional roles at least, uninterested in the question whether God exists.

In terms of this division, the present book is clearly the product of a philosopher of religion who works in the religious studies style. I do see my discipline as properly in conversation with the other disciplines in the academic study of religion. In fact, I see the location of philosophy of religion as one disciplinary approach among several in the academic study of religions simply as a feature of its location in the university—even when it is practiced

24

in a philosophy department. Moreover, I agree with other scholars of religion that the meaning of religious phenomena depends on its cultural and historical context, and in this respect the work of philosophers of religion is already dependent on the interpretive work of others. Nevertheless, like the philosophers of religion in the philosophy department style, I also judge that the distinctive contribution of philosophy of religion has to do with the evaluation of truth claims, which means the assessment of reason-giving and arguments. Thus, my aim is that this book can be read as a proposal for how the two styles of philosophy of religion can be related without excluding the value of either. Specifically, the proposal is that the religion department style of philosophy of religion is the more inclusive model in the following sense: given what I am calling the first task of philosophy of religion, normative questions about theism are appropriate, but they are part of the larger task of evaluating the truth claims of all religions. This first task is distinct from—though, again, part of—the philosophical study of all religious phenomena which would include not only the philosophical study of doctrines and arguments but also what I call the second task of the discipline, namely, the philosophical study of the experiential, practical, and institutional aspects of religions. Then, finally, these two philosophical tasks (my so-called X- and Y-axes) are distinct from though again part of an even more inclusive, "three-dimensional" model that includes critical refection on the categories of the study of religion itself. Thus, the overall aim of the book is to provide a model that can serve as an ideal for an integrated or holistic philosophical study of religions in way that that gives a coherent place to every important question in the discipline.

Bibliographic Essay

The first chapter of the book contrasts what I call traditional philosophy of religion—which I characterize as the focus on the rationality of theism—with the three more inclusive tasks that I recommend for a more inclusive philosophy of religion. I discuss several options for how to label the more inclusive view. The most popular label is "comparative philosophy of religion" (Reynolds and Tracy 1990, 1992, 1994; cf. Neville 2000a, 2000b, 2000c; Wildman 2010), a label that parallels the increasingly popular subfields of comparative religious ethics (see, e.g., Yearley 1990; Stalnaker 2006; Fasching, deChant, and Lantiqua 2011) and comparative theology (see, e.g., Thatamanil 2006; Roberts 2010; Clooney 2010; Nicholson

2011). Purushottama Bilimoria argues that philosophers of religion should avoid the term "comparative" because it has an imperial genealogy in that it emerged as a pseudo-scientific attempt to create a pseudo-evolutionary hierarchy of religions from the primitive to the higher (see Bilimoria 2009); the texts listed above, however, are not guilty of that charge. The other alternatives I mention are "cross-cultural philosophy of religion" (Dean 1995); "global philosophy of religion" (Runzo 2001; cf. Phillips 1995, Kessler 1998); "post-colonial philosophy of religion" (Bilimoria and Irvine 2009), and "post-secular philosophy of religion" (Blond 1999). Some of the best work embodying the first task of philosophy of religion that I recommend puts Buddhist philosophy into conversation with contemporary analytic philosophy; as examples, see Arnold (2005) and Siderits (2003).

I argue that to make the case for theism today requires engagement not only with naturalism but also other religious philosophies. Robert Neville has long championed this view, writing that "this discipline has almost incorrigibly insisted upon an eighteenth century angle of vision on religion, which sees little more than Christianity and through only epistemological perspectives. Ignoring the vast amount of information about other religions now available in English it is embarrassingly parochial, and innocent of so many other philosophical approaches to religion, many learned from other religiophilosophical traditions, that it is out of the loop for understanding religion in late modernity" (Neville 2002: 5–6; cf. Ch. 12).

The "anatomy" of religion I give in the chapter is similar to five of the seven dimensions on Ninian Smart's well-known map of religion: (i) the doctrinal dimension, (ii) the experiential or emotional dimension, (iii) the ethical and legal dimension, (iv) the ritual dimension, and (v) the social dimension (see Smart 1995, 1996). The primary differences are that I see all of the dimensions as "embodied and embedded" and I therefore see Smart's narrative and material dimensions as tools for teaching proper ethical, political, ritual behavior and not as distinct dimensions of religion in their own right. For alternative anatomies, see Livingston (2005) and Cannon (1995). As I mention in the chapter, there has been some interest among philosophers in religious experiences (e.g., Alston 1991) and there has been some interest in the practice of prayer (e.g., Phillips 1965). My suspicion that religious communities are preeminently interested in ethical, political, and ritual concerns, and not speculative concerns, is shared by John Cottingham who argues that "it is in the very nature of religious understanding that it characteristically stems from practical involvement rather than from intellectual analysis" (2005: 6).

Endnotes

1. It is intriguing to read the introductions to traditional philosophy of religion textbooks and to watch for the shift from an understanding of philosophy of religion as the philosophical study of religions in all their variety to philosophy of religion in the restricted sense as only the philosophical study of God. Usually this shift is unmarked and undefended. To take one illustrative example from many, on the first page of his long in print and widely used textbook, Louis Pojman speaks sweepingly of the Vedas, the Bhagavad Gita, the Bible, the Koran, and the Dhammapada. He refers to the pyramids of Egypt, the Parthenon in Greece, the Hindu Juggernaut, and the cathedral of Chartres. "What is the truth about religion?" he asks. But then in the very next paragraph he says: "At the heart of the great theistic religions—Judaism, Christianity and Islam—is the idea that the universe was created by an all-powerful, benevolent, and providential God" (Pojman and Rea 2008: xv), and once he has introduced God as a topic of discussion, he never looks back. Of the seventy-four essays included in the anthology, seventy-one are on theism. The other three include Plato on the existence of an eternal and immaterial soul and the Dalai Lama on what Buddhists think of the possibility of Christian truth. There is one chapter on Hindu philosophy, and the rest of the religions of the world are not included.
2. The two quotes from Ludwig Wittgenstein in this paragraph come from Wittgenstein (1966: 56, 48).
3. This example is found in James' essay, "The Sentiment of Rationality" (1956: 96).
4. This idea is the theme of the first section of Lewis 1952.
5. See Paley (1819: esp. 16–28) and Behe (1996). In addition to his own sub-cellular examples, Behe discusses the biochemistry of vision (18–22) and the strengths and weaknesses of Paley's case (211–6).
6. For Caputo's definition of religion, see Caputo (2001:1). For Gschwandtner's argument about French philosophy of religion, see Gschwandtner (2013).
7. I develop this definition of religion, along with the idea of "superempirical" realities, in Ch. 5.
8. See Richard King (2009: 40).
9. Another way to put this is to say that the series of arguments between theism and atheism over the *existence* of a reality worthy of worship is half of philosophy of religion. The other half, now emerging, is the engagement between religions over the *nature* of a reality worthy of worship.
10. An interesting question concerns the extent to which religions develop this doctrinal interest not simply as a result of speculation about the nature of things but rather a response to challenges, alternatives, and doubts that come from rival religious paths. In other words, the dimension of religions that has

traditionally been the central object of study for philosophy of religion may not be the "essence" or even a necessary dimension of religion but rather a method employed by some religious communities to respond to religious diversity and conflict. Of course, this does not make doctrines any less a religious phenomenon, but it underlines that there are other religious interests and that those interests, though slighted in traditional philosophy of religion, may be more central to religions globally.

11. These quotes can be found in Covington (1995: 167, 168).

Chapter 2

Are Religious Practices Philosophical?

i. Toward a Philosophy of Religious Practice

In the opening chapter, I argued that philosophers of religion should take as the object of their study not only the religious philosophies that have been the traditional object in the discipline but also the diversity of religious rituals, ceremonies, sacrifices, pilgrimages, and disciplinary and contemplative regimens. In my geometrical metaphor, I suggested that the future of philosophy of religion should grow not only to include the doctrines and arguments of all the religions of the world (so to speak, along the first axis) but also to include all the performed aspects of those religions (so to speak, along a second axis). In short, philosophy of religion should include the philosophical study of religious practices.

It would be unfair to say that traditional philosophers of religion have ignored the fact that religions are not merely sets of beliefs but are also forms of life, with all the affective, social, and historical implications thereof. Philosophers of religion in general have known that religious beliefs are not simply propositions entertained in the head but arise and draw their sense from particular religious communities, their practices, and their institutions. The belief in God, to take the traditional theistic example, informs acts of worship, prayer, and spiritual disciplines, it motivates acts of charity and acts of war, and it has shifted and evolved from one culture or historical period

Philosophy and the Study of Religions: A Manifesto, First Edition. Kevin Schilbrack.
© 2014 Kevin Schilbrack. Published 2014 by John Wiley & Sons, Ltd.

to another. Most philosophers of religion have not forgotten the social and historical matrix in which religious beliefs find their home.

Nevertheless, the philosophical study of religious practices is a relatively unexplored field. The traditional division of labor in the academic study of religions seems to have followed a tacit rule that the discipline of philosophy of religion studies religious *beliefs* (the mental) and the social scientific disciplines study religious *practices* (the bodily), reflecting an implicit but pervasive mind–body dualism. This dualism has been critiqued from numerous postmodern perspectives, however, and we now have the intellectual tools to replace it with a more adequate understanding of the ways in which minds and bodies, practices and beliefs, weave together. Moreover, the mind–body division supports a view that religious practices lack the properties found in cognitive activities and are simply mechanical or thoughtless. As a consequence, most philosophers of religion leave religious practices for others to study on the assumption that the practices themselves are not philosophical. In this chapter, I want to undermine this assumption and to contribute to the nascent conversation between philosophers and others who study religious practices.

But what would a philosophy of religious practice (or of lived religion or of ritual embodiment) look like? How might religious practices be of interest—specifically—to philosophers? And how might the traditional division of labor be shifted so that philosophers of religion can engage the performed aspects of religions practices in a way that is in conversation with and yet distinct from other disciplines? To be sure, some philosophers of religion have been interested in the body. But I don't think that religious practices will attract wide interest among philosophers unless the practices can be seen as cognitive, that is, unless they can be seen not only as ways to communicate, teach, or inculcate the claims that a religious community wants to make but as sites of inquiry, exploration, and creativity in their own right. Anthropologists have long objected to the assumption that rituals are thoughtless (and have pointed out that this assumption reflects the Protestant background of the study of rituals generally), but how to speak of religious practices as philosophical is not yet clear. In this chapter, I make three suggestions about how philosophers of religion can address this issue. These suggestions are not the only way in which religious practices can be studied by philosophers, but they are ways that permit scholars to see such practices not merely as symbolizing but as exploring and inquiring, which is to say, as cognitive activities.

My first recommendation is that philosophers of religion adopt what the anthropologist of religion Thomas Csordas has called a paradigm of embodiment, that is, a methodological perspective that takes the body as not solely as a passive object but as the condition for both subjectivity and intersubjectivity. I then recommend two theoretical tools for philosophers interested in religious practice: a theory of conceptual metaphor according to which one's ability to reason develops out of one's bodily engagement with the physical world, and a theory of cognitive prosthetics according to which the mind is "scaffolded" in the sense that human beings off-load cognitive work onto their physical and cultural environments. The next three sections of this chapter put these three proposals on the table—the embodiment paradigm, the theory of conceptual metaphor, and the theory of cognitive prosthetics—and the final section then shows how the three proposals fit together to contribute to a philosophy of religion practice.

ii. Embodiment as a Paradigm for Philosophy of Religion

In their traditional focus on doctrines and arguments, philosophers of religions have focused almost exclusively on the study of texts. They have focused, in other words, on explicit written statements made by sages and theologians, seers and teachers—the representative intellectuals of religious communities. This focus on texts has in fact characterized the academic study of religion in general for most of its history. When the study of religion began as an academic field, about 150 years ago, it was dominated by the translation and the interpretation of books. The reasons are not surprising. On the one (conceptual) hand, the focus was the result of Christian assumptions that scripture was essential to the nature of religion and, on the other (physical) hand, the *Sacred Books of the East* are easier to transport to the classroom than, say, the 12-day Agni fire ritual. In the years since, and especially in the past two generations, there has been a shift of focus from the study of religious texts to the study of religious practices.

As scholars of religion turned to study practices, however, they have often understood the practices as *like* texts: the practices "said" something, and those who knew what the symbolic gestures stood for could "read" them. This semiotic paradigm opened up the study of practices to hermeneutics and the study of culture to discourse analysis. But as Thomas Csordas nicely puts it, textuality is a "hungry metaphor," crowding out the study of

33

embodied experiences and "swallowing all of culture to the point where it becomes possible and even convincing to hear the deconstructionist motto that there is nothing outside the text" (1999:146). Csordas therefore recommends that those who study culture should complement the semiotic paradigm with what he calls an embodiment paradigm. From this perspective, the body is not simply a passive object on which cultures write their variable meanings, but is also that source from which one engages the world. Here the body is the very condition of subjectivity and the prereflective ground of self and culture.

The philosophical roots of the embodiment paradigm are in existential phenomenology, a philosophical approach that distinguishes between reflective and pre-reflective modes of experience. In the pre-reflective mode, one finds oneself invested in a situation—say, climbing a hill or cooking a meal—and the body is the ground from which one perceives and acts in the world. The body is not originally an object in one's awareness but the means though which the world becomes present and one's projects become possible. It is only in the reflective mode that the world is constituted in terms of objects, including one's own body as another "thing" among the rest. On this approach, then, one's body is not in the first place simply raw material on which culture operates or writes upon as a text or a sign but rather the seat of one's active being in the world.

As Csordas develops the embodiment paradigm, he combines the phenomenology of perception developed by Maurice Merleau-Ponty with the analysis by Pierre Bourdieu of the role of social practices in shaping one's embodied habits. Csordas notes, "For Merleau-Ponty, perception begins in the body and, through reflective thinking, ends in objects. On the level of perception, there is not yet a subject-object distinction—we are simply in the world."[1] Merleau-Ponty recognized that the pre-objective act of perception was always embedded in a cultural world (so "pre-objective" does not mean "pre-cultural"), but he did not develop an account of how perception is shaped by culture. Csordas therefore turns at this point to Bourdieu's analysis of the socially informed body. Csordas joins Bourdieu's understanding of the "habitus" as an unselfconscious orchestration of practices, grounded in collective life, with Merleau-Ponty's notion of pre-objective perception in such a way as to clarify how the embodied subject's pre-reflective experience of the world is shaped by culturally various styles of moving and attending to the world. In this way, the embodiment paradigm is relevant not only to the analysis of an individual's I-it or I-Thou relations but also to the lives of social collectivities. Csordas calls this approach "cultural phenomenology."

The embodiment paradigm therefore lets scholars complement the idea of culture as text, discourse, and representation with the idea of culture as a mode of being in the world.

As I see it, the embodiment paradigm has both negative and positive uses for the philosophical study of religious practices. The negative value of the embodiment paradigm is that it gives us a vocabulary for critiquing those approaches to the study of religious practices that assume that they are thoughtless. Many scholars in the academic study of religions take it for granted that religious practices are more characterized by indoctrination, rote learning, or authoritarianism than other kinds of practices. It is not unusual to see religious practices described as inculcating certain ideas and shaping participants as if the practitioners are in thrall. Most of the studies of ritual inspired by Michel Foucault, for example, treat the body as a blank text on which one's culture inscribes, the body as merely an effect of discourse. Perhaps it is the influence of Protestant opposition to Catholic sacraments and "works righteousness" or perhaps secularist opposition to superstition that leads scholars of religion to take embodied religious practices as unthinking, and this leads to the assumption that such practices do not involve the kinds of cognitive activity that deserve philosophical attention. The embodiment paradigm is then not a specifically philosophical tool but rather a general outlook that can be shared by those in any discipline who seek an alternative to the approaches that treat the body as solely passive.

The positive value of the embodiment paradigm is that it lets us see religious practices not only as the means with which a religious community inscribes religious bodies with certain values (treating the body as a passive text) but also the means with which the practitioners themselves can investigate the world (with the embodied subject as an active inquirer). With this view, the activities of religious communities—the ethical, political, and ritual practices described in the previous chapter—may appear as examples of active engagement in the world in which participants gain *knowledge-how*, or even as opportunities for cognitive inquiry in which participants gain *knowledge-that*. Such practices can be seen as opportunities for religious practitioners to investigate the nature of self, other, and environment (a topic to which I return in the next two sections of this chapter).

Adopting the embodiment paradigm does not replace or undermine the philosophical study of texts. Texts have a representationalist function—that is, they can make and justify claims about what exists—in a way that practices cannot. But the embodiment paradigm complements the study of texts

35

because it focuses on the ways in which perception is shaped by religious culture and so it can illuminate the ways in which religious objects are constituted for reflection. It thereby approaches the philosophical study of religious subjectivity and intersubjectivity in a manner that opens questions relevant to and in conversation with the anthropological and other approaches to the study of religious practice. This idea of embodiment has not yet had much an influence on philosophy of religion. But philosophy of religion is especially well suited to contribute to the study of embodied practice since religious practices often provide powerful paths that cultivate modes of inhabiting the world. This permits philosophers of religion to speak of ritual experience, ritual worlds, or even ritual metaphysics.[2] In both its negative value as a critique of the limits of the semiotic paradigm and its positive value as a productive approach to experiential aspect of religious practices, therefore, the embodiment paradigm can serve as a bridge that puts philosophy of religion in conversation with the interpretive and explanatory approaches in the academic study of religions, insofar as they take embodied subjectivity seriously.

iii. Conceptual Metaphors and Embodied Religious Reason

The embodiment paradigm is a general methodological perspective in which the body is the pre-reflective seat of subjectivity. If one accepts this perspective, how then does one come to see religious practices in particular as thoughtful? Toward this end, I recommend two theoretical tools, the first of which is the theory of conceptual metaphors.

According to this theory, human abilities to reason are prefigured in and develop out of structures of our embodied activities, such as perception, manipulation of objects, bodily spatial orientation, and movement of our bodies through our environments. These kinds of sensorimotor activities begin at birth (or even before birth), and they are the means by which even the tiniest newborn begins to develop structures of understanding and a sense of self. As the child engages in manipulation of objects and movement of his body—pulling his hand to his mouth, watching the ball roll from where it starts to where it stops, putting a ball into a box—the child begins to learn what we might call the spatial logic of the world. The child learns the spatial logic of LINEARITY: if something moves along the path to that end point, it reaches the end point, but if it moves along another path, it reaches a different end. The child learns the spatial logic of CONTAINMENT: if the balls are in the box, then they are not outside the box. These are examples of how

36

objects behave, and the child also first learns about herself in an embodied way. She learns the spatial logic of BALANCE: if she leans too far from her center of gravity, she falls. She learns the spatial logic of VERTICALITY: when she stands upright, she can see further. In all of these cases, the basic unit of meaning is an "image schema" (written in small caps) of how the world works or responds to action in it. It is worth underlining that these image schemas are unreflective and nonpropositional. Even before one learns a language, therefore, one has inculcated such patterns or structures of embodied experience, and they are learned—necessarily—though physical movement and interaction with one's environment.

When people come to think about more abstract aspects of life, they can recruit these basic units of meaning, these patterns that characterize one's bodily movements and interactions, to structure more abstract concepts metaphorically. Because one has put objects together into the same container, such as the toy box, one can imagine *categories as containers*: one can ask whether tomatoes are "in" the fruit category or "in" the vegetable category. Because we reach end points in our movements when we achieve our purposes, such as when we reach the doorway to leave the house, one can imagine *purposes as destinations*: we speak of getting "closer" to the goal, making "progress," or getting "sidetracked" even when reaching the goal involves no physical movement. Because when one is intimate with someone else, one is physically close to that person, one can conceive of *intimacy as closeness*: we speak of those who are our "close" friends even when they are not physically close, or we speak of friends "drifting apart," even when this is not literally the case. In short, when thinking about general qualities or characteristics, we build metaphors that draw on the spatial logic of our most basic patterns of experience, thereby projecting characteristics that we have learned in the sensorimotor domain of our life to the conceptual domain. Eventually these metaphors can be put into language and such conceptual metaphors permeate not only poetry but everyday speech. And even before they are spoken aloud, these metaphors shape the ways that people think about and relate to friends and enemies, purposes and obstacles, and categories and objects. In this way, reason is dependent upon our embodied engagement in the world and would not be possible without it. "Reason" is therefore a name not for a property that exists independent of embodiment, but rather the name for an emerging and developing capacity, a capacity that emerges through one's physical interaction with one's environment.

It is worth underlining that since image schemas are templates for engagement with the world, they are not static but carry expectations and entailments. Even the perception and conceptualization of objects are typically tied to plans for action. The logic of LINEARITY, mentioned above, for instance, enables one to think, "If I want to catch the ball, I should move in this direction, at this speed," etc. Accepting the validity of a conceptual metaphor then commits the listener to a certain course of action and, therefore, thinking in terms of such dynamic schemas tends to be value-laden and affect-rich. For example, if one thinks in terms of the metaphor that *purposes are destinations* and one judges that one's nation is *headed in the wrong direction*, then one is likely to agree that we should return to our original principles, that those who lead us in this direction betray those principles, and that social change is desirable. As Edward Slingerland puts it, thinking in terms of such metaphorical patterns gives rise to normativity-bestowing emotional reactions and this is why metaphors are arguably the primary tool of religious, political, and moral discourse.[3]

What contribution can this idea of conceptual metaphors make to the philosophical study of religious practices? Conceptual metaphor theory proposes that people appropriate the structured patterns that they learn in sensorimotor activity (the "source" domain) to conceptualize and reason about other, relatively unstructured aspect of life (the "target" domain). For example, from the concrete bodily activities of moving along a path to a destination one takes the SOURCE-PATH-GOAL pattern and uses it to structure how one thinks about some abstraction about which one wants to think, such as one's progress in one's career. I would argue, then, that this theory has two benefits for the philosophical study of religious practices, insofar as religious practices straddle both the source and the target domains. That is, first, insofar as religious practices are physical activities, they can serve as the concrete "source" experiences on which religious thought can then draw. Practices like lighting candles in which illumination spreads can provide the source experiences that then fund and structure religious teachings about insight, discernment, or enlightenment. Practices like prostration in which one makes oneself smaller and lower provide the source experiences that fund and structure religious teachings about humility, submission, and sovereignty. Practices like fasting in which one denies one's biological cravings inform religious teachings about desire, discipline, and self-sacrifice. And so on. In these ways, one can see that religious teachings about the purpose of life or the nature of true virtue or about the source of existence—teachings of the greatest abstraction—are inevitably grounded in and draw their sense from the patterns learned in embodied religious practices. Participating in such practices with an understanding of the teachings of a religious community can then "feel right," giving participants the sense that the experiences one has in the practice confirm the teachings.

The second benefit of conceptual metaphor theory is that it gives philosophers of religion the tools to see that insofar as a religious practice houses metaphors about a "target" domain—that is, the practice is designed to draw attention to some general feature of life—then participating in the practice is itself an exercise in abstract thought. Religious practices can thereby harness bodily experiences of up and down, darkness and light, strength and weakness to develop metaphors for thinking about abstract concepts. In this respect, the physical activities of a religious practice are not simply raw material for later reflection, activities that wait on thinking done elsewhere. Nor are they merely the expression of a myth or a text or theorizing done previously. Religious practices themselves can be examples of (and not simply the products of) imaginative, creative thought. The philosopher interested in religious practices can therefore look to see: what metaphors does the practice teach? Does it draw on and assimilate the experience of being physically upright and balanced to the spiritual goal of being morally upright and balanced? Does it draw on the experience of being in the dark to being ignorant or sinful? In this way, one can see that no matter how abstract are the topics of religious philosophy—topics such as guilt, duty, God, karma, attachment, or other "spiritual" themes—religious thought may be prefigured in and may draw on the interactive structures of movement and manipulation found in religious practices.

Let me illustrate this important point. Conceptual metaphor theory distinguishes between the physical experiences that generate patterns of understanding and the conceptual metaphors that deploy those patterns in order to reason about the world. I am saying that structured religious activities participate in both, so that they can not only provide the patterns of experience on which religious teachings draw but can also deploy those patterns to develop and to teach one way of life or another. Take mortality as an example of a target domain. Religious communities practice rituals that frame this feature of human existence according to different metaphors. A given funeral ritual might frame the experience of death as if it is a departure for a journey. This conceptualization would be conveyed by how the body is handled, what is buried with it, and the physical markers that are used. If one sees death as a departure for a journey, then ritual participants will think of the deceased as a kind of traveler, they will feel that he needs to be equipped with the accessories needed for the journey, and the question of his final destination will become central. A different funeral ritual might teach that death is a

39

release from pain and bondage, and this metaphor will entail a different set of activities. Another might teach that death is going to a permanent sleep, another that death is a return to one's proper home, or another that death it is simply the end of life and that nothing comes after. The point is that—even apart from any theological commentaries—the gestures, architecture, implements, and words of the practice itself can teach metaphorical frames that shape the affective and cognitive responses to the phenomenon. In this light, one can see religious practices as both the raw experiential material for thinking done elsewhere and as modes of thinking in their own right. In fact, it seems plausible that the metaphorical thinking embodied in practices like funerals would typically antedate and shape any reflective account of the nature of souls, other worlds, or what determines one's final end.

iv. Religious Material Culture as Cognitive Prosthetics

The second theoretical tool I recommend for developing a philosophy of religious practice is the idea that the material aspects of religious rituals—the implements, the art, the offerings, the incense, the buildings themselves—can serve as what we might call cognitive prosthetics or scaffolds. I borrow this idea of "cognitive prosthetics" or "scaffolded minds" or "extended cognition" from embodied cognitive scientists who observe that, when people are solving cognitive problems, they often "lean on the environment" and off-load their thinking processes onto physical and cultural implements in the world. People exploit external structures in their environment or they create aids that reduce the computational load on their brains and help them remember, process information, and solve cognitive problems.

This idea of off-loading cognition onto physical media refers to a common occurrence. A few examples should make the idea clear. First, imagine that someone runs out of, say, milk, and to remind himself to buy more, he puts the empty milk carton on the counter by the front door. The carton serves as a reminder, a memory pump. Landmarks perform a similar operation marking other kinds of memory. Bookmarks serve to mark another.

A second example involves more interaction between the problem-solving person and the physical world. Take the process of multiplying numbers. Most adults can solve simple multiplication problems like 7×4, as we say, "in our heads." But calculating larger sums is harder. When we need, for instance, to multiply four digit numbers, like 7262×9428, most of us turn to paper and pencil. We can then break down the complicated problem into a sequence of simpler problems, beginning with the units digits. We use the pencil to store the partial and provisional answers on the paper until we are able to complete all the steps and arrive at a final answer. In examples like this, the thinking process "leaks" out of the head and onto the extra-cranial environment and the physical aids become an extension of one's cognitive abilities. In fact, in interactive cases like this one, the physical prosthetics often become an extension of one's abilities to the extent that one cannot solve the problem without them.

A third example involves not only looking to one's environment for help with memory or with the provisional steps in problem solving, but also manipulating the external tools themselves. As an example, consider the way that players operate in the game of Scrabble. In Scrabble, as in many games and other intellectual puzzles, one's ability to reach a solution does not emerge solely from inner cogitation. Instead, one arranges and rearranges the Scrabble tiles in order to create a variety of fragmentary inputs that will prompt the recall of whole words from one's ability to see and complete patterns. There is a sustained and iterated process of interactions between one's brain and the external physical props. In sum, then, the three examples of cognitive prosthetics illustrate an increasingly dynamic, active engagement with one's environment. The example of the milk carton illustrates how regularly and casually people use physical objects to spur a single thought. The example of doing math problems on paper illustrates the back-and-forth interaction that is sometimes needed to use one's cognitive prosthetics and how difficult or impossible it would be to find the right answer without them. And the example of the Scrabble pieces illustrates how thinking may use cognitive prosthetics not solely as an aid to memory, but in some cases involves their manipulation to find the best solution, a solution that does not merely help one recall what one already knows but rather fits one's situation best. Thus, when one finds the best arrangement in games like Scrabble, one does not say: "Ah, now I remember," but rather: "Ah, there you go."

The cognitive scientists who have developed this idea of extended cognition do not claim that *all* thinking involves one's environment: remembering what one ate this morning is not typically an intellectual process that requires the use of physical prosthetics. Nevertheless, the use of extra-cranial mind tools is ubiquitous. Drawing maps or diagrams lets one represent and streamline one's plans. Clocks and calendars can be seen as prosthetics that help one solve problems that require keeping track of duration or synchronizing activities. Slide rules can be seen as tools that help one solve problems of fit. Knots used for record-keeping, the abacus, Post-it notes, calculators, and computers all extend mental faculties. In fact, the emergence of language itself can be seen as the product of developing extra-cranial problem-solving tools. Speaking one's views and goals publicly not only allows one to communicate them to others but also to make one's views and goals available for inspection, evaluation, and improvement. In light of this kind of linguistic interaction, some scholars point out that cognition can be socially distributed in that *other human beings* can also serve as one's cognitive prosthetics. Think of one member of a couple who relies on the other to remember the names of acquaintances; or the ship or airplane that is piloted by a crew that divides the navigational problems. In this vein, one can also see institutions (say, the judicial system) as socially distributed problem-solving devices stretched out over time. In the judicial system, for instance, the cognitive work required to distinguish different kinds of criminal activity and appropriate levels of punishment, the kinds of admissible evidence and the procedures for adjudicating a case, not to mention the actual determination in a given case, are distributed among judges and juries and lawyers and law schools. The individual juror who is asked to come to a decision, then, is part of a larger cognitive system. Most of the cognitive work is not done by the individual.

These examples of cognitive prosthetics illustrate how in some cases the process of cognition is extended into the physical, linguistic, and social environments and would not be possible without using the external aids. But there is a live debate about what such examples imply. On the one hand, there are those who say that such external aids should be seen simply as the mind's tools. "Just as you cannot do much carpentry with your bare hands, there is not much thinking you can do with your bare brain."[4] The cognitive work is not possible without the tools and therefore cognitive prosthetics play an essential role in what we are able to think. On this view, we should not see the mind as an internal, immaterial thinking substance but rather as the subject's embodiment and embeddedness in the world. This interpretation inherits from the existentialist and phenomenological traditions (introduced above in the discussion of the embodiment paradigm) that argue against Cartesian mind–body dualism and for the thinking subject as originally engaged in the world. Call this the *embedded mind* hypothesis.

On the other hand, a more controversial interpretation is that the cognitive prosthetics ought to lead us to redefine what is meant by the mind. Call this the *extended mind* hypothesis. The extended mind hypothesis is that mental states (such as believing) can be realized, in part, by structures outside the human head. The most debated example is the fictional case of "Otto," a man who suffers from a mild form of Alzheimer's and who therefore writes down in a notebook the information that he thinks that he may need. When he wants to go to the museum, for example, he consults the external note-book for the address just as if it is his internal memory. The question here is whether we should define the mind functionally as a coupled system that includes both the biological person and the nonbiological prosthetic. Those who say Yes make the following argument: if all the components play an active causal role, jointly governing behavior, so that if one were to remove the external component, the person's behavior would drop just as if one removed part of her brain, then we should see cognition as constituted in part by that external component in the organism's environment. Philoso-phers Andy Clark and David Chalmers propose what they call the Parity Principle which states that "if, as we confront some task, a part of the world functions as a process which, were it to go on in the head, we would have no hesitation in accepting as part of the cognitive process, then that part of the world is (for that time) part of the cognitive process."[5]

When we see the mind as embedded in the physical world, we see cog-nitive prosthetics as tools of the mind, but not part of the mind. When we see the mind as extended into the world, we take the boundaries between mind, body, and world as permeable and evolving, and what counts as the mind is seen as open to transformative restructuring by incorporating new cognitive equipment. On the embedded mind hypothesis, the physical tools of thinking are enabling conditions for cognitive work. On the extended mind hypothesis, they are constitutive conditions.

Where to draw the boundaries between the thinking person and her pros-thetics is a fascinating question.[6] But the important point for a philosophy of religious practice is that, whether one sees the thinker as extended into and part of the ritual environment or merely as embedded in but still distinct from the ritual environment, attention to cognitive prosthetics in religious contexts opens a path for the study of religious practice as a cognitive enter-prise. On this approach, one can see the religious participants' interaction with the implements and environment of a ritual not as thoughtless and not as merely expressions of thought done elsewhere, but rather as the enabling or constitutive parts of a cognitive process.

This idea of extended cognition has not yet played a significant role in religious studies, but the role that it can play will turn on what one judges that religious people think *about*. There are those who define religion as interaction with beings that are not available to the senses. Let's start with that "animist" definition. If religious cognition is about invisible beings, then icons, statues, and others aspects of the ritual material environment can be seen to help religious practitioners visualize such beings, to discriminate between them, and to track one's interactions with them. In those religious practices that involve treating spiritual beings as if they are guests or rulers who are physically present, for example, the ritual implements transform the cognitive work of religion from "off-line" imagination to "on-line" perception.[7]

My own sense, however, is that religious cognition is not limited to inter-acting with invisible beings, and so the religious use of cognitive prosthetics goes beyond simply helping participants visualize them. Religious practices promise a wide variety of benefits to those who participate in them. In some cases, the benefits of the practice are concrete—like recovery from an illness, finding love, or being successful in an endeavor. In other cases, the bene-fits are less concrete—the community may hold that participating in their practices is the way for one to learn propriety or to become an adult. And even less concretely, some religious practices are said to lead to liberation or salvation. It may be that, like work, such religious practices pursue an end outside themselves or it may be that, like play, they are done as an end in themselves. But on either interpretation, they can be seen as opportuni-ties for cognition about health, love, duty, maturity, sovereignty, purpose, or—at the most abstract—the nature of human existence.

I do not want to exaggerate the idea that religious practices are a source of novel thinking. Many religious practices are repetitious or routine. And there is no doubt that the practitioners are often passive in the face of tra-ditions, authority, and training. Nevertheless, the practices can still serve as opportunities for inquiry. Here is a nonreligious example that can serve as an analogy: think of two people involved in a social practice like cutting a tree down with a two-person saw. What one learns in the activity of such a practice might be distinguished into three topics. First, one learns about oneself: how physically strong am I? How much perseverance do I have? Second, one learns about those with whom one works: is this other person co-operative? Lazy? A quick learner? And third, one learns about the world: is the wood of this tree harder than that one? Is the blade getting dull? Even when a practice does not explicitly aim to answer such questions, it is hard to imagine how one could engage in the practice without learning these answers. The questions are answered by the practice itself, and in this respect we can see that no matter how little the context of cutting wood resembles that of a laboratory, the practice need not simply be mechanical or thoughtless but can also provide an opportunity for inquiry.

I recommend that philosophers of religion take the same interpretive approach to religious practices and see them as social practices that cannot fail to involve learning and exploration. The questions that get answered are analogous to the tree-cutting example. Some of the things that one learns by participating in ritual will be about oneself. When I engage in this practice, what about me is changed? My original desires? My will? My habits? What in me resists this change and needs to be surrendered? Some of the things one learns will be about those with whom one interacts: who among us is unreliable? Who among us can serve as a role model? And some of the things one learns will be about the world as the context of one's action: about storms and diseases and about food and music—and ultimately practices can serve as opportunities for inquiry about the superempirical resources that make the practice successful. It is this last element that distinguishes religious practices from nonreligious ones. What superempirical reality sustains the practice or makes it effective? The point of this analogy is not that religious communities might come to ask these questions, so to speak, afterward, explicitly reflecting on practices that they have done, though of course they might. The point is rather that the practices themselves can provide the cognitive prosthetics that let practitioners explore these questions. My hypothesis, then, is that religious practices can serve as occasions of thoughtful inquiry when they provide the physically, linguistically, and socially extended cognition that enables participants to ask and answer questions about the features of and the conditions for their normative paths.

If this analogy is sound, then we can say that religious practices do facilitate cognition about invisible beings. But they also deal with other cognitive problems. For instance, initiation rituals teach participants about adulthood, responsibility, and gender. Pilgrimages teach participants about land, memory, and persistence. Funerals teach participants about the physical body, detachment, and mortality. Other rituals may treat health, pleasure, and reward; still others, dignity, shame, and privacy. There is not one problem that is "the" religious problem. Nevertheless, following the tree-cutting analogy above, one can see religious practices as giving participants the opportunity to work on and to inquire into self, other, and world. The inquiry into how one should understand oneself rightly is in service to the cultivation of integrity. The inquiry into how one should understand community rightly is in service to the cultivation of justice. And the inquiry into how one should understand reality rightly is in service to the truth. My hypothesis, then, is that religious practices can provide the physically, linguistically, and socially extended cognition that enables participants to explore such normative questions.

I want to return now to the question of cognitive prosthetics, and ask: how might ritual implements help one think?

The contribution of some ritual prosthetics is relatively simple, helping prompt one's memory, analogous to the milk bottle example above. Prayer beads, for example, help one to keep track of one's progress in a cycle of prayers, and circumcision serves as a sign of the covenant between Yahweh and the descendants of Abraham. But other religious practices involve more interaction between the practitioner and the ritual environment, analogous to solving the math problem with pen and paper or to moving around the Scrabble tiles. As illustrations of a way in which participants might interact cognitively with their ritual environment, consider these two examples. The first is the Stations of the Cross, fourteen images that depict for contemplation and devotion the events in the crucifixion and burial of Jesus. Here is a treatment for children of the fifth station (picked at random) in which Jesus is helped by Simon the Cyrene.

Fifth Station: Look at Jesus
Jesus is so tired that the soldiers know he cannot carry the heavy cross by himself. So they look around and see someone who looks strong enough to help Jesus carry this cross. This person's name is Simon.

Jesus just looks at Simon and quietly whispers, "Thank you" to Simon. Then they continue on the long road, carrying the cross together.

Look at Your Heart
Sometimes helping someone can be difficult, for so many different reasons. Maybe you haven't finished something that you like to do, when someone asks you for help. Or maybe you just don't feel like helping that person.

Can you think of a time when you were asked to help someone and did not want to help? Show Jesus what it was like when that happened, and picture Jesus loving you as you show him your heart. Maybe you can even hear Jesus whisper, "Thank you for helping." When you are ready, you can ask Jesus to help you to have a helping heart.[8]

The second example is a mural that stretches along a wall depicting scene from the Ramayana, the epic story of Vishnu's incarnation as Lord Rama, his virtuous wife Sita, and their struggles and eventual victory over evil rak-shasas. The tableaux show tests of virtue, heartbreaking exile, loyal family and friends, and manly leadership and martial skill. In the serial pictures, Rama sacrifices his personal desires to the wishes of his father and to the public good. Sita submits to the challenge of her faithfulness. Lakshmana epitomizes the loyal younger brother and Hanuman the devoted servant who has Rama and Sita, literally, in his heart.

To say that the depicted scenes from the Ramayana and the Gospels help the ritual participant to imagine invisible beings is not false. But the scenes are also fragments of larger stories that exemplify and are intended to help one inculcate ideal behavior. These ritual devices therefore use a series of images as memory pumps to remind participants of their dramatic narra-tive contexts. But exactly which images are those with which one should identify, which ideal action should be emulated, and how that action could be interpreted to fit one's own life are left to the practitioner. Ritual par-ticipants contemplate the images of the Gospel or of the Ramayana and it requires work to correlate them to one's own tests, sacrifices, obligations, and loyalties. And, like the tiles in the Scrabble game, there may be a best answer about which scene is most fitting to one's life, or what interpretation of that scene to draw, but a fair amount of freedom is necessarily left to the ritual participants regarding how to apply the norms represented in images to their own situations. In fact, to render proper behavior visible in this interactive way is also to court multiple interpretations and disagreement. But the point is that the physical representations can be seen as cognitive to the extent that, like the game tiles, they provide fragmentary prompts that are meant to engage participants to think in a certain way about them-selves, others, and the world of which they are a part. From the perspective I am proposing, the ritual environment provides the conditions for making progress on the normative problem as the paper and pencil do for solving the math problems, and religious rituals can be seen as an opportunity for inquiry that merits attention from philosophers of religion.

v. A Toolkit for the Philosophical Study of
Religious Practices

This chapter has run quickly through three proposals for the philosophical study of religious practices. I proposed, first, that philosophers of religion adopt the embodiment paradigm according to which the religious body is

47

not simply a biological or material object "inscribed" by culture but also the pre-reflective condition of perception and engagement with the world. I proposed, second, that philosophers of religion investigate whether religious practices are examples of embodied reasoning in that they both draw on pre-linguistic image schemas and also use them to develop conceptual metaphors that frame how participants conceptualize abstract features of their lives. And I prosed, third, that philosophers of religion investigate whether the material culture of religious practices serve as cognitive prosthetics with which practitioners solve intellectual problems. My hope in each case is that these theoretical approaches gives philosophers of religion tools with which to see religious practices as having a cognitive function. But in closing this chapter, it is worth noting how well the three approaches complement each other.

Conceptual metaphor theory has already been used to study religious texts. In the study of religious texts, the question is: on what embodied experiences does the religious text draw? Asking this question connects an instance of religious language (in all its specificity) to basic conceptual metaphors (which are shared much more broadly) and then connects these metaphors to the physical movements and experiences that generated them. For instance, the text of *Journey to the West* describes the allegorical quest of a Buddhist pilgrim and his piggish and monkeyish companions as they overcome hazards on a journey from India to China to secure Buddhist scriptures. A particular text like this draws on the metaphor that *life is a journey*, a metaphor that informs multiple religious texts in many religious traditions, a metaphor which in turn draws on the SOURCE-PATH-GOAL pattern that is typically learned even before a person can speak.[9]

By digging down in this way from texts to metaphors and then from metaphors to widely shared embodied experiences, the conceptual metaphor approach provides a means for cross-cultural understanding and comparison. In fact, this "embodied realism" provides an alternative both to a naïve realism in which there is one objective description of reality that is right, independent of observers, and to a post-modern antirealism in which all ideas are social constructions, and there is no way the world is. Conceiving of people as biological material organisms, navigating through a shared environment, embodied realism provides grounds for assuming that different cultures will have much in common.[10]

However, conceptual metaphor theory has two shortcomings. The first is that, by showing how different ways of conceiving the world share common metaphors, and how those metaphors arise in universal or near-universal patterns of embodied activity, conceptual metaphor theory tends to explain different cultures in terms of common or shared experiences. Conceptual metaphor theory has relatively less to say about cultural particularities in their specificity. Happily, however, precisely this is the contribution of a theory of cognitive prosthetics. That is, the theory of cognitive prosthetics considers the environmental and cultural scaffolds in terms of whatever local cognitive problem the practitioner is trying to solve (such as remembering their shopping, multiplying numbers, or winning a game of Scrabble). The two theoretical tools can thus complement each other by focusing on two different aspects—the general and the particular—of any given practice.

The second shortcoming is this. The conceptual metaphor theory illustrates how embodied activities are harnessed by the mind in order to create metaphors with which one can conceptualize abstract features of the world. But this approach treats embodied practices as raw material for thinking, but not as thinking themselves. As Csordas has said, conceptual metaphor may show "the body in the mind" (to use the title of Mark Johnson's book), but they do not show how the bodily activities themselves are thoughtful or inquiring; they do not show "the mind in the body." But precisely here, the embodiment paradigm can help. The embodiment paradigm holds that the physical activities are not only resources for a mind's or a culture's symbolizing but also exploratory, inquiring, investigative. As Csordas puts it, "to embrace the paradigm of embodiment as a move from representation to being-in-the-world would be to endorse a further step in the progression from 'culture from the neck up' to 'the body in the mind,' moving finally to recognition of 'the mind in the body.'"[11]

I therefore judge that these three ideas support each other, balancing each other's weaknesses, and together provide a promising three-pronged tool for those scholars of religion who want to study religious practices as thoughtful.

Bibliographic Essay

In this chapter, I recommend three theoretical tools that can help philosophers—and perhaps scholars of religion in general—to move away from a Cartesian assumption that embodied religious practices are mechanical or thoughtless and toward a view that such practices can be opportunities for cognitive inquiry. The three tools I recommend are the embodiment paradigm, the theory of conceptual metaphor, and the theory of cognitive prosthetics. Thomas Csordas introduced the idea of an embodiment

49

paradigm in Csordas (1990), and elaborated it in 1993 and 1994. I describe this paradigm as a synthesis of Maurice Merleau-Ponty's phenomenology of perception (esp. Merleau-Ponty 1962) and Pierre Bourdieu's analysis of social practice (esp. Bourdieu 1990). For the methodological approach that Csordas calls "cultural phenomenology" (which I also mention in Ch. 7), see Csordas (2011) or, even better, Csordas (1999).

The second tool I recommend is the idea of conceptual metaphor. George Lakoff and Mark Johnson introduced this idea and demonstrated the ubiquity of metaphor even in everyday thought in Lakoff and Johnson (1980) and showed its philosophical relevance to the position they call "embodied realism" in Lakoff and Johnson (1999). Lakoff and Turner (1989) show the role of metaphor in poetry and give an extended treatment of poetic metaphors for conceptualizing life as a journey (Ch. 1). Mark Johnson (1987, 1999, 2007) provides a clear account of the philosophical relevance of conceptual metaphor, including the contribution of imagination and emotion to cognition. Ted Slingerland applies this idea conceptual metaphor to understanding religious ideas of classical China in Slingerland (2003), he recommends it as a tool for comparative religious studies (Slingerland 2004), and he provides the best critical discussion I know of this theory and its value as a bridge between the humanities and the sciences (Slingerland 2008: esp. Ch. 4).

The third tool I recommend is that of cognitive prosthetics or scaffolding. The primary philosopher writing on the topic of extended mind has been Andy Clark (1997, 2003, 2008), and I borrow from him the examples of the bottle left as a shopping reminder (1997: 201), that of solving math problems with pencil and paper (1997: 60–1; cf. 2003: 1991), and that of the manipulation of Scrabble tiles (1997: 64). For good discussions of language as a cognitive prosthetic, see Dennett (1996: Ch. 5) and Clark (1997: Ch. 10). The examples of socially distributed cognition in the piloting of a ship or a plane come from Hutchins 1995a and 1995b, respectively. For an excellent discussion of the role of embodied social action in cultural memory, see Connerton (1989).

The extended mind hypothesis, introduced by Clark and David Chalmers (1998), has generated an enormous amount of discussion in cognitive science and philosophy of mind (see Clark 2008, 2010, and Menary 2010). For a discussion of socially extended cognition that will be of relevance to the study of religious institutions, see Gallagher (2013). Few scholars have applied the idea of extended mind to the study of religion, and even fewer to religious ritual, but see Matthew Day (2004, 2005) and the special issue of

Zygon: Journal of Religion and Science on "The Extended Mind and Religious Thought" (September 2009).

Endnotes

1. See Csordas (1993: 137).
2. I develop the idea of ritual metaphysics in Schilbrack (2004).
3. See Slingerland (2008: 188). This paragraph is indebted to Slingerland's insightful discussion of conceptual metaphors (2008: Ch. 4).
4. This quote is from Bo Dahlbom and Lars-Erik Janlert (quoted in Day 2009: 720).
5. This quote is from Clark (2010: 44). In response to criticisms that the Parity Principle includes too much, Clark has proposed more stringent criteria that would have to be met by nonbiological candidates for inclusion into an individual's cognitive system. They are: "[First, that] the resource be reliably available and typically invoked. (Otto always carries the notebook and won't answer that he 'doesn't know' until after he has consulted it). [Second, that] any information thus retrieved be more or less automatically endorsed. It should not usually be subject to critical scrutiny (unlike the opinions of other people, for example). It should be deemed about as trustworthy as something retrieved clearly from biological memory. [And third, that] information contained in the resource should be easily accessible as and when required" (Clark 2010: 46).
6. On whether to count the scaffolded mind as embedded or extended, my own sympathies lie with Lynne Rudder Baker (2009).
7. This suggestion is explored by Matthew Day (2004). However, Day himself later points out that this understanding of the cognitive value of religious props may be of limited value since children do not seem to need material artifacts, like dolls, to "anchor" their relationships with imaginary companions (2005: 251).
8. Lucille Perrotta Castro, *Stations of the Cross: Children and their Families walk with Jesus*. Accessed May 28, 2013. <http://www.cptryon.org/prayer/child/stations/index.html>
9. The epic is available in an abridged version (Wu 1943) or in a more recent complete version in four volumes (Wu 2012).
10. On the concept of embodied realism, see Lakoff and Johnson (1999; cf. Slingerland 2004).
11. See Csordas (1999: 151).

Chapter 3

Must Religious People Have Religious Beliefs?

i. The Place of Belief in the Study of Religions

The concept of *belief* has been absolutely central to the discipline of philosophy of religion. It is possible that no other concept has been more so. As I said in Chapter 1, philosophers of religion have traditionally focused on the rationality of theism, pursuing a set of interconnected questions concerning the evidence, logic, justifiability, or warrant for belief or lack of belief in God. But even if one were to expand the scope of the discipline so that it takes into account the variety of religious beliefs all around the world, a change that would be a central part of the transformation of philosophy of religion that I am proposing in this book, it seems that it would still be—and that it would still have to be—beliefs that philosophers of religion study.

The concept of belief has been central to the study of religions even among nonphilosophers. Edward Tylor, the early anthropologist of religion, defined religion as belief in spiritual beings; and William James, the early psychologist of religion, defined religion as belief in an unseen order. These belief-centered definitions reflect the intellectualism that has pervaded the study of religions and in that respect they are altogether ordinary. And even if today anthropologists, psychologists, comparativists, and philosophers are developing the tools to study religious performances, practices, experiences, material culture, and "lived religion," many still assume a priority to belief

Philosophy and the Study of Religions: A Manifesto, First Edition. Kevin Schilbrack.
© 2014 Kevin Schilbrack. Published 2014 by John Wiley & Sons, Ltd.

so that it is precisely the beliefs of the participants that give the religious performances, practices, experiences, artifacts, and lives their sense.

But the role of the concept of belief in the study of religions has been increasingly criticized as misleading or distorting, if not completely illegitimate. Doesn't the focus on belief distract us from religious emotions, practices, art, laws, and rituals? Increasingly, scholars of religion have been calling for more attention to the material aspects of religion, and some argue not only that we should redress the balance between the material and the cognitive but also, more radically, that one can completely explain religious behavior without the concept of beliefs. This eliminativist position proposes that religious behavior can be exhaustively understood in terms of nonmental causes. For these belief-averse scholars, belief is a concept that should be—as one scholar put it in an introduction to a panel of critics of belief—bound, gagged, and dropped into the sea.[1]

In this chapter, I consider and assess two important objections to the concept of belief in religion. The first objection has to do with access. The student of religions can observe what religious participants do, and she can listen to what they profess. But if beliefs are inner mental states, then how can one ever really know what another person believes? The permanently hidden character of what others believe seems to saddle the study of religions with an impossible goal. A second objection to the place given to belief in the study of religion has to do with cultural bias. The Christian tradition has often made the confession of belief a sign of membership in its communities, and the definitions of religion as a kind of belief then emerged, predictably, in parts of the world where Christianity was the dominant cultural force. But for a religious community to ask its members to believe or to insist that they believe rightly is not typical. Most religious communities do not give belief this privileged role. The assumption that belief is universal or essential in religious lives therefore seems to saddle the study of religions with a distorting presupposition.

It is the goal of this chapter to address both of these objections. Before I do so, however, I want to underline that what this chapter is doing—namely, drawing on the tools of philosophy to solve conceptual problems involved in the study of religions—enacts the kind of philosophy of religion that I think is most useful for religious studies. That is, as I see it, philosophy of religion can serve as a kind of bridge, a connection between the problems that arise in the study of religious lives and the philosophical tools that are available which, in the case of this chapter, come from the philosophy of mind. Ideally, this bridge-building project will have value for those who are on both sides of the bridge, both for the scholars of religions frustrated by problems implied by traditional concept of belief and for the philosophers of mind who are working on exactly that concept but who rarely consider its relevance to the study of religions. This chapter makes a constructive proposal about how students of religion should think of belief. But my hope is that, even if I am wrong about the specific proposal I make, other philosophers of religion will agree that the bridge-building project is worthwhile and will begin to give attention to questions that arise for those who study religion in addition to the questions that arise for those who are members of a religion.

ii. Objections to the Concept of Religious Belief

The first objection to the role of belief in the study of religions has to do with access. If a religious belief is an inner mental state, then it is something that the observer of religions cannot … well … observe. Given that understanding of belief as private and interior, one seems ineluctably led to the conclusion reached by the anthropologist Edmund Leach: "I claim that the anthropologist has absolutely no information about what is inwardly felt by any professed believer."[2] The historian of religions Bruce Lincoln also raises this objection and proposes a solution. He gives two reasons why those who study religions should abandon the study of belief: "First is an epistemological consideration. Students of religion have no unmediated access to the beliefs of those they study, nor to any other aspects of their interiority. Rather, we come to know something of those beliefs only as they find external (always imperfect and sometimes quite distorted) expression in acts of discourse and practice. Regarding that of which one can have no direct knowledge, scholars cannot speak with any confidence and should—in their professional capacity, at least—perforce remain silent. Second, an ontological and ontogenetic observation: Belief almost never arises *de novo* in pristine interior reflection and experience, but generally follows exposure to the discourse of significant others. These include parents, above all, but also friends, family and clergy, who signal what they believe and what they (also the institutions and traditions to which they belong) believe ought be believed. As these statements are received and metabolized by those to whom they are addressed, they are internalized as beliefs, but in this process, discourse is both logically and chronologically prior to belief." As a solution to the problem of access, Lincoln proposes that scholars of religion replace traditional

57

belief-centered definitions (like those of Tylor and James) with a definition of religion in terms of data that are publicly accessible, and he outlines an alternative anatomy of religion in terms of discourse, practice, community, and institutions. Let me call this an *exclusively public model of religion*. This first objection, in short, then, complains that to attribute a belief to someone is like saying that there is something in a box that one can never open. Even if the attribution of belief is true, beliefs are not available to us in our efforts to understand and explain religious phenomena. If religious beliefs are private and therefore not something to which one can have direct access, then the scholars of religion would do better to shift their understanding of the object of study on religion to the kind of data that is available to the historian. This proposal for an exclusively public model of religion does not claim that beliefs do not exist, but it removes them from the study of religion. Lacking any access to what religious practitioners believe, this model gives up on the project of trying to guess what they are.

The second objection is that it reflects a cultural bias to assume that what religious communities centrally care about—what religions *are*—is a set of beliefs. As anthropologists and comparativists have increasingly recognized, the Christian tradition has emphasized doctrines, creeds, and statements of faith, but finding this focus in other traditions is rare. What religious communities typically ask their members to do is not to believe, but rather that one promise oneself, be loyal, trust, or pledge one's allegiance. Religious people then typically commit themselves to serve or to be obedient, and not (or not merely) to believe some proposition. Moreover, what it means to believe has evolved over time. The idea that believing is religiously important is, even in Christianity, a modern development that does not accurately describe the interests of the early church. The historian of religions Wilfred Cantwell Smith sums up the evolution of the meaning of "believing" over the centuries as a story of loss: "The affirmation 'I believe in God' used to mean: 'Given the reality of God as a fact in the universe, I hereby pledge to Him my heart and soul. I committedly opt to live in loyalty to Him. I offer my life to be judged by Him, trusting His mercy.' To-day the statement may be taken by some as meaning: 'Given the uncertainty as to whether there be a God or not, as a fact of modern life, I announce that my opinion is 'Yes'. I judge God to be existent."[3] The assumption that religious people must have religious beliefs therefore seems to reflect a view of religion that is Christian and modern, not universal.

Taking to heart the claim that religious belief is not universal, several scholars have turned their attention away from religious belief and towards the social and linguistic conventions in the modern west that led people to define religion in terms of belief. They ask the reflexive questions: what are the conditions under which we came to think that the most important thing about religious people is that they hold certain private beliefs? What ideological purposes does the concept of private religion serve? Answers to these questions reveal that the modern focus on interiority that assimilates religion to beliefs has a genealogy: perhaps it has its roots in the Platonic idea of a soul, in Augustine's narrative confession of his own sinful journey, and in the Reformation focus on emphasis on faith apart from works. But the idea that religion is a matter of beliefs about what cannot be publicly proven one way or the other comes to dominate the way that people in Europe think of religion only in the political and philosophical and legal transformations that led to the privatization of religious belief and the secularization of the public sphere. John Locke is often taken as the protagonist of this story. But for these genealogists, to define religion in terms of privately held beliefs is not to get at the core of religion, but rather to accept a modern vision that has already excluded religion from the public world. As the anthropologist Talal Asad says, "the suggestion that religion has a universal function in belief is one indication of how marginal religion has become in modern industrial society as the site for producing disciplined knowledge and personal discipline."[4]

If the identification of religion with "belief" is an invention of the modern west, then perhaps the scholar of religions should not only leave beliefs to the side when one studies them, as Lincoln suggests, but should also challenge the assumption that to be religious one must have religious beliefs. In a widely read essay, Donald Lopez calls into question what he calls the pervasive "belief in belief." Lopez suggests that the modern idea of interior, private belief—beliefs that are not the same as what one does or says but must be somehow ferreted out—is an idea that emerged in the power struggles of the Inquisition. Until they were exposed to modern westerners, he points out, Buddhists understood their own tradition in terms of a set of practices and disciplines, not in terms of belief. He comes to the view that beliefs are an index of or a surrogate for material concerns; that is, what people call beliefs stands for some aspect of the outer life, not the inner life. Beliefs do not explain behavior but are invented only as an "afterthought" to justify positions taken for political or economic reasons. As a consequence, the modern focus on beliefs does not capture how religious people understand their own religious lives and, worse, the reference to inner states of the mind ignores and obscures the non-intentional forces that could actually explain what religious people are up to.

59

At this point, it is worth introducing a term from philosophy of mind: eliminativism. Eliminativists about beliefs are those who argue that the assumption that beliefs lie behind people's actions is false and pernicious; beliefs are fictions. Eliminativism comes in two flavors. First (so to speak, from the Anglophone side), there are those who call themselves eliminative materialists and who predict that understanding and explaining people's actions by reference to beliefs will be undermined and abandoned just as reference to the four humors was, and we will get along as well without one as we have with the other. Beliefs, they say, are simply part of folk psychology, the theoretical account of the mind that arose before we had any real sense of the complexity of the material world. But as we learn more about the physical causes of human behavior, especially from the neurosciences, beliefs will drop out. The second kind of eliminativists (so to speak, from the Continental side) are postmodern philosophers who argue that the very idea of belief is a rhetorical construction or an ideological fiction that hides and thereby serves material interests. They see themselves as following Derrida's deconstructive and Foucault's genealogical efforts to overcome the idea of the Cartesian or transcendental subject. For these postmodern philosophers, the focus on beliefs reflects an uncritical adoption of modern liberal humanism.

Now, the theorists of religion I have cited are not eliminativists. On the contrary, Lincoln says (in the quote cited above) that as people participate in discourse and practices, they internalize statements as beliefs; Asad also believes in beliefs. Lopez is more skeptical: he calls beliefs "elusive" and "nebulous" and says that it is difficult to determine whether beliefs really exist or not.[5] These theorists of religion are not philosophers and they don't take any explicit position on the ontology of mental states. Nevertheless, the latter are at least methodological eliminativists and, like the eliminativists in philosophy of mind, they seek to replace mental causes with materialist ones. Moreover, there is this useful analogy: just as in philosophy of mind there is an argument between realists who hold that beliefs exist and eliminativists who deny this, there is a parallel argument in religious studies between those who seek to understand and explain religious phenomena in terms of beliefs and those, like Lincoln and Lopez, who propose eliminating beliefs from the field. In fact, this may be more than an analogy, since those who seek to eliminate the concept of beliefs as they study the mind and those who seek to eliminate the concept of beliefs as they study culture no doubt influence and support each other.

The rest of this chapter gives my response to these two problems of belief and to the suggestion that the best solution is to eliminate the category. The next two sections explore two proposals about beliefs drawn from contemporary philosophy of mind that can, I judge, help scholars of religion deal with the problem of access, and then the last section returns to the problem of cultural distortion.

iii.   Holding One's Beliefs in Public

The critics of belief in religious studies rarely show an awareness of the ways in which belief is discussed among philosophers of mind. It is probably fair to say that most philosophers assume that belief is universal in the sense that all persons have beliefs (a point to which I will return at the end of this chapter), but it is not accurate to say that most philosophers assume that belief is inner, private, and inaccessible. I therefore want to consider ways in which contemporary philosophers of mind see beliefs as intimately and intricately participating in—and not merely "expressed in"—our public lives.

For philosophers of mind, no matter what camp they are in, the concept of believing refers to holding that something is true. If someone holds it as true, for instance, that the earth is round, then she believes that the earth is round. A belief is therefore a kind of commitment or attitude that a person takes on. But beliefs in this minimal sense of propositional attitudes (what I will call "beliefs in the taking true sense") are not something that a human person might or might not have. Beliefs in this sense are, rather, something that one must have in order to be an agent, and they are something that one must attribute to others if one is to see them as agents. Having beliefs is therefore an *a priori* aspect of agency. Philosophical camps then develop and divide as philosophers disagree over the question of how one should make sense of this attitude of taking true. For the sake of simplicity, I want to examine what I take to be the three main contemporary philosophical answers to this question.

The first philosophical position on belief to consider is representationalism. Representationalists argue that to hold that something is true requires one to have a mental representation of it. If one believes that the earth is round, for instance, then one must have a representation of this state of affairs, perhaps as an image or perhaps as a sentence, in one's mind. This view that a belief is an inner representation of some external reality turns

61

on a strict distinction between one's inner mind and one's outer body. On this account, one's public words and gestures and one's beliefs may operate completely independently of each other. What a person says and does may not reflect what that person believes at all.

It seems clear that the majority of those in religious studies who criticize belief as inner, private, and inaccessible assume something like the representationalist understanding of belief. What they object to is the idea that beliefs are invisible, ghost-like, and "in one's head."[6] This makes their critique valuable since representationalism has been the dominant view in philosophy of mind in the modern world, the one closest to the everyday, "folk" ways of speaking about the mind, and the one that has often been assumed in the study of religions. However, it is fair to say not only that representationalism is a beleaguered position in philosophy but also that the previous century of philosophy has been postmodern precisely in the variety of ways that it has opposed mind–body dualisms and has therefore sought to develop nonrepresentationalist accounts of mental states. Certainly, the pragmatist tradition—running from Pierce and Dewey to Brandom that has sought to understand cognition as an element of practical inquiry that is embodied and social—has been explicitly an attack on the concept of the Cartesian subject. The same is true of the phenomenological tradition that runs from Heidegger and Merleau-Ponty to contemporary embodied cognitive science that has sought to reconceptualize subjectivity as being-in-the-world. And it is again true of the philosophers influenced by the later Wittgenstein, a lineage of thinkers that runs from Ryle to Dennett and Davidson who take the impossibility of private language as the starting point in their understanding of meaning, truth, and reference. Almost all philosophers of mind today seek to develop accounts of belief that reconceive the mind as necessarily in the body, embedded in the world, and woven into social networks. To be sure, representationalism is still a live issue in philosophy of mind. The idea that beliefs require representations of the world that are somehow stored in the mind may be necessary, and this may be most apparent when we want to understand how people make judgments about realities that are not present. And the representationalist idea that beliefs are composed of structured elements, just as a sentence is or a map is, may also have advantages when it comes to understanding how changes to one belief affects one's other beliefs. Perhaps then the most successful accounts of belief will not completely abandon representationalism. Nevertheless, contemporary philosophers of mind have widely sought to repudiate the picture of the mind in which beliefs are in the head and have sought to develop post-Cartesian and nonintrospective accounts that see believing as, in part, a public activity that is embodied, embedded, and intersubjective. I turn now to two positions on belief—dispositionalism and interpretationism—that seek precisely this.

Dispositionalists see believing not as something a mind does but rather as something a *person* does. They identify a belief not with something private in one's mind or brain, but rather with a range of dispositions that a person adopts to act, feel, and think in certain ways. Say that a person comes to take it as true that I live in the house he saw me exit. To say that he takes it as true or that he believes it is equivalent to the fact that he is disposed to certain thoughts like drawing conclusions about my mail and my keys, to certain actions like giving directions there when asked where I live, and to certain feelings like surprise if he hears that I live somewhere else. These at least partly public dispositions constitute what we mean when we say that a person has a belief. From the dispositionalist perspective, therefore, it is not right to think of a belief as a concrete "thing" at all. Instead, to have a belief is to have a propensity or a tendency, or a set of them, typically shaped by one's social context, to interact with the world and with others according to a more or less specifiable pattern. Moreover, given a dispositionalist understanding, it is possible that the believer may not be the best judge of what he himself believes. Recognizing a pattern of dispositions is not always easy, and it is not always obvious or transparent, even to the agent himself.[7] •

Granted, a dispositionalist account of belief does not make the work that is required to identify what someone else believes completely evaporate. Dispositionalism cannot reduce what we mean by "she believes such-and-such" to "we see her do or say such-and-such." It also does not eliminate the difference between the first-person access one has to one's own beliefs and the third-person access one has to another's beliefs. Nevertheless, dispositionalism can help us to see that what we mean by a belief need not refer to an invisible entity stashed away in the person's head, but refers instead to a pattern of activities at least some of which are public.

One of the best known dispositionalists is Gilbert Ryle, and we can use two of his terms to bring out the public aspects of dispositional beliefs.[8] First, Ryle famously argues that the assumption that beliefs are in one's head is a "category mistake." According to Ryle, those who speak of beliefs as stored in the mind assume that just as physical language is about physical objects, mental language must be about mental objects. But for Ryle, a person who sees, for example, a child shrinking back, crying and saying that the dog might bite him, but says that we still have not seen what the child believes about the dog is like a person who goes to tour a university and visits the classrooms, libraries, playing fields, and offices but says that we still have not seen the university. Or he is like a person who thinks that team spirit is an invisible member of the team. The category mistake is to think that a belief is some entity in addition to the way that one's living is shaped by the belief. For Ryle, those who picture the mind as a kind of space and a belief as a kind of object inside that space are (to use the Wittgensteinian phrase) captured and misled by a picture, namely, the picture of language in which sentences to be meaningful must refer to objects.

Here is Ryle's second useful term. To attribute a belief to someone is not to describe an occult object in her head but rather to make a statement about a person's capacities, tendencies, or propensities over time. It is, to use Ryle's phrase, an "inference-ticket" in the sense that it lets one make predictions about how alleged believers will answer questions, how they have acted in the past and will act in the future, and in general to explain their behavior. Ryle compares attributions of belief to attributions of capacities like the ability to speak French. In both cases, the descriptions do not aim to report what is occurring right now, in someone's mind, but rather to describe a feature of a person from which one can draw expectations about how the person might act under certain circumstances. To attribute a belief is therefore not to describe an invisible "vaporous" something but rather to make a prediction about a relatively indeterminate and open-ended but coherent range of behavior. Attributions of beliefs are then counted as accurate to the extent one's predictions are satisfied.

What would it mean for the study of religion to adopt a dispositionalist view of belief? The primary advantage is that dispositionalism emerged as an alternative to the Cartesian idea of the ghost in the machine, which is to say that it emerged as a solution to the problem of access. Dispositionalism would move part of what we call religious belief from the occult space inside the head to empirically available words and actions. Thus, to say that so-and-so believes that Muhammad is the seal of the prophets would be based on observations of (and would in turn make possible further inferences about) how that person acts, what he values, whom he associates with, what he is likely to say, and so on. A religious belief therefore cannot be separated from a religious pattern of behavior. To paraphrase Ryle, going on a pilgrimage is both a physical process and a mental process, but it is not two processes.

One should note that when dispositionalists say that a person believes something (e.g., that he believes that the earth is round), they do not mean that he is consciously believing this. Believing that the world is round does not mean that the idea is presently "on one's mind." In fact, although one can become conscious of one's beliefs, some have said that one never consciously believes. One might *think* about the idea that the world is round for, say, half an hour, and then stop thinking about it and move on to other things. But once a person has judged that the world is round, then (whether or not he is thinking about this) he still is in the state of taking it as true and so he still believes it.

Let me develop this idea one last step. Since on this account beliefs are not conscious mental events but rather dispositional states of persons, the dispositionalist approach lends itself to those in the study of religions who are interested in the ways in which such states come to be formed. Some beliefs may be formed through a conscious judgment, but others are the product of relatively automatic perception or unconscious inference. Thus the idea of dispositional beliefs can serve those who judge that people's sensibilities and modes of thinking are formed through their public participation in religious practices, institutions, and other kinds of training. As Susan Harding puts it in her discussion of the witnessing done by Evangelicals that leads to people to convert: speaking is believing. That is, "belief ... involves an unconscious willingness to join a narrative tradition ... [and] generative belief, belief that indisputably transfigures you and your reality, belief that becomes you, comes only through speech."[9] The dispositional account of beliefs therefore fits well with the view that subjectivity itself is constituted intersubjectively.

In sum, for the dispositionalist, to have a belief—to take something as true—is to live with a certain understanding of the world. This does not make beliefs public in the sense that one's understanding of the world is displayed like a sign on one's shirt, but it does, I hope, shift the conversations about studying religious beliefs away from the talk about intuiting mysterious objects in the head and to the processes involved in grasping different patterns of living. Moreover, given a dispositionalist account of belief, to say that a religious person or community does not have beliefs would be to say that he or they take nothing as true. It would be to say that they are committed to nothing and they make no judgments. There may be some religious phenomena for which understanding behavior in a thoughtless way is advisable, but the overhaul required to study religion without the concept of belief is wildly underestimated.

iv. What We Presuppose When We Attribute Beliefs

The previous section considers ways in which simply *having* a belief is, in part, a public activity. This section considers ways in which the practice of *interpreting* another person as having a belief also reveals a dimension of belief that is public, and necessarily so. These requirements of attributing propositional attitudes have been explored by a philosophical approach that has come to be called interpretationism.

As we have seen, the representationalists define a belief as an information-bearing structure in the mind or brain of the individual, and the disposition-alists took a view of belief that what we might think of as "broader," in that they argue that one cannot ascribe a belief to another person's mind with-out taking into account that person's dispositions, in a certain specifiable but open-ended pattern, distributed over time. One way of appreciating the interpretationists' contribution is to see them as pulling the conceptual lens back further in order to bring into the picture not only a pattern of dis-positions, but also what the interpretationists consider crucial to the iden-tification of beliefs, namely, the involvement of the one attributing belief. The interpretationists want to draw our attention to the conditions for the possibility of interpreting the beliefs of another person. They agree that to attribute belief requires one to recognize a pattern of dispositions, but they focus on the fact that pattern recognition is an act that requires interpretation on the part of the observer. Their contribution to this discussion might be put this way: if dispositionalists hold that beliefs are public to the extent that they are patterns of living, interpretationists add that these patterns are nec-essarily intersubjective, both in their generation and in their intelligibility.

Consider two everyday illustrations. In the first one, imagine that an adult is teaching a toddler. "The cat is in the tree," he says, pointing, or "these apples taste good," taking a bite. Of course, the child may not grasp the meaning or the referent of the sentences at first. But over time the teacher can instill proper performance in the verbal behavior of the learning child by repeating lessons and by correcting misapplications of "cat," "tree," and "apple." Now, imagine a second case in which an observer is trying to understand someone speaking a language she does not know. Is the infor-mant referring to the cup or what is in the cup? Is he indicating that it is healthy or that it is sweet? It is crucial that in both the case of the child and of the linguist, an interpreter looks for regularities in the verbal behavior of the informant by correlating it with events and objects in their com-mon environment. In both cases, the interpreter's beliefs emerge in a social situation that involves reference to a shared world. This observation points to a general rule: to interpret the beliefs of another involves joint recognition of public facts.

Here is an analogy: when one is trying to determine what another person is looking at, one imagines his lines of sight to see where the other's perspective and one's own meet. Similarly, when one tries to identify what another person believes, one looks for the object that is the cause of his behavior. The philosopher Donald Davidson calls this everyday process "triangulation."[10] To make a hypothesis about the intended connections between the sounds that others make to the events and objects in our common environment is a necessary condition for attributing beliefs to the person observed. In this way, the attribution of beliefs *presupposes* a shared environment. Human beings could not have the practice of attributing beliefs to each other without it. The point is not that if one wants to know what another believes, one can try matching up distal causes. The point is that if people did not already match up distal causes, they would have no beliefs. Without shared reactions to common stimuli, we could not say that anyone had beliefs at all. The interior life that is private *depends on* an exterior world that is public. As Davidson says, "Knowledge of another mind is possible ... only if one has knowledge of the world." Or as Daniel Dennett similarly put it, "one must be richly informed about, intimately connected with, the world at large, its occupants and properties, in order to be said with any propriety to have beliefs." A shared, public world is a condition for the possibility of interpreting the beliefs of others. If we do the latter, then we already have the former.

This observation has an important implication. In the examples, the child can come to learn "cat" and "tree" and "apple" by means of the adult's identification of elements of their shared world, and the linguist can come to learn the informant's words for "healthy" and "juice" and "offering" by means of the informant's identification of elements of their shared world. If this is right, then it follows that for an individual to come to have beliefs requires not only that she interact with the publicly available objects in the world but also that she grasp what another person believes about it. It is not true that one person, with his or her solipsistic interests, generates beliefs about the world and then hopes that others can read his or her mind. On the contrary, one has beliefs about the world only because and to the extent that one has already successfully and repeatedly navigated what others believe. The content of one's beliefs derives from what one gathers from others. One's beliefs about the world, one's beliefs about what others believe, and one's beliefs about one's own mind come into existence as an interlocking set. In short, then, interpretationism holds that the very existence of beliefs presupposes a public world and intersubjective understanding of it.

From the fact that one's beliefs are dependent on one's interpretations of other's beliefs, it follows that people have to agree with each other on some of their beliefs before they can intelligibly disagree. In fact, the two sides will always have to have much more agreement than disagreement. (Think of how much agreement two people would need to have in order to disagree about whether a pitch is a ball or a strike, whether a reptile is a crocodile or an alligator, or whether a boat is a ketch or a yawl.) There are at least two implications of this for the study of religious beliefs. First, dis-agreement about religious beliefs cannot lead to a complete relativism. The difficulties involved in interpreting the religious beliefs of another person are real enough, but given the massive agreement about primary beliefs about cats and trees and cups, the difficulties cannot lead one to conclude that religious believers live in "different worlds" or that "we can never know what they believe." As scholars of religion seek to interpret the religious beliefs of others, there are limits to diversity and so there are constraints on interpre-tive despair. Second, the interpretationists underline that people learn their primary beliefs about the world in their interactions with others. Beliefs are then collective in the sense that in the first instance they are common to and shared by members of a discursive or interpretive community. It is of course individuals who believe, but they do so primarily in their capacity not as individuals but as members of a collectivity. Dissent and dissimulation com-plicate any study of collective beliefs, but it is not inappropriate to generalize about a group by saying that "they believe" in the collective rather than the distributive sense. As I said above, there is no way to give an account of belief so that the problem of access completely evaporates. But in these two ways the interpretationist approach puts limits on the negativity: we will not be able to say both that others have religious beliefs and that one can never figure out what they are. We live in a common, shared world with Daoist alchemists, Christian crusaders, Lakota dancers, and so on.

The critic of belief may respond that belief may be public in what one might call these presuppositional or "transcendental" ways, but these general truths do not solve the problem of access. The problem was that religious practitioners may make public declarations that they believe, and they may publicly act as if they believe. But we do not know—and we cannot know—whether privately they really do believe. The solution proposed by some critics of belief was to develop an exclusively public model of religion that shifts the study of religion away from religious belief and to the study of religious discourse, practice, community, and institutions.

The dispositionalist–interpretationist approach gives us tools to develop a different solution to the problem of access. Since dispositionalists understand beliefs not as private mental entities but rather as dispositions to act, feel, think, and speak in certain ways, they only attribute beliefs where the belief would make such a difference. This is not to say that beliefs are always manifested, but there has to be at least what philosophers call a counterfactual difference: that is, the belief *would* make a difference *if* the relevant circumstances arise. But if there is a counterfactual difference between believing and not believing something, then there is a real difference between them, and the difference can be relevant both for understanding and for explaining religious phenomena.

Here is an illustration. Imagine two religious people, Peter and Paul, whose religious discourse and practice are identical. Peter (consciously or unconsciously) takes the religious discourse as true and takes the religious practice to be justified by that truth. Paul does not take it as true but (consciously or unconsciously) judges that it is in his interest. *Ex hypothesi*, their public performances are immaculate and the only difference between them is their beliefs. Treating belief as an inner entity which one can never check, the exclusively public model of religion leaves belief aside and declines to discriminate between those motivated by religious beliefs and those motivated by self-interest or other factors. For a great deal of religious phenomena, this approach is sound; it often will not matter whether religious speakers believe their discourse. But failing to include belief as an analytic category for the study of religion impoverishes one's work to the extent that one can make counterfactual predictions about behavior. One can predict: if circumstances change so that religious participation is no longer in their interest, then Paul's performance will change but Peter's will not. Or one can predict: if the circumstances do not change, but Peter and Paul are both convinced by a defeater for their beliefs, then Peter's performance will change but Paul's will not. Belief is thus one way that we explain and predict behavior. Even if the circumstances do not change, and so one never observes their behavior diverge, attributing beliefs in this counterfactual way is coherent and meaningful, and it does not saddle the interpretation of religion with the problem of access. This illustration is admittedly brief, but it does indicate, I hope, how discriminating between beliefs is both possible and relevant for the study of religious lives. Moreover, explaining and predicting behavior in this way are everyday occurrences. They do not assume Christian views of the soul or modern Western views of liberal humanism but are instead part of the folk psychology that has been practiced since at least Homer, Kongzi, and Valmiki. And such explanations and predictions of behavior are not possible without the category of beliefs.

The exclusively public model of religion and the dispositionalist–interpretationist account of religious belief I have sketched both seek to bring the study of religion out of the head. According to either approach, the study of religion would focus on publicly accessible data. In this respect, the two approaches resemble each other. The difference, however, is that the exclusively public model of religion assumes that when one studies religious discourse and practice, one is not studying religious beliefs at all. It holds (with the representationalists) that beliefs exist in some unobservable inner space and so it maintains a Cartesian mind–body dualism with regard to human activity. Unlike that model, the account of beliefs proposed here does not shift the study of religion to the study of religious discourse and practice *as opposed to* belief. Instead, it takes a holistic view of human agent as embodied and social, but nevertheless also with the capacity to imagine, to make judgments about, and to live according to certain beliefs.

v. The Universality of Belief

With these public aspects of having beliefs and interpreting beliefs in focus, we can return to the question: Must religious people have beliefs? Is belief universal to religions? As we've seen, there are those who argue that, when we look at the different ways that people have been religious around the world and throughout history, belief has not been something in which all religious communities have shown an interest. For that reason, to approach the study of religions via the category of belief, they say, is distorting. But the question whether belief is universal to religions is ambiguous and the critics of belief often collapse two senses that we should keep distinct. The positive answer that I want to defend requires me to disambiguate the two senses.

The first sense of the question is: Do all religions explicitly teach their members to believe certain things? In other words, is the category of believing religiously important to all religious communities? Here I think that the work by anthropologists, comparativists, and historians has shown that the answer is clearly No. Religious communities typically offer a path for people to follow. A religion may ask its members to dress, eat, marry, or

70

have sexual relations in a certain way, or it may seek to cultivate in them certain affections, virtues, and sensibilities, but religious communities usually do not ask their members to believe certain things and they usually do not seek to regulate the members' beliefs. The notion that a religion *is* a set of beliefs misrepresents what religious communities typically care about. Belief in the sense of doctrines and statements of faith is not a universal feature of religious interests. The second sense of the question is this: when people engage in religious behavior, do they take certain propositions as true? Do religious people commit themselves to a certain view of things by engaging in their religious lives? Here I think that the answer is Yes. All human behavior—and therefore all religious behavior—involves attitudes of taking some propositions as true. But if I am right that religious practices must involve beliefs in the sense of what analytic philosophers call propositional attitudes (from here on, "beliefs in the taking true sense"), then all religious people have religious beliefs. In this way, belief in the taking true sense is a universal feature of religious life. For the rest of this chapter, I want to clarify what this claim implies for the study of religions.

Most contemporary philosophers do assume that belief in the taking true sense is universal. If such beliefs exist at all, then they are something that pervades our lives. The philosopher Donald Davidson speaks for the majority of contemporary philosophers when he writes, "Belief is central to all kinds of thought. If someone is glad that, or notices that, or remembers that, the gun is loaded, then he must believe that the gun is loaded. Even to wonder whether the gun is loaded, or to speculate on the possibility that the gun is loaded, requires the belief, for example, that a gun is a weapon, that it is a more or less enduring physical object, and so on."[11] Beliefs in the taking true sense are universal in that they are a contemporary philosophical account of what it means to feel, calculate, act, or speak with an understanding of one's environment.

From my perspective, Wilfred Cantwell Smith correctly distinguished my two questions and got both answers right.[12] As I mentioned above, Smith was one of the first to show that the concept of religious belief, widely assumed as essential for something to be called a religion, has not had a uniform or stable meaning. What Christians have meant by belief has evolved. Statements like "I believe in God" had originally been references to putting one's trust in God or swearing allegiance to God, but only in the modern era had they come to refer to something less engaged and less personal, namely, what I am calling belief in the taking true sense. Smith points out that the word for belief does not occur in the Bible and he concludes that

71

"[t]he idea that believing is religiously important turns out to be a modern idea." Coming to the defense of the concept for the study of religion, however, Donald Wiebe argued that the use of belief for the study of religions cannot be eliminated. He accused Smith of saying that in Biblical days people did not have beliefs. We might say that Wiebe saw Smith confusing the contingent question whether religious people have beliefs *qua* religious and the necessary question whether they have beliefs *qua* people. In effect, Wiebe, like me, wants to keep the two senses distinct and he accused Smith of collapsing them. But Smith answered clearly: he never denied that anyone lacks belief in the taking true sense—that is, religious people have always taken certain claims and not others to be the case—even while he was pointing out that the contemporary concept of belief was not shared in premodern times. As a consequence, both sides can be right; Smith is discussing belief as an element of orthodoxy that one finds in some religions but not in others, whereas Wiebe was interested in belief as an element of cognition and theorizing that one finds in all human beings. As Smith nicely put it: Jesus manifestly believed in devils even if there is no way of saying in Biblical Greek that he believed in devils. In this way, Smith disentangles the two questions and argues that it is not wrong to say that religious people universally take certain propositions to be true, even if it is wrong to say that religious communities universally call on their members to do so.

But that debate was in 1980. Since then, one increasingly hears that scholars *should* collapse my two questions. That is, critics of belief—especially the eliminativists of the continental, social constructivist variety—argue that the global spread of modern Christianity exported a set of modern liberal humanistic assumptions about individuality and agency, thereby shaping assumptions not only about what it is to be religious but also about what it is to be a person. Spreading belief in God, they say, simultaneously spread a belief in belief. These opponents of belief see their critical project in this way: several decades ago, anthropologists and historians like Smith undermined the assumption that beliefs are an essential part of being a religious person, but now the contemporary critics are interested in undermining the assumption that beliefs are an essential part of being human. The critics accuse universalists about belief in the taking true sense (like me) of buying into and projecting globally an ideology of belief. The universalists about belief, they allege, fail to see that modern western ideas of subjectivity are themselves part of a particular worldview that emerged only under certain political and institutional conditions and that was developed to serve modern western interests. In response to this kind of conceptual colonization, the critics of belief seek to purge from theories of religion any constructive account of belief and other subjective categories.

Although it seems to me that the capacity for being a subject capable of reflecting on and deliberating about one's beliefs is a precondition of human agency, religious or otherwise, I don't have space to give a full response to those who wish to theorize religious activity without the concepts of subjectivity. But I can point out that this claim that belief in the taking true sense is not universal but rather a particular ideology is again ambiguous. It is unclear whether the critic is saying that the concept of belief in the taking true sense *emerged* only under certain political and institutional conditions or whether the concept *applies* only to some particular place. The claim about the concept's emergence is, I grant, surely correct. Belief in the taking true sense—belief in the sense of having a propositional attitude—is a concept of modern western provenance. This means that almost none of the members of the religious communities that scholars study had the concept. Moreover, had they known about the concept, it is likely that they would not (*qua* religious people) have been especially interested in it. But it does not follow that the concept is only useful for studying those of the modern west, any more than this would follow for the modern concepts of economy or gender.[13] The truth about the concept's emergence is therefore not an obstacle to the universalism in which I am interested, which is whether the category of belief in the taking true sense is relevant outside its place of origin. Does the concept of belief in the taking true sense help us to understand and explain people's religious behavior? Is this western invention useful? The fact that religions do not typically consider belief central does not mean (and if I am right about the ubiquity of belief in the taking true sense, then it cannot mean) that some religions lack the category of belief. No religion lacks a cognitive element or fails to proffer a vision of the nature of things. To hold that belief in the taking true sense is universal is therefore to say that the practices of any religious people can be illuminated by analyzing them as taking certain propositions as true.

From the fact that the concept of belief in the taking true sense was developed in the modern west, it does not follow that what the concept names is not operative elsewhere. The only thing that follows is that those who employ this concept should recognize that they are analyzing people with a concept that those they study may not share. This is not an objection since the study of religion does not merely seek to describe the lived worlds of religious people in a way that they will accept, but also to redescribe them according to one's own lights. (I develop this point more fully in Chapter 7.) This means that when the scholar gives an interpretation of a religious community's discourse and practice in terms of propositional attitudes, the scholar may not be replicating what the community explicitly teaches. Rather, like the child seeking to understand the adult's beliefs about the cat or the linguist seeking to understand the informant's beliefs about the cup, the scholar may be abstracting from religious discourse and practices the propositions that make the most sense of what their informants are saying and doing. To be sure, the scholar's interpretation is fallible and may need to be corrected in the future, and one's interpretation of belief will be underdetermined in the sense that other interpretations may be possible, but this is always true of attributions of beliefs. In sum, I am arguing that even if the label of belief as an attitude of taking-as-true is an especially western or modern label, the attitude itself is not.

Like the critics of belief, I have been frustrated by disembodied or solipsistic treatments of belief. But my hope is that the dispositionalist and interpretationist approaches provide some direction for those of us who consider some concept of belief ineliminable but also see the need to develop more tractable approaches to it. Those approaches let us propose an answer to the question of universality, namely: whether or not religions explicitly teach beliefs in the representational sense, all religions do at least implicitly teach beliefs in the dispositional sense. That is, even when religious communities do not explicitly require orthodoxy, they teach their discourse and behavior *as true*, which is to say that they seek not only to get their members to perform the discourse and behavior properly but also get those who perform the discourse and behavior to take them as natural, warranted, grounded in reality, or corresponding to the way things are. In other words, even when they do not use this language, religious practices inculcate religious beliefs in the taking true sense.[14]

The concept of belief has been central to the study of religions. Given the approaches explored in this chapter, the concept could keep some parts of its traditional role but would have to give up others. One part of its traditional role, seen in all the disciplines involved in the study of religion, is the use of beliefs in explanations of religious phenomena. If it is right that religious communities typically teach their practices as true, then one can use beliefs in the taking true sense to explain religious behavior. For example, one might judge that the Daoist adept practices internal alchemy because he believes that doing so will improve the flow of energy from his cinnabar fields. One might judge that the Crusader left to fight the Saracens because he believed that God willed it. One might judge that the Lakota performed the Ghost Dance because they believed that it would hasten the event when war and violence would be ended. Other explanations of such behavior are possible, including explanations in terms of nonreligious beliefs or explanations in terms of nonintentional structures such as the economic system or genes. But the variety of explanations of religious behavior does not undermine the idea that religious discourse and practice can sometimes be explained by the fact that the practitioners believe it.

A second part of belief's traditional role is particular to philosophy. The very idea of belief implies that what one believes may not be the case. That is, to have the concept of belief is to have the concept of truth and falsity independent of one's attitudes. And this is the primary reason why the concept of belief is of interest to many philosophers of religion: they want to ask about what is true and false. But if belief in the taking true sense is present whenever one takes something to be the case, and therefore it is a universal aspect of religions, then philosophers of religion can take as their task to interpret and then to evaluate the attitudes toward the world taken by those who participate in religious communities. (This would be the first task of philosophy of religion, as described in Chapter 1.) The claim that religions include beliefs in the taking true sense thus makes their philosophical evaluation possible.

The criticisms of belief, however, require those who keep the concept of belief to be clear about what belief is not. The account of belief that is, I judge, most useful for the study of religions is one in which a belief is an attitude of taking true that is a socially informed pattern of thinking, feeling, speaking, and acting. On this account, beliefs are not mysterious inner objects. And however beliefs are understood, they are not the essence, let alone the whole of a religion. Religious beliefs are not immune from explanation in nonreligious terms. Religious communities speak and act in ways that can be redescribed in terms of what they take as true, a redescription that makes certain kinds of explanation and evaluation possible. But my primary goal has been to take seriously the material aspects of religious life without eliminating the concept of belief. The critics are right that public affirmation that one takes something as true is not the same as taking it as true; belief is not equivalent to practice. Nevertheless, practice and belief, like body and mind, do not swing completely free of each other and the best account of religion will include both.

Bibliographic Essay

In this chapter, I weigh (and, in the end, reject) the views of those scholars who hold that the study of religions should not include the category of belief. The label "new materialists" I take from David Chidester who describes them as scholars who hold that beliefs are "out" and "embodiment and materiality are in" (Chidester 2000: 369) and who illustrates this movement with the best-selling collection by Mark Taylor (Taylor 1998). Against that perspective, I argue that the attention to the material dimensions of religion should lead scholars of religion not to abandon but rather to improve our understanding of beliefs. I see allies, respectively, with regard to belief, subjectivity, and experience, in Godlove (2002); Furey (2012); and Bush (2012). Bell (2008) and Bivins (2012) both use the category of belief as a theme with which to interrogate the state of theorizing in the study of religions.

In the chapter, I consider two reasons to drop the category of belief: first, that belief is inaccessible to the scholar and, second, that scholarly focus on belief reflects an implicitly Christian assumption about what religion is. The latter point that the role given to creedal belief by Christians is not found in other religions seems to me undeniable; for support, see Wilfred Cantwell Smith (1962); Robert Bellah (1970); Malcolm Ruel (1982); and Talal Asad (1983).

The claim that the identification of religion with a set of beliefs is a modern development is often credited to genealogists of religion, and especially to the work of the anthropologist Talal Asad (1993), but it is worth pointing out that Asad believes in beliefs (Asad 2011, which also speaks of religions as existing). Donald Lopez (1998) is often read, like Asad, as a genealogist of religion, but when he complains that attributions of belief "cannot be submitted to ordinary rules of verification" nor "judged by the criteria used for other kinds of utterances" and when he calls belief an "afterthought" and not a cause of behavior (1998: 33, 24, 34), he seems to be assuming, like the positivists, that there is just one set of rules or criteria for verifying all claims about what exists or, like the eliminative materialists, that beliefs are fictions.

I suggest that the critics of belief in the academic study of religions parallel the eliminative materialists in philosophy of mind who argue that beliefs and other mental states do not exist. The best known statements of eliminative materialism are Richard Rorty (1970); Paul Churchland (1981); Stephen Stich (1985); and Patricia Churchland (1986); for a powerful critique of this form of eliminativism, see Baker (1989). The critics of belief in the study of religions may also hold that their opposition to belief is in line with contemporary Continental philosophy, especially Foucault and Derrida. For example, Mary-Jane Rubenstein proposes that "belief does not come into play except insofar as it remains the perpetual target of what Foucault called 'permanent critique'" (2012: 68–9). And there is some textual support for the claim that these philosophers sought to do away with subjectivity altogether. For example, here is Foucault: "One has to dispense with the constituent subject, to get rid of the subject itself, that's to say, to arrive at an analysis which can account for the constitution of the subject within a historical framework. And this is what I would call genealogy ..." (1980: 117). And Derrida: "The subject is a fable" (1991: 102). I would argue, however, that deconstruction and genealogy do not have a purely negative or corrosive approach to the subject. That Foucault and Derrida did not aim to purge theories of the subject is suggested in their statements like these: "it is not power, but the subject, which is the general theme of my research" (Foucault 1982: 209; cf. Allen 2000) and "The subject is absolutely indispensable. I don't destroy the subject; I situate it. That is to say, I believe that as a certain level both of experience and of philosophical and scientific discourse one cannot get along without the notion of subject" (Derrida 1972: 271).

In the chapter, I divide the philosophical accounts of belief into three camps: representationalists, dispositionalists, and interpretationists. Daniel Dennett (1991) slices the pie in a slightly different way, distinguishing five positions on the ontology on beliefs. My chapter then foregrounds non-representational accounts of belief. For a tremendously influential account of the development of a nonrepresentational theory of knowledge in the work of Dewey, Heidegger, and Wittgenstein, see Richard Rorty (1979). Richard Bernstein (1988) then builds on Rorty and adds Gadamer, Habermas, and Arendt. And Warren Frisina (2002) adds the process philosopher Whitehead and the neo-Confucian Wang Yang-ming. For an argument that accounts of belief should not completely abandon the idea of representationalism, see the philosopher of embodied cognitive science, Andy Clark and Josefa Toribio (1994) and Clark (1997: Ch. 8), and for a response to Clark that defends a completely nonrepresentational or "radically embodied" cognitive science, see Chemero (2009). A nice piece on the possible futures of representationalism is Chalmers (2004).

The anthropologist Benson Saler points out that the critics of belief rarely show an awareness of how belief is discussed in philosophy of mind (2001: 48). This may explain why, as I argue in the chapter, they tend to assume a representationalist account of belief. By contrast, I recommend to scholars of religion an account of belief that focuses not on inner mental representations but rather on (i) one's dispositions and (ii) what must be true for one to interpret the agency of another. Dispositions are best understood counterfactually: that is, dispositions are what a person would do if the relevant circumstances were to arise. The sharpest account of counterfactuals I know is Baker (1995: Ch. 6). Although early dispositionalists like Ryle (1949) tended to link belief only with dispositions to *behave* in certain ways and were accused of reducing mental states to physical ones, more recent versions like Schwitzgebel (2002) add phenomenal and cognitive dispositions, as I do here.

The most prominent interpretationists are Donald Davidson and Daniel Dennett. I use the interpretationists, first, to make the point that recognizing a pattern of behavior is an act that requires interpretation on the part of the observer (see Davidson 2001: 212; Dennett 1991). Dennett describes himself, not inaccurately, as loosely following Wittgenstein, but for an analysis of their differences on the issue of pattern recognition, see Hark (2001). Terry Godlove (1989) uses the work of Davidson to argue persuasively that for interpretation of another person to be possible, there must be limits to diversity of belief. I use the interpretationists, second, to make the point that beliefs are learned intersubjectively. For examples of religious belief as the dispositional product of unconscious social practices (in addition to the forms of religious speaking mentioned in the chapter), see Griffiths (1999) on religious reading and Hirschkind (2006) on religious listening (cf. Asad 2011; Mahmood 2005).

My argument that one cannot make sense of religious practice without the category of belief is shared by Donald Wiebe 1979 and 1992. Wiebe writes, "it is not possible to write an adequate 'history of religion(s)', or to undertake a 'comparative study of religion' without the use of the concept (category) of belief... the *concept* of belief (in the modern sense) is necessary in an analysis of medieval [and other non-modern] religion" (1979: 235, 236). Terry Godlove (2002) also argues persuasively that if one cannot attribute religious beliefs to another, then one cannot attribute a religion to that person. Catherine Bell, sometimes seen as one of the belief-averse theorists of religion, concurs, saying, "without 'belief,' it is not clear what we mean by 'religion'" (2002: 115). As I argue in the text, despite the fact that Wilfred Cantwell Smith brought attention to the historical evolution of the importance of belief, he concurs with the position I defend that all agents have beliefs in the taking true sense. Similarly, although Malory Nye is a critic of belief who has harsh things to say about the assumptions that religions must have beliefs, that beliefs explain actions, and even that people have beliefs in the minimal sense of statements internalized "on the basis of being true or false" (2008: 119), in the end he agrees with the position I defend, saying that "religious belief… is something that permeates the whole of a person's body" and that believing and doing "cannot be separated" (2008: 124).

My claim that one can speak of collective beliefs is shared by the anthropologist Martin Southwold (1979; cf. Bell 2002). I agree with Southwold's defense of belief, though not his recommendation that one take religious beliefs as symbolic beliefs. In the chapter, I point out that although one can become conscious of one's beliefs, some have said that one never consciously believes (Crane 2001: 105–8). Though this point is controversial, it fits with the dispositionalist account of beliefs I defend.

I note in the chapter that it is not only possible but usual that a person will join a religious movement, participate in its practices, and identify with that community for reasons that have nothing to do with its beliefs. I therefore interpret Robert Orsi's question "What do beliefs have to do with it?" (1998: xxi) as foregrounding noncognitive reasons for religious membership and not as a rejection of the category of belief. For a nice account of the relative unimportance of religious beliefs in religious conversion, see Michael and Healy (2012).

It may be worth clarifying that belief in the taking true sense is not the same as what Ninian Smart calls the doctrinal and philosophical dimension of religion (1996). Belief in the taking true sense operates whenever religious people make judgments about their world, and such judgments would shape all the dimensions of a religious life, not just explicit statements or defenses of orthodoxy. In fact, I think that the distinction I develop between belief in the creedal sense and belief in the taking true sense is equivalent to Pierre Bourdieu's distinction between "adherence to a set of instituted dogmas and doctrines ('beliefs')" and what he calls practical belief, that is, "a quasi-bodily involvement in the world that presupposes no representation of the body or of the world, still less of their relationship" (Bourdieu 1990: 66, 68). Bourdieu also concurs that practical belief—that is, the taking true sense—is universal: "an inherent part of belonging to a field" (67).

It may be that many academics want to purge the study of religion of beliefs not because they really judge that there are no beliefs, but rather because they do not think that scholars of religion should make negative judgments about cultures other than their own. The "focus on truth claims tempts an evaluative response" (Bivins 2012: 55), and many scholars see the evaluation of religion as an element in the cultural imperialism of the west. Rubenstein says that we should abandon the concept of belief because it leads to social ills. Belief, she writes, is at the root of everything that deconstructive postmodernists do not like: "the ontotheological God, the transcendental subject, the metropole, the phallus, capital, the nation-state, progress, presence, the sovereign—none of these lynchpins of what Derrida called the 'globalatinized' order can said to be independent of belief. They are all massively powerful phantasms (*eidôla*) whose violent operations are sustained solely because we believe in them" (2012: 68). However, I see no way around the conclusion that those who take it as true that this is a list of problems are equally guilty of believing.

Endnotes

1. See Lofton (2012: 51). Lofton describes herself as taken aback that anyone would try to resuscitate the concept of belief.
2. Leach (1968: 655). The quotes in this paragraph from Bruce Lincoln are from Lincoln (2003: 111, n.15; cf. Lincoln 2005: esp. 65–7).
3. This quote comes from Smith (1977: 44; cf. Ruel 1982: esp. 22).
4. See Asad (1993: 46).
5. See Lopez (1998: 21, 27, 34).
6. The critics' opposition to the concept of beliefs is typically constructed with a dualistic rhetoric of a private inside and a public outside. In his critique of belief, for instance, Lopez describes belief as "interior … contained in the mind … inner and not outer … invisible content of the mind … an inner state … inner and not visible … inner … inner" (1998: 21, 22, 24, 27, 27, 27, 33, 34). The same interior way of describing belief is seen in Bivins (2012); McCutcheon (2012); and Rubenstein (2012).
7. To say that dispositional beliefs are "patterns" does not imply that one's beliefs must be coherent with one another, and this is likely true even within religious micro-systems such as Catholics at Mass or Muslims at prayer or Buddhists making offerings. That is, people doing these sorts of things very likely have incompatible dispositional beliefs about them. I owe this point to Paul Griffiths.
8. The concepts in the next two paragraphs come from Ryle (1949). The comment that the mental and the physical are not two processes can be found on 1949:33.
9. See Harding (2001: 58, 60).
10. For Davidson's notion of "triangulation," see Davidson (2001: esp. Ch. 7, 14). The two quotes in this paragraph come from Davidson (2001: 213) and Dennett (1987: 189), respectively.

11. This quote is from Davidson (1984: 156–7; cf. 2001: 98–9).

12. In this paragraph, I discuss the debate found in Smith (1977); Wiebe (1979); and Smith (1980; cf. Wiebe 1992). The Smith quote about the modernity of the importance of belief is from Smith (1977: v), and the quote about Jesus and the devils is from Smith (1980:252).

13. Any scholar of religions who would reject even belief in the taking true sense would have to state their case carefully. There is a danger that the argument that "propositional belief is a Christian preoccupation" slides into a romantic view that nonChristian religions (perhaps premodern religions or the religions of indigenous peoples or Zen) are mystical or noncognitive ways of life that lack reason or judgment. Distinguishing between belief in the taking true sense—a sense which is inexpungeable for understanding any intentional behavior—and belief in the sense of a creed or a confession, one can say that Christianity has been more invested in the latter sense than have other religions, but not that Christianity has been more invested in the former sense than have other religions.

14. One more distinction is relevant here. It is not only possible but usual that a person will join a religious movement, participate in its practices, and identify with that community for reasons that have nothing to do with its beliefs. Members often join, participate in, and identify with a religion because of affective bonds to other members, material benefits, and other noncognitive reasons. I take it that this is what Orsi means when he says "What do beliefs have to do with it?" (1998: xxi). But even when one is unpersuaded by or ignorant of a religion's "belief system," instead believing that a religious community is welcoming or fun or expected by one's family or a good way to make business contacts, one's actions are still interpretable in terms of what one takes as true.

Chapter 4
Do Religions Exist?

i.   The Critique of "Religion"

Several scholars have recently argued that the concept of "religion" is manufactured, constructed, invented, or imagined, but does not correspond to an objective reality, "out there" in the world. If one thinks of deconstruction in a nontechnical sense as an approach which takes meanings that are unreflectively taken as real and seeks to reveal them as conceptually unstable, historically emergent, and ideologically motivated, then these critics are pursuing the deconstruction of the concept of religion. In this chapter, I evaluate that critique and seek to defend the reality of religion. In the next chapter, I propose my own definition of religion.

Here is a summary of this chapter's trajectory. There is an unreflective but widespread view of religion that takes religion as something that exists independent of the concepts with which it is described. From this perspective, religion has a certain objective character and the scholar's task is to discover it. Call this view of religion "naive realism." I believe that in the face of the critique, a naive realism about religion is indefensible. Nevertheless, some of the critics draw the conclusion that "there is no such thing as religion" or "there are no religions," and I argue that this anti-realist view of religion does not follow from the critique. I seek instead to develop a chastened view of the concept of religion, a critical realism, that takes into

Philosophy and the Study of Religions: A Manifesto, First Edition. Kevin Schilbrack.
© 2014 Kevin Schilbrack. Published 2014 by John Wiley & Sons, Ltd.

account the contribution of the modern western provenance of the concept but nevertheless sees the study of religion as the study of a social reality that is in the crucial respects independent of the scholar.[1]

In my judgment, the critique of the concept of religion can be profitably sorted into three distinguishable levels.

The first level of the critique is that the term "religion" is a social construction. Whether or not religion has always existed, critics say, the concept of *religion* is a relatively recent invention. According to them, the concept of "a" religion as a particular system of beliefs embodied in a bounded community was largely unknown prior to the seventeenth century, and the concept of "religion" as a generic something which different cultures (or all cultures) share was not thought until the nineteenth. Before the modern age in the West, what is now called religion permeated the culture and was inseparable from other aspects of the culture. There was no term for the so-called religious aspect of a culture as opposed to the so-called nonreligious aspects. Moreover, there was no term for the religion of one's own culture as opposed to the religions of another culture, and so there had been no term for something of which Christianity was but one type of several. One may speculate about whether modern Europeans developed the concept of religion because of the fragmentation of the Christian church in the Reformation or because of the explosion of information about nonEuropean cultures, but the main point of the social constructionist critique of *religion* is that the concept is not universal. There is no word in classical Sanskrit for the concept and so "religion" does not appear in Hindu scriptures. There is also no word in Pali and so it also does not appear in Buddhist scriptures. There is no term for religion in Chinese or Japanese or Egyptian or in Native American languages. There is not even a word for religion in the Hebrew Bible or in the Greek New Testament. It is only modern European Christians who generalized or abstracted from their own practices and developed the word "religion" as a term for sorting a certain kind of activity. The term "religion" in its modern sense is thus not a concept shared universally but rather a product of a particular modern, European, and Christian history.[2]

The second level of the critique of "religion" is that the term distorts, it is said, the cultural phenomena on which it is imposed. (One might say: if the accusation on the first level is that the term is a social construction, the accusation on second is that it is a *flawed* social construction.) The critics argue that the term "religion" is flawed because it is not and cannot be culturally neutral but rather carries with it connotations derived from its modern, Western, Christian origins. To summarize this complaint, they argue that the term is flawed in three specific ways. In the first place, it is flawed simply because to use a single generic term for a variety of beliefs and practices hides differences and essentializes disparate ways of life. To say that scarification in a coming of age initiation is the same kind of thing as separating meat and milk dishes in accord with Biblical rules, and that both are the same kind of thing as believing that the cosmos is approaching the Last Days—that all of these are religion—implies an ahistorical, monolithic homogeneity. In the second place, the critics argue that the term is flawed because to use a word that distinguishes the religious aspect of a culture from the political and other aspects of a culture reflects a modern "separation of church and state" understanding of what religion is, an understanding that has not been shared by most religious people in history. To use this word therefore implies that what "religion" describes is something distinct from economics, politics, and issues of power. And the critics argue that the term is flawed in the third place because the word still carries the Christian sense that what is described as religion is one's "faith" or one's "beliefs," that is, something private and interior. In short, the critics hold that the term carries so much conceptual baggage that it is inevitably misleading.

The third level of the critique of "religion" is that the construction of "religion" is ideologically motivated. If the previous points were that "religion" is a social construction, and a distorting one at that, the third point is that the distortions are deliberate and the definition of religion serves the purposes of those who developed it. Specifically, the development of the concept of religion serves the purposes of modern western power. As Daniel Dubuisson says, with the emergence of the concept *religion*, "[a]t a single stroke, imperialism and colonialism were equally justified and even, with the impetus of missionary activity, received an unanticipated moral guarantee."[3] The concept *religion* as an ideological weapon can be used in multiple ways. One use has been for Europeans to argue that other people have no religion. They are without spiritual values, understanding, or morals, and are closer to animals. Consequently, they are unable to govern themselves and to colonize them is a benefit to them. Another ideological use of the term has been for Europeans to argue the reverse, that nonEuropeans are actually too religious, and that unlike the west where secular politics and science are separated from the religious, other cultures are premodern and superstitious. In either strategy, the development of the concept of religion is a part of an orientalist and imperialist project. Defining religion is thus not innocent or apolitical but grows from and serves material interests. "Religion" is a social construction developed in a certain time and place in history, and it is developed for the purposes of those who needed that conceptual tool. The concept was developed not by someone musing about the nature of words, but rather as a tool in order to accomplish certain goals. And it was developed as a tool in a period when Europeans were seeking an ideological justification for their expansion into the New World of the Americas, the race for Africa, and the gunboat diplomacy in Asia.

In sum, then, the critique of "religion" points to constructivist, historicist, and ideological problems with the concept. The argument of the critics is that if religion is socially constructed, then religion is not a thing in the world but rather a product of Western imagination. This use of language distorts what it describes and is ideologically motivated to be pejorative toward nonwestern cultures.

Given this multifaceted challenge to the legitimacy of the concept of religion, what should students of religions do? Answers to this question can usefully be divided into abolitionist and retentionist responses: on the one hand, as seen above, the abolitionists argue that the term "religion" is so biased, so theologically and ideologically laden, that the best thing for scholars to do is to abandon it. They argue that the concept "religion" should be replaced with other concepts, and that therefore religious studies programs should be disbanded or reconceived. According to the abolitionists, in other words, reflexivity in the study of religions means deconstructing or dissolving both the object of study and the field erected to manage it. On the other hand, there are retentionists who agree that the concept of religion is problematic, but argue that it can be refined or redefined more carefully or more broadly, so that it is less distorting, less Christian, or less privatized, so that it is suitable for cross-cultural study.

In the remainder of this chapter, I will give reasons for resisting the abolitionist view. In terms of a typology of social constructionists drawn up by Ian Hacking, abolitionists are "rebellious" social constructionists: they believe not only (1) that religion as it is understood in the modern West is not determined by the nature of things, and (2) that the concept is distorting or harmful or both but also (3) that we would be better off if we did away with the idea altogether. They are rebellious in the sense that they want not only to unmask the concept of religion—to undermine the practical effectiveness of the term by exposing the function it serves—but also to disabuse others of the concept. In contrast, I am a "reformist" social constructionist: I agree that the term is a social construction, and that some uses of the term are problematic, but I argue that the criticisms of the term should lead scholars to refine and not abandon the term. I turn now to my critical realist defense of the concept.

ii. The Ontology of "Religion"

My response to the first level of the critique is that the concept of "religion" *is* socially constructed, but religion nevertheless exists, "out there" in the world.

It is not unusual to hear some of those who point out that "religion" is a social construction draw the conclusion that "there is no such thing as religion," that "religion does not exist," or that religions are "nonexistent objects." The critics suggest that social constructions (or at least this social construction) are projections or illusions that correspond to nothing outside the modern Western imagination. We can call this a deflationary account of social construction, and the argument is that scholars should drop the term because "religion" denotes or designates or refers to nothing, and religion has no ontological status. On a deflationary account, there is no religion and no religions in the actual world. Religions are like chimeras, mythical animals that will not be found, no matter what stone one overturns.

Clearly, however, when one says that there is no such thing as religion, a great deal turns on what is meant by "thing," or what it is to be "real," and so it is a shame that these critics usually say so little about this. In fact, there is an irony here that theorists who are postmetaphysical in so many ways are raising and making central this ontological question. So the ontological question is where I would like to start: if "religion" is a social construction, and I am agreeing that it is, then what kind of reality does the referent have?

Since "religion" is a social construction and a product of human history, it clearly follows that religion does not exist as a natural kind—like lightning, say, or frogs. That is, religion does not exist apart from human ways of thinking, speaking, and acting. Since religion is a social construction, the only reality that religious phenomena have, they have by tradition or convention or agreement. It follows that if people had never thought, spoken, and acted in religious ways, or if they ceased to think, speak, and act in these ways, then what are often described religious phenomena would not exist. If everyone were to cease to recognize holy days, for instance, there would be no more holy days. If everyone were to cease to recognize priests, there would be no more priests. The deflationary account is right about the socially constructed and relatively fragile ontology of religion. But to say that something exists merely by convention (or merely rhetorically, or merely by linguistic agreement) is not at all the same as saying that the entity does not exist.

To clarify how religion exists, it helps to distinguish between "socially dependent facts" whose existence depends upon human behavior and "socially independent facts" that would exist even had no human beings ever lived. The existence of religion is clearly a socially dependent fact: it would not exist if there were no people. This dependence is something religion shares with other social patterns of behavior like politics and sports and the economy. "Jacob Zuma is the president of South Africa" is another example of a socially dependent fact. Its existence depends on a cluster of human institutions, concepts, and actions. If people ceased to recognize presidents, then they would no longer exist. "The batter struck out" is another example of a socially dependent fact. Its existence depends on a different cluster of institutions, concepts, and actions. But "Jupiter is closer to the sun than Saturn" and "Triceratops was an herbivore" are examples of socially independent facts. (The English sentences describing these facts are socially dependent, of course, but the realities described are not.) The situations that those sentences describe were the case long before and whether or not any humans existed. But the point is that socially dependent facts are nonetheless facts. They are "out there," in the world. As John Searle concisely puts it, even though socially dependent facts are ontologically subjective, they are also epistemically objective. They are ontologically subjective in the sense that they require human subjectivity in order to exist; they are brought into existence by and continue to depend on collective human agreement. But socially dependent facts are also epistemically objective in the sense that the facts that make them true are independent of what any individual person thinks. One may wish that Zuma was not elected president, or that the last pitch was not a strike, or that one's rent is not due on Wednesday. But noting that elections and baseball games and private property are social constructions will not change these facts. They are independent of one's preferences or beliefs. And this independence is also part of the general ontology of any social fact, something that religion shares with politics, economics, sports, and other human institutions.

An anti-realist critic might argue that religion does not exist because the term is only an abstract term created by academics for their own sorting and comparing. In a well-known statement that is often read in this way, Jonathan Z. Smith says, "Religion is solely the creation of the scholar's study. It is created for the scholar's analytic purposes by his imaginative acts of comparison and generalization. Religion has no existence apart from the academy." Russell McCutcheon, who often cites the Smith quote just given, agrees, saying, "the category of religion is a conceptual tool and ought not to be confused with an ontological category actually existing in reality."[4] Here "religion" exists as a way of thinking and speaking, but—to use Smith's slogan—map is not territory, and it is a mistake to confuse one's concepts with the actual world.

From the critical realist perspective I am developing, this claim that "religion" is only a scholar's word is doubly misleading. It is misleading in the first place in that the word has a history of employment by monks and theologians and princes outside the academic study of religion. More importantly, this claim is misleading in the second place because religion is not merely a word or a concept or a taxon or a label. This latter point deserves some discussion.

What is the ontology of social realities? What is the relation between human words and the human world? In my judgment, religion is a social construction, but this social construction is in the first place performed rather than spoken, and as it is performed it transforms bodies. The Thai boy, for instance, is not merely called a monk; he becomes a monk. His religious status—his monkhood—exists not merely because a religious word is used to describe him, not merely because he is seen, so to speak, though the lens of a religious vocabulary. He embodies this religious status because his hair has been cut in tonsure, because he has been given and wears his robes, because of the creation of the monastery and the arrangements of the finances and laws to support it, because of its Vinaya code and the discipline he takes from it, and because of the boundaries of the sangha as a group distinct from the householders and exclusive of women. In this way one can speak of religious hair, religious clothes, religious buildings, religious behavior, and religious communities as social realities in the world, and one can speak of religion as the abstraction that refers to the set of such things. In these ways, religions are not merely concepts but also inhabited worlds. Analogously, "nations" is the abstract or general sorting term that refers to the set of inhabited worlds or imagined communities that includes Japan, Ireland, and Senegal. As Talal Asad says, "This construct [i.e., the nation] is no less real for being ideological."[5] Someone who is committed to a materialist ontology might still insist that only physical things like laptops or chairs are real, and that words for socially dependent entities like religions or nations are merely heuristic tools for organizing the physical world. But for the critical realist, a religion is a practice that includes words, and is not solely a word.

To say that there are no religions (or that there are no nations) is therefore either false or a misleading way to make a point about the performed nature of social realities.

To say that religion is a social construction is important because it introduces reflexivity into one's study. It lets scholars of religion raise the questions of who gets to define what religion is and what purposes their definitions serve. This attention to the history and politics of one's concepts is what makes a critical realism critical. But to show that a concept is a social construction says nothing about whether or not that concept identifies something real. The concept of "molecule" and "magnetic field" are socially constructed but this alone does not show that the entities so labeled are chimerical. Or, to take cultural examples, "gender" and "sexism" and even "colonialism" and "imperialism" are social constructions but nevertheless indicate social realities that exist in the world. This view is what makes critical realism a form of realism.

iii.   Can There be Religion Without "Religion"?

There is, however, a problem in the account I am developing. In all of my examples of social facts, the people involved in the practices themselves use the concepts that are at issue. People who are voting for a president understand themselves as participating in an election; pitchers and batters themselves use the term "baseball game." Similarly, people involved in religious practices today in mosques and temples and churches and gurdwaras understand themselves as practicing religions. For this reason, my argument so far only amounts to this: we can describe a practice as X when the practitioners themselves understand themselves as practicing X. But as many of the critics of "religion" have pointed out, most people in history and around the world who are now said to have practiced religion did *not* understand themselves that way. The contemporary concept of religion was invented in Europe roughly in the seventeenth century, it is said, and then the concept was spread by European travelers, missionaries, and colonial administrators and imposed on the rest of the world. The abolitionist might grant that many today do understand what they do as religion, but might nevertheless insist that there were no religions before that time, or outside that spreading circle of European proselytizing and imperialism. If it is inappropriate to impose a label on someone who does not understand themselves under that description, then it is inappropriate to speak of religion outside modern Europe in

China, India, Africa, South America, and so on. In fact, on this view, there were no religions even in Europe before the concept emerged.

Now, it is absolutely true that to identify a human practice under a description not used by the practitioners themselves is unacceptable.[6] There is an obvious confusion in saying that someone is voting when they do not have the concept of an election, or that they are striking out when they do not have the practice of baseball. To identify a practice, or properly to describe it, one must restrict oneself to concepts and beliefs that inform that practice. An action performed by a person is informed by the understanding of that person, and this understanding of the action is what makes it the action that it is. Put philosophically: because practices are intentional behavior, the participants' self-ascription is normative for identifying the practice. Nevertheless, one *can* employ the concept of "religion" in ways that are appropriate, even if the people in question themselves do not use the term. Even when the practices so labeled do not include that idea, one can legitimately redescribe a practice as religion. I want to develop this idea.

One might think that if the term "religion" is not native, then it will be by that fact alone inappropriate to impose it. In order to describe a practice properly, one must be faithful to the concepts that inform it, and to fail to respect the distinctiveness and integrity of the culture under description is a form of "conceptual violence" or "symbolic violence." There should be little question that people have sought to legitimate physical forms of violence through the use of concepts, not least "religion." Nevertheless, scholars of religion can employ the concept of religion even when it is not indigenous if they distinguish between the conceptual work of *identifying* a practice and that of *interpreting* it. It is true that one must identify a practice using native terms, for the reason given above. However, once one has identified a practice, it can be fitting and illuminating to interpret or redescribe or translate that practice into nonnative terms. In fact, redescribing something in terms not used (or not even known) by the speaker is commonplace. We say, "When he said 'the woman with the baby,' he was referring to Maria." Or: "When you climbed K2, you climbed the second tallest mountain in the world." To apply this distinction to a religious example: one might identify what certain participants are doing using their own terms, say, as honoring the ancestors. If one then wants to redescribe what they are doing in one's own terms, in terms that the practitioners do not know, then one is redescribing or interpreting that practice. One is arguing that "honoring the ancestors" is a form of religion. In situations when the term is not known, then, ascriptions of religion are elliptical, in the sense that to say "The people practiced religion" really means: "The people practiced (something that they describe as X but that I would interpret as) religion." Scholars of religion should recognize that the parenthetical comment is always implied, even when it is not made explicit.

This is the point at which how one defines religion becomes important. For instance, if one defines religion as a kind of social formation, then to interpret honoring the ancestors as religion is to argue that honoring the ancestors is a kind of social formation. By contrast, if one defines religion as experience of the sacred, then to interpret honoring the ancestors as religion is to argue that honoring the ancestors is a kind of experience of the sacred.[7] The question for scholars of religion then turns on whether these interpretations of honoring the ancestors fit and illuminate the practice, or whether they distort it. Either is possible. To make this distinction between identifying a practice and interpreting is crucial, I judge, because it highlights the fact that ascriptions of religion in conditions when the word is not used are always a step removed from the description proper. They are paraphrases, elaborations. The term "religion" is being used as a model or a template in order to interpret the phenomena, but since the term is not internal to the practice, misinterpretation is possible. The redescription may fail to fit. Either insiders or outsiders to the practices being interpreted may reject the label. An interpretation is open to challenge *as* an interpretation and therefore those who interpret, unlike those who describe, have to be able to give reasons in support of their labels. And so the distinction between describing or identifying on the one hand and redescribing and interpreting on the other opens up a space for challenge and highlights the fact that the meaning of "religion" is not self-evident.

The critics of "religion" might grant all this and still be skeptical. They might question whether the practices redescribed as religion—the pilgrimages and prayers and sacrifices and so on—have any *unity* independent of the sorting done by the term. Perhaps, as Ian Hacking has analogously argued about the label "schizophrenia," the term "religion" gathers disparate social phenomena together in an external and arbitrary way. I judge that this is a legitimate worry. The retentionist therefore needs to show that the use of a nonnative sorting term is not arbitrary.

Let me illustrate how one might make the argument that the concept of *religion* does not sort cultural forms arbitrarily. I will use a minimalist (Tylorean) definition of religion as a set of rituals, stories, and institutions connected to belief in superhuman beings. Now, I agree with the critic that it would not be appropriate to lump together the rituals, stories, and institutions from some culture into a set and then call this their "religion," if these elements are in the eyes of the practitioners themselves unrelated. If these elements are always simply cobbled together by outsiders, then I would agree that it is more accurate to say that there are no religions outside modern European influence. What a retentionist needs to show, therefore, is that the elements in the set are not arbitrary but are instead connected to each other by the practitioners themselves. A retentionist needs to show that there is a structure to these elements that exists independent of the label. That is, if the practitioners themselves relate their rituals to the stories they teach—for instance, they hear the stories as the source or the model or the justification for the rituals—and if the rituals and stories are in turn linked to the institutions, then there is a structure to the phenomena that antedates the label. Whether some particular rituals are connected to some particular stories and whether rituals or stories are connected to the institutions are not things that one can know *a priori* or declare by fiat; these are questions that would have to be asked in each case. But the retentionist hypothesis is that even if a culture does not have the concept of religion, the connections that constitute the cultural pattern are indigenous and not imposed by the use of the external label. Let me give two examples. If the Nuer tell stories that dramatize what they see as the relationship between ethical lapses and the loss of purity, and they connect these teachings to expiatory sacrifices, and they also connect their story-connected sacrifices to the social roles of the leopard skin priests, then it may be fitting and illuminating to redescribe this complex of teachings and rituals and institutions as Nuer religion, even if the Nuer themselves do not use the term. Similarly, if the Huichol tell stories about the journeys of ancestor spirits, and these journeys are imitated in peyote rituals conducted by a shaman, then it may be fitting and illuminating to redescribe this complex of stories and rituals and institutions as Huichol religion, even if the Huichol themselves do not use the term. In such cases, the interpreter is claiming two things: (1) that there is a cultural pattern or structure that exists independent of the label of it as a religion and (2) that the label of "religion" fits or illuminates that pattern.

One can therefore distinguish between sets of cultural elements that are arbitrary and those that we might call kin. It is inappropriate to impose the label "religion" on a set of cultural elements if they are an arbitrary set. In his discussion of mereology (i.e., the study of parts and wholes), Hilary Putnam creates a set that includes his nose and the Eiffel tower,[8] and if a random grouping like that is all that speaking of religion as a set of elements amounts to, then retentionists should let the term go. But if the elements that make

95

up a religion are kin to each other, taught by the participants as an interconnected complex, then it may not be inappropriate to interpret that complex as a religion—even if cultural insiders lack a corresponding term. And to be clear, if one argues that a culture lacking the term religion nevertheless has practices that are aptly interpreted as a religion, she need not be claiming that they are "unconsciously" religious nor that they are "latently" religious, but only that one can legitimately redescribe what they are doing as religious, for one's own purposes, when the label fits. On this approach, people have practiced what many people today call religion without abstracting from that practice in order to develop either an explicit name for that practice or a common term for that practice as a generic type of which there are others. On this approach, in other words, religions, like dinosaurs and sexism, have existed even without the term.[9]

To sum up my argument to this point, I have argued that one can use the label "religion" if the people so labeled themselves use the term and that, in some cases, one can also use it even if the people so labeled do not use the term themselves, as long as the elements so labeled are kin to each other and one recognizes that one is importing an etic term that redescribes indigenous practices. To mark the difference between these two situations in the study of culture, it may be worth underlining the distinction between the practice of "describing" on the one hand and "redescribing" or "interpreting" on the other. In this context, to describe is to give a practice a name that the practitioners themselves use; thus one is simply describing what they understand themselves to be doing, and one describes a practice as a religion when the practitioners themselves use or import that concept. But when one gives it a name not used by the practitioners themselves, one is redescribing or interpreting their practice. Interpreting involves another level of analogical imagination, and so the interpreter is imposing a label, though this may be a fitting label.

iv. "Religion" as Distortion

The second level in the critique of "religion" is that the use of this term typically distorts the cultural phenomena on which it is imposed. Whether or not religion exists in the world, the critics' second, historicist argument is that the term in its modern western sense carries so much conceptual baggage that it is misleading to use it to redescribe other cultural examples.

The meaning of the term is derived from and only properly fits its own historically particular situation.

I take this critique seriously. The most important conceptual problems with the concept "religion," in my judgment, are the following. In the first place, nouns carry with them the implication that the reality described is a bounded and even static object. Call this *the problem of reification*. This conceptual ossification was detailed by Wilfred Cantwell Smith, who argued that the history of the word "religion" began with attention to the way that people struggled to live, a living response to a vision, and shifted over time to an abstract and hypostatized noun. Smith points out that the early term *religio* was used to refer not to a cultural entity but to whether a person was pious, faithful, and observant: "What began ... as designating a quality of life, eventually came to refer to the formal pattern or outward system of observances in which that quality found expression."[10] Reification is also problematic because a collective noun homogenizes. The term conceptually gathers together historical realities that are diverse and in process and occludes both the differences between them and the changes within them. With social realities there is also the implication that the reality described is discrete and coherent rather than a contested space in which different groups struggle and negotiate with each other. This process of reification occurs at the level of generalizing about "religion" and then it can occur again at the level of individual religions: the idea of Hinduism, for example, also suggests that there is something ahistorical and monolithic about being Hindu, and the same is true of the labels of "Buddhism," "Christianity" and so on. This opposition to *religion* thus draws on the widespread philosophical rejection of essentialism.

The second kind of distortion is that the word "religion" distinguishes between religion and the nonreligious aspects of culture. But if "non-religious" is meant to refer to politics, economics, and other so-called secular aspects of a culture, then this division clearly reflects the modern understanding of the term, epitomized by John Locke and the Constitution of the United States, in which religion is restricted to the private or in which church and state are separated. Call this *the problem of autonomy*. To label something as "religion" implies that it is distinct from those other cultural processes, but for most of human history, the people who are now called religious did not make these distinctions. Take, for example, a sacrifice that is offered as part of the installation of a king. It distorts the phenomenon if one classifies the ceremony (the participants involved, the objects used, the social effects of the ritual, or the feelings experienced) as religious-not-political or as political-not-religious. The use of the label "religion" suggests the view of religion found in the modern west where religious and political aspects of culture are treated as distinct spheres. At a minimum, therefore, the use of the word suggests that religion and politics are separate aspects of culture; at worst, it can suggest that religion is isolable, sui generis, and irreducible.

The third kind of distortion is that the dominant religion in the west puts great emphasis on internal states of piety, and the term therefore carries with it the sense that what religion refers to is faith or belief understood as a mental state. Call this *the problem of privatization*. Christian practice has long included a central focus on creedal statements, the Reformation and its repudiation of Catholic sacraments and "works righteousness" underlined this focus on belief even more, and the Enlightenment ideal of a rational faith underlined it still again. Typically, as a consequence, "religion" is implicitly heard or explicitly defined in terms of voluntary belief. This internal focus is also seen if one defines religion as an experience of the sacred, that is, as a distinctive kind of experience that cannot be reduced to social or psychological feelings. In both cases, this focus reflects an especially modern and an especially Christian perspective.

The term "religion" is thus weighted with multiple connotations and these can distort our understanding of what people do and think. Given the inevitability of abstractions for any kind of thinking, however, it seems that there are only two choices open to us. We can develop new terms, a new taxonomic vocabulary, or we can refine the old ones.

If one decides to develop new terms and replace the term "religion," I see two general strategies. One is to develop a "bigger" concept, a concept that is even more inclusive than "religion." A good example of this strategy comes from Daniel Dubuisson who proposes the idea of "cosmographic formation." Unlike "religion," which Dubuisson says is ethnocentric, cosmographic formation is "truly universal." It connects the formation of a character and a way of life to a vision of the cosmos; it unites "comprehensive ideas of the world" with "the practices, the rules for living, and prescriptions that they imply." Unlike definitions of religion that include divine beings, this open-ended notion can apply to all cultures. As he says, "This notion can also apply to the cosmographies of atheists, agnostics, and materialists," and this lets one use it to illuminate Confucianism, communism, Stoicism, and Theravada Buddhism and (I would add) those indigenous traditions that do not imagine a supernatural realm separate from the natural world.[11]

In my judgment, "cosmographic formation" is a useful phrase because it draws attention to human agents and their purposes and thereby avoids the suggestion that the process of formation is reified, autonomous, or private. Dubuisson's term also undermines the near-automatic assumption that religions are inherently moral, pious, or spiritual. I limit my critical discussion of this proposal to one point. Dubuisson claims that "religion" is a parochial idea, local to and indeed definitive of the Christian West, but that his idea of "cosmographic formation" is better because it is "less European." This is dubious. The notion of cosmographic formation is made of two elements, the idea that all things can be imagined as a totality (*kosmos*) and the practice of writing (*graphein*), both of Greek origin and both of which have been widely used as the markers of European superiority to non-European cultures. Moreover, the true parent of Dubuisson's idea is Immanuel Kant. Kant holds that all human beings construct a world through the categories of their understanding. Dubuisson is clear about his respect for Kant's first critique and how it informs his own work: Kant's distinction between the world in experience and the world in itself shows us how one can speak of the cosmos without speaking of the world as it is in itself.[12] In brief, for Dubuisson, Kant's turn to the subject shows how the study of the comprehensive ideas can eschew metaphysics. But this claim—that the study of different views of reality should follow Kant in the sense that it should presuppose that premodern and nonwestern cosmographers were always confused when they believed that they were describing the nature of things—hardly seems less ethnocentric than the more philosophically neutral term "religion." Kant's project is a quintessential part of the European Enlightenment. Kant is perhaps the premier representative of modernity in the West. Phenomenology, existentialism, critical thought, deconstruction, all grow from Kantian soil. In this way, it is hard to imagine a *more* European concept. And so Dubuisson's proposal, though pedagogically valuable for its ability to unsettle entrenched ideas, seems just as ethnocentric as the term it is supposed to replace.[13]

The other strategy for replacing the term "religion" is to develop concepts that are "smaller"—that is, more particular and less inclusive—than "religion." One example of this strategy is the proposal of Timothy Fitzgerald, who breaks the concept of religion down into three elements: ritual, politics, and soteriology. Ritual refers to standardized actions, he says, politics to the different means for the legitimation of power, and soteriology to a release from life's ills, in either this-worldly or other-worldly terms. Fitzgerald claims that these three categories let us analyze contemporary

Indian Buddhism, for example, in greater specificity than the fuzzy and over-determined word "religion." And, as with Dubuisson, the terms he has chosen do not suggest that what is being analyzed is a reified object, autonomous from political struggles, or an internal mental state. Of course, other approaches to the study of religion also break the concept of religion down into constituent elements: Ninian Smart famously analyzes the seven dimensions of religion, and this process is central to every "family resemblance" approach to religion. But what is distinctive about Fitzgerald's deflationary approach is his argument that the more specific terms substitute for *religion* so adequately that that the term "religion" can be dropped. His argument is that there is nothing to religion over and above ritual, politics, and soteriology. In fact, he says, the ideologically motivated invention of the term "religion" is precisely what mystifies the phenomena that one is seeking to analyze.

I limit my critical discussion to one point. There will be some cultural phenomena that do not include all three of the elements Fitzgerald focuses on. A birthday party, for instance, may involve ritual but have little or no political or soteriological significance. A local election may be analyzed as both political and ritual but not soteriological. Yet there will be some aspects of a culture that are so semantically rich that they combine all three, the ritual, the political, and the soteriological. The movements, events, institutions, behavior, or traditions that combine all three will be aspects of a culture that are especially complex. Two well-known examples include the Babylonian New Year (Akitu) festival and the Lakota ghost dance. What label should scholars give to phenomena like these that combine ritual, politics, and soteriology? Any answer to this question reintroduces "religion" or an equivalent. There seems to be a conceptual need not only for the small, particular, local terms but also for generalized abstractions, for the imagined whole of which the small terms are parts. Fitzgerald recognizes this, I believe, but he considers "religion" too distorting, and therefore proposes the word "culture." But this answer returns us to the previous strategy of more inclusive terms and, with its close ties to the idea of civilization and its employment in distinctions between high and low culture, the word "culture" is no more politically innocent than the word "religion." Both the more inclusive and the more particular replacement strategies therefore seem to become entangled in the fact that no language is pure.

If replacement terms become mired in the same conceptual and ideological problems that bedevil "religion," and one therefore chooses to retain the term, then one still needs to confront the problems of reification, autonomy, and privatization. The problem of the semantic drag of "religion" is real, and those who retain the term have to recognize and combat the entrenched view of religion. They have to make it clear—perhaps especially to themselves—what parts of the term's semantic history they endorse and what parts they are rejecting.

But at least they are not alone. This process of trying to stretch the word "religion" to include new meanings and of trying to excise unwanted meanings is not new. Anthropologists and historians have long been central in the evolution of the word away from its Protestant roots. Those who use the label "religion" have to make it clear that a set of practices and beliefs may be a religion not only if it lacks a belief in God, a Bible, or a Sabbath, but also, more radically, even if it has not been articulated as a system, does not have a distinct community, makes dances more central to membership than creeds, and is inseparable from the public life of the culture. To combat the problem of autonomy, with its assumption that religion and politics are independent, one can make it clear, with Bruce Lincoln, that religion has both minimalist forms that seek to separate church and state and maximalist forms in which religion is used to ground ethical, aesthetic, and political values. To combat the problem of privatization, with its assumption that religions are a matter of interior beliefs, one can make it clear, with José Casanova, that religion has both personal and intellectualist forms and, increasingly, social and public forms.[14] And to combat the problem of reification, with its assumption that a religion is a holistic entity, one can specify that religions exist on a spectrum from unsystematized set of practices and beliefs that are diffuse in a culture to a systematized theology with a distinct religious community. Religion may not be a structure as much as a space of contestation between different constituencies who use the stories, rituals, and institutions that mark off that space as tools to establish their own norms as the authoritative ones. In fact, those who continue to use the label "religion" should clarify that something may be a religion without a name, and therefore may not exist in the minds of its practitioners as an entity separate from the rest of their culture.

v. The Ideology of "Religion"

The third level of the abolitionists' critique is that the term "religion" is part of an orientalist and colonialist program and therefore ideologically poisonous. The abolitionists argue that the invention of the term in the Enlightenment was not an innocent neologism but was politically motivated, as Europeans sought a justification for imperialism. One response to this argument is that the original use of a word does not determine its future use. To conflate the origin of the term with its applicability is the genetic fallacy. Another response is that discourses of power can always be reappropriated and put to the service of subversive interests. The same is true of the discourse of "religion." Both of these responses are sound. But in this closing section of this chapter I want to develop a critical realist response to the root question of the relation between ideological interests and descriptions of reality. My goal is to keep in mind the critics' awareness that religion is a social construction without giving up the possibility that the thing which the term refers nevertheless exists.

There is no denying that our concepts are the products of our interests. And this is likely to be true both in the sense that the development and use of certain concepts will reflect what people find interesting and in the sense that people develop and use the concepts to promote their own interests. But this does not settle the question about whether the concepts correspond to the world. Let me apply this observation to the invention of "religion." It is true that the interests that people have may lead them to notice certain facts about the world, and to label them, whereas those with other interests may overlook or ignore these states of affairs. Perception itself is driven by interest. In broad strokes, then, a critical realist account of "religion" would be that the Reformation led Europeans to notice or realize that there were structural and functional similarities between the beliefs and practices of the different Protestant and Catholic churches. Given this perception, Zwingli and Calvin (but not Luther) took the term "religion" and began to stretch it so that it might serve as a type of which there could be more than one token. This new conceptual tool served the polemical purpose of distinguishing between the authentic piety of the reformers and the spurious piety of the Roman Church. Subsequently, the enormous growth of information about the diversity of cultures around the world in the age of colonialism led Europeans to notice or realize that non-European cultures had elements functionally or structurally analogous to what were now called European religions. Given that perception, Herbert of Cherbury and the Enlightenment *philosophes* stretched the word "religion" again to broaden it further, first to seek to include nonChristian and later to include nontheistic types. This development served the polemical purpose of distinguishing the so-called natural religion of the *philosophes* from the so-called revealed religions of those around the world deceived by priestcraft.

An account of "religion" like this one focuses on the interaction between self-interested perceptions of the world and the ideologically driven history of the concept. My critical realism therefore does not deny that "religion" is a product of the European *imaginaire*, nor does it claim that the term is ideologically innocent. On the contrary, it foregrounds the issue of the historical context and the purposes of those who developed the terms. Nevertheless, it does not follow that the word is substantively empty or refers to nothing.

One can imagine the reasoning that leads the critics to make this deflationary claim. What "religion" means shifts according to the ideological interests of those using the term. What Zwingli refers to with the term differs from what Herbert refers to, which differs again from what Tillich refers to. This seems like evidence that "religion" is simply an ideological marker and that religion (without the scare quotes) is a not a reality but merely a product of the way that the world is described. The label apparently gets applied not because the term corresponds to something that "is" religion, but because it is in the interests of those who apply the term. On this view, it seems that, as Russell McCutcheon argues, the study of religion might better understand itself not as the study of a real thing but as the investigation into who gets to decide what counts as religion, that is, not as the investigation of rituals, stories, and institutions connected to belief in superhuman beings but rather as the study of a disciplinary concept. On this account, there is no fact of the matter concerning what religion really is. When one follows this line, the ideological critique of religion blocks the ontological question about what kind of thing religion "is."

The deconstructive idea that facts about the world are *created* by how one describes the world may lead the critic of "religion" to argue that, outside of language, there are no religions. It is crucial to a critical realist account to distinguish between this deconstructive idea (which he does not accept) and the very different idea that which descriptions of the world are accepted depends upon one's interests (which he can). One can endorse the latter without in any way accepting the former. It is true that "religion" is a modern and European and Christian word and that it has been imposed on other cultures. But labels for social realities like religions typically presuppose a certain conceptual distance. It is therefore not surprising that labels for religions are so often created by outsiders. "Hinduism" may be an invention of Muslims. "Confucianism" may be an invention of the Jesuits. "Shinto" can arise as the Chinese word for the religion of Japan. The *philosophes* distinguished "revealed religions" that claimed revelation from "natural religion" based on reason. William James invented labels for "healthy-minded" and "sick-souled" religions. "Civil religions" is a label created by Robert Bellah. Today scholars debate the appropriateness of "fundamentalism" as a sorting word. Perhaps all of these terms for categorizing human beliefs and practices were created by outsiders to label the practices of other people. Does this make them inadmissible? Often insiders then adopt the labels to describe themselves. Does that then make them acceptable?

The view I am arguing for in this chapter is different: there are innumerable ways that any cultural phenomenon can be described. When one sees the world a certain way, one develops a label to mark that part of the world as such, uses that label, and recommends its use. The label reflects the purpose of the labeler. When it comes to religions, often (perhaps even typically) the labels groups have been deprecatory or pejorative. But this does not mean that the labels never correspond to distinctions in how people are living. This is complicated by the fact that all of the terms being discussed— such as "religion" and "Hinduism" and "healthy-minded"—are "interactive kinds" in the sense that once they are connected they can be picked up and embraced by those so described. With social realities, if people find the term useful and live in its terms, this agreement is all that is needed for the alleged thing to exist. To recall the quote from Talal Asad, "This construct is no less real for being ideological."

Some of the critics have emphasized that the word "religion" is inevitably a Christian concept. They often claim that the term is covertly theological or ecumenical, and that their critique of the term is part of a naturalistic, non-theological approach to the study of cultures. But I find the critics confused about the relation between their critique and Christian theology. Presumably, according to the critics, theologians or theologically inspired scholars want the concept of "religion" in order to flatten differences between various ways of life and to suggest that the members of every culture have the same spiritual needs or the same contact with the transcendent. But the truth is that plenty of contemporary theologians welcome the critique of "religion." This is as true of conservative theologians like Karl Barth and Paul Griffiths as it is of liberal theologians like John Hick and John Thatamanil. Griffiths endorses the critique because if there is no way to distinguish between a religion and a secular ideology, as Fitzgerald puts it, then there is no way to distinguish between theological and secular theorizing, and so there are no grounds for excluding theology from the public sphere or from the academy. And John Hick wrote the laudatory foreword to Smith's critique expressly to oppose the essentialism and reification of religion as a modern and distorting western view.[15] In my judgment, the critique of "religion" can at the least be perfectly put to theological or ecumenical use. At the most, the critique of "religion" is simply part of theology in its post-modern incarnation.

I write this chapter defending the concept of *religion* with ambivalence. I agree with the critics that the concept is not innocent. "Religion" was used and is still used to classify and judge as inferior cultures other than the dominant ideology of the modern west. And that means that I am myself implicated in this discussion: the concept of religion was used and is still used to classify and judge as inferior cultures other than my own. But, as suggested above, there are no terms whose history or implications are free of politics. None of our thinking is without ideological baggage. None of our perspectives are neutral. There is no way to study what we now call religious rituals, stories, experiences, institutions, and so on, without the acts of classification that make possible value judgments between cultures. This is why I argue for retaining the word "religion," though now conscious of the shadows it casts.

Bibliographic Essay

In this chapter, I argue against those who hold that religion is a concept that does not correspond to anything in the world and I argue for a critical realist view in which religion exists, like money or politics, as a social reality. Some scholars of religion have reminded us that the concept *religion* depends on ways of thinking and acting that emerged only in the modern West, and some of these scholars have therefore proposed that we should recognize that religion is an invented concept that does not correspond to something that exists in the world. These include Wilfred Cantwell Smith (1962); J. Z. Smith (1982, 1998); Asad (1993); Lease (1994); Balagangadhara (1994); McCutcheon (1997, 2001); Fitzgerald (1997, 2000, 2007); Arnal (2000, 2001); Dubuisson (2003); Webb (2009). Representative statements such as "there is no such thing as religion," "religion does not exist," and religions are "nonexistent objects" are by Arnal (2000: 32 and 2001: 4), Webb (2009: 35); and Fitzgerald (1997: x), respectively. Similarly, Wilfred Cantwell Smith writes: "there is no such entity ... In any case, the use of a plural, or with an article, is false" (1962: 326, 194; cf. 144), and Gary Lease writes: "there is no religion" (1994: 472). The analogy of religions to make-believe chimeras can be found in both Dubuisson (2003: 11) and

Fitzgerald (1997: 49). Masuzawa (2005) critiques the construction of the idea of "world religions." Insightful discussions of the issue can also be found in Wax (1984); Wilson (1998); and King (1999).

In the chapter, I quote Jonathan Z. Smith's widely cited statement that "Religion is solely the creation of the scholar's study. It is created for the scholar's analytic purposes by his imaginative acts of comparison and generalization. Religion has no existence apart from the academy" (Smith 1982: xi). Smith's dictum that "map is not territory—but maps are all we possess" (1978: 309) also suggests that the reality to which scholars' words refer is either nonexistent or unavailable because noumenal.Russell McCutcheon follows Smith here, both in the quote in the chapter and when McCutcheon says that "the notion of myth, ritual, and even religion do not refer to real things in the human environment; they are, instead, comparative categories of our making ... part of our scholarly toolbox" (2001: 63). But Smith and McCutcheon overstate the case when they suggest that that tool is the invention of scholars. Peterson and Walhof detail a variety of ways in which "inventing religion was never purely an academic project. Creating, redefining, and standardizing religion has long been a political strategy linked to the making of national identities and the exercise of colonial power" (2002:1). The historical essays collected in Fitzgerald (2007a) make the same argument (see explicitly 2007a: 10–1).

On the question whether religion exists, McCutcheon wavers. He has written that "'religion' has no analytic value whatsoever" (McCutcheon 1998: 56), but he later writes that it does: "Although I would be the last to suggest that such things as 'society' or the 'nation-state' were real in the same way that my laptop, or the chair I'm now sitting in, are real, unlike the humanist or theologian, I see 'society' 'economy,' and 'the nation-state'— not to mention 'God,' 'sin,' or 'heaven'—as *analytically or heuristically useful, everyday fictions* that people in certain groups use to organize and negotiate the complex world around them" (2003: 150). He has recently said that, encouraged by Tomoko Masuzawa, he no longer speaks of "religion" as having analytic value (personal communication).

I describe the antirealist position on "religion" as a form of deconstruction. Though the critics of "religion" do not embrace the entirety of Derrida's project, McCutcheon points out that his critique of the *sui generis* concept of religion resembles Derrida's deconstructive method in that, in Derrida's words, it "reads backwards from what seems natural, obvious, self-evident or universal, in order to show that these things have their history, their reasons for being what they are, their effects on what follows them, and that the starting point is not a given but a construct, usually blind to itself" (McCutcheon 1997: 73; quoting Derrida 1981: xv). Arnal and Fitzgerald likewise recommend the deconstruction of "religion" (Arnal 2000: 30; Fitzgerald 2000: 12, 245; 2007a: 8, 14).

Some critics of "religion" question whether the practices redescribed as religion have any *unity* independent of the sorting done by the term. Dubuisson makes this argument: "the ordinary definition [of the word 'religion' refers to] a complex set of distinct elements and conceivable relationships. The fact that it may be possible to find elsewhere, in other cultures and in an isolated state, one or other element that is comparable to one of those contained in the western system in no way authorizes us to infer the existence of the structure itself" (2003: 13). For a critical discussion of Dubuisson's project, see the Review Symposium in *Religion* 36 (2006): 119–78. In the chapter, I argue that the elements on such lists can be kin to each other. My position is therefore similar to that of the retentionist Bruce Lincoln, who argues that religious discourse is linked to religious practices that are in turn linked to religious communities and institutions (Lincoln 2003: Ch. 1).

One weak tactic for arguing that the concept of religion is incoherent and not referential (not covered in the chapter) is what I label *the disparate list argument*. Here, the critic lists a panoply of allegedly religious phenomena and then asks rhetorically: what could the items on such a list have in common? As an example, Dubuisson writes, "The trance of a participant in a voodoo ceremony, a Benedictine monk praying in his cell, a Brahman bathing in the Ganges, a Christian's examination of his conscience before confession, the butchered victim of an Aztec sacrifice, the conclusions of a canonization process, a Byzantine icon, the prayer wheel of a Tibetan pilgrim, the myth of Oedipus, the pope's ban on contraception, the cabbalistic exegesis of a verse of Scripture, the solitary practice of yoga by a devotee of Shiva, an extract from Hesiod's *Theogony*, the morning breathing exercises of a Taoist master, peasants' midsummer festival and bonfire, the personality cult devoted to the emperor of China, a Roman seer reading the future in the entrails of a dead bird, a pilgrim in Mecca, the Buddhist expression sarvam duḥkham, 'all is suffering,' the cosmogony outlined in Plato's *Timaeus*, the symbolism of the Sacré Coeur cathedral, the collective suicide of the members of the Order of the Solar Temple, the genealogical list of Egyptian pharaohs, the gnosis of the Upanishads ... Can we identify a common denominator ...?" (Dubuisson 40–1; cf. 24, 28–9, 44, 205; see also Fitzgerald). Those who use this tactic do not mention the attempts to answer that question.

Another weak tactic for rejecting the category of religion which I find irritating but kept out of the chapter is to take proposed definitions of religion and to add unnecessary exaggerations to them. If one says that realists claim not only that religion exists but also that it exists "universally" or "self-evidently," then the proposed definition is then easier to scoff at or reject. But clearly one can be a realist without holding that religion is universal (self-evidently or not): it may be that some cultures have a kindred set of beliefs and practices having to do with superempirical realities and others don't. To offer a definition of religion also does not imply that what is being defined has a "changeless" or "ahistorical" essence, nor that there are "indisputable" criteria (Dubuisson 2003: 47). This tactic aims at straw men.

I agree with the critics, however, that the concept of *religion* typically reifies the conceptualized phenomena. This problem of reification is stressed especially by Wilfred Cantwell Smith (1962). Most of the historians see the shift to understanding religion as a set of beliefs as a joint product of the Reformation and the Enlightenment. Harrison (1990: 61–73) and Smith (1962: 40) both point at Herbert of Cherbury as emblematic. I also agree with the critics that the concept *religion* often distorts the beliefs and practices it is used to interpret. Balagangadhara (1994), for example, argues that the concept distorts the traditions of India; Fitzgerald 2000: Parts II–III that it distorts Buddhism, Hinduism, and—his best example—Shinto; and Asad (1993) that it distorts Islam and medieval Christianity. On the construction of the concept of *religion* as an ideological tool useful for European imperialism and the spread of capitalism, see especially McCutcheon (1997: Ch. 1, 6) and Fitzgerald (2000, 2007a, 2007b). For multiple examples of denying that Africans have a religion, see Chidester (1996).

In my account of the ontology of religion, I draw on some of the ideas of John Searle (1995). Crucial to my argument is Searle's point that socially dependent facts are ontologically subjective but epistemically objective (1995: 7–9). For an excellent account of the ontology of religion that complements this one but does not use Searle, see Stowers (2008). Also crucial to my position is the rejection of linguistic determinism, the notion that, as Dubuisson expresses it, "our language is also our world" (2003: 31). I argue that although one's perceptions are led and shaped by one's interests (which are themselves socially and linguistically given), it does not follow that one's world is determined or exhausted by one's language. On this I follow Paul Boghossian (2006), who distinguishes between these two positions clearly and labels the valid one the "social relativity of descriptions" and the invalid one the "description dependence of facts."

The typology of different kinds of social constructionists is borrowed from Hacking (1999). In addition to the two kinds mentioned in the chapter, Hacking also recognizes a more radical position, "revolutionary" social constructionists, who actually seek to change the world to eliminate the pernicious social construction—in this case, religion. The abolitionists considered here by contrast are "rebellious" because their recommendations remain within the domain of ideas. The idea of "interactive kinds," that is, categorizations that are picked up and embraced by the people who are so described also comes from Hacking. My examples of Nuer and Huichol religions were suggested by Evans-Pritchard (1956) and Myerhoff (1976).

Given the influence of Michel Foucault, Pierre Bourdieu, Judith Butler, and others, the idea of the body as a socially informed or culturally inscribed representation is perhaps the reigning paradigm in cultural studies, though I am persuaded by the work of Thomas Csordas that a more adequate account of embodiment should complement this idea with the idea of the body as also the intersubjective ground of experience (see Csordas 1994, 1999; cf. Schilbrack 2004).

I also agree with the critics of "religion" that the scholar must describe or identify a practice in terms accepted by those described. To fail to do this is the error that Wayne Proudfoot labels "descriptive reductionism" (Proudfoot 1985: Ch. 6). To avoid that error, Proudfoot draws this rule: "In identifying the experience, emotion, or practice of another, I must restrict myself to concepts and beliefs that have informed his experience. I cannot ascribe to him concepts he would not recognize or beliefs he would not acknowledge" (193). To fail to respect the distinctiveness and integrity of the culture under description is a form of "conceptual violence" or "symbolic violence" (Daniel Dubuisson; Richard King).

Timothy Fitzgerald seeks to replace "religion" with three terms that give us greater analytic specificity: ritual, politics, and soteriology (Fitzgerald 2000: esp. Ch. 6). In this approach, Fitzgerald follows Talal Asad, who writes, "The anthropological student of *particular* religions should therefore begin from this point, in a sense unpacking the comprehensive concept which he or she translates as 'religion' into heterogeneous elements according to its historical character" (1993: 54). For a critique of Fitzgerald's project, see Schilbrack (2012).

The sociologist Martin Riesebrodt makes an important argument that when one turns attention from the natives' language to their actions, one sees that cultures which lack the explicit word "religion" can nevertheless act with the implicit concept. That is, cultures distinguish (what others call) their religious activities from their nonreligious activities, their religious specialists from their nonreligious specialists, and so on. Moreover, even without the word, religious traditions have perceived other religions as rivals, debating them, polemicizing against them, and appropriating their sacred places. And religiously heterogeneous empires have developed a "politics of religion" that recognizes and seeks to manage the different traditions. Riesebrodt concludes that "the distinction between religious and nonreligious is lacking neither in the premodern west nor in nonwestern cultures, and the religious in the sense of institutions that are associated with superhuman powers has existed in all ages and cultures" (Riesebrodt 2010: 1).

Endnotes

1. The heart of critical realism is the distinction in one's inquiry between one's "transitive" cognitive materials and the "intransitive" reality those materials let one investigate. The classical statement is Roy Bhaskar's *A Realist Theory of Science* 1975, the opening sentence of which states: "Any adequate philosophy of science must find a way of grappling with this central paradox of science: that [people] in their social activity produce knowledge which is a social product much like any other, which is no more independent of its production and the [people] who produce it than motor cars, armchairs or books, which has its own craftsmen, technicians, publicists, standards and skills and which is no less subject to change than any other commodity. This is one side of 'knowledge'. The other is that knowledge is '*of*' things which are not produced by [people] at all: the specific gravity of mercury, the process of electrolysis, the mechanism of light propagation. None of these 'objects of knowledge' depend upon human activity. If [people] ceased to exist sound would continue to travel and heavy bodies fall to the earth in exactly the same way, though ex hypothesi there would be no-one to know it" (1975: 21).

2. This paragraph draws on Wilfred Cantwell Smith (1962: Ch. 1.)

3. See Daniel Dubuisson (2003: 115).

4. These two quotes come from J. Z. Smith (1982: xi) and Russell McCutcheon (1997: viii).

5. The quote is from Asad (2003: 194).

6. I argue for this view more fully in Chapter 7, section ii.

7. The definition of religion as a kind of social formation comes from Russell McCutcheon (1998); the definition of religion as an experience of the sacred comes from Mircea Eliade (1959).

8. This example of a mereological sum comes from Putnam (2004: 36).

9. Wilfred Cantwell Smith has commented that "in some ways, it is probably easier to be religious without the concept" (Smith 1962: 19).
10. Smith (1962: 72).
11. The three quotes in this paragraph from Daniel Dubuisson come from 2003:90, 2003: 17, and 2006: 175, respectively.
12. The quote in this paragraph from Dubuisson comes from 2003:90; the comment about Kant is from 2006: 169.
13. "Department of Cosmographic Formation" would also be hard to sell to university administrations.
14. For Lincoln's distinction, see Lincoln (2003: Ch. 4); for Casanova's, see Casanova (1994).
15. For Fitzgerald's statement that one cannot distinguish between the religious and the secular, see Fitzgerald (1997: x). Griffiths shows the theological relevance of this point in Griffiths (2000). For Hick's introduction to Smith, see Smith (1962).

Chapter 5

What *Isn't* Religion?

i. Strategies for Defining Religion

The previous chapter argued that despite social constructionist arguments about the invention of the concept of religion, one can legitimately use the term "religions" to refer to certain kinds of social patterns that exist in the world. Naturally, then, the next question is how we should understand the character of those social patterns. How should we define "religion"? In this chapter, therefore, I shift from a defense of the concept to risk making a positive proposal of how, in my judgment, one might best think of what religion involves.

It is important to note at the outset that one implication of the previous chapter is that any definition of religion will have to be what I will call a *strategy*. By this I mean that one cannot define the word "religion" simply by looking at that to which the word allegedly refers. Since the very existence of religion depends on historically emergent concepts and since the reality of religion is itself a social construction, what religion is depends upon social recognition. The concepts of those who observe religion (whether practitioners or not) are therefore entangled, Schrödinger-style, in the nature of their object. As a consequence, what one decides is the "best" or the "right" definition of religion will depend on and be indexed to one's purposes. The criterion of a good definition is therefore its practical value. In other words,

Philosophy and the Study of Religions: A Manifesto, First Edition. Kevin Schilbrack.
© 2014 Kevin Schilbrack. Published 2014 by John Wiley & Sons, Ltd.

to call a definition of religion a strategy is to agree with the sociologist Peter Berger's statement that "Definitions cannot, by their very nature, be either 'true' or 'false,' but only more useful or less so."

The definition that I will propose, therefore, is not offered as a discovery of the sole truth about religion, but as a heuristic tool that lets us see religious studies as a field that permits a plurality of interpretive, explanatory, and evaluative projects with their divergent foci and methods. Towards that end, I outline a particular kind of functional definition that I call promissory and a particular kind of substantive definition that I call superempirical, and I then propose that the most useful definition for the study of religions will be an intersection of both. To be sure, some have suggested that the study of religion is now so diverse and fragmented that we can no longer expect theorists to have a common purpose, and so we cannot expect them to agree on a definition of religion. Although I recognize (and, in fact, insist on) a variety of purposes in the study of religions, I remain hopeful that students of religion can see themselves as sharing a common purpose or set of purposes to the extent that they might agree on the utility of a given definition. Indeed, I hope that they see greater utility in mine.

So: what is the best way to define religion for the practice of study of religion across cultures? Most of the answers to this question can be divided into two opposed strategies.

On the one hand, *functionalist strategies* seek to define certain beliefs, practices, institutions, and communities as religious in terms of what such phenomena do for the participants. These functional—or, as I will also call them, pragmatic—definitions of religion identify cultural phenomena as religious when they address a certain problem or need that is defined as distinctive of religious phenomena. On functionalist–pragmatist approaches, religion is, for example, what unifies a people, or integrates an individual's conscious will and unconscious drives, or provides guidance in the question for life's meaning. The best known and most popular functionalist definition of religion is that of Emile Durkheim and his followers, who identify beliefs and practices as religious when they unite those who adhere to them into a single community. On this account, the focus of a religion can be God, but it can also be one's nation or a sense of team spirit—whatever generates the sentiments that integrate a collective. When some concern brings people together and unites them as a moral community, the beliefs and practices related to that function would be religious, according to this strategy. The required marker of religion here is that the phenomena in question address that specific problem or need.

116

By contrast, *substantive strategies* seek to define certain beliefs, practices, institutions, and communities as religious in terms of their focal object. These substantive—or, as I will also call them, ontological—definitions of religion identify cultural phenomena as religious when they refer to a certain content or reality that is defined as distinctive of religious phenomena. On substantive–ontological approaches, religion is an engagement with supernatural, spiritual, or superhuman realities. The best known and most popular substantive definition of religion is that of Edward Tylor and his followers who identify beliefs and practices as religious when they involve spiritual beings. If a person believes that there exist spiritual beings—such as God, bodhisattvas, or ancestral spirits—then on this account that would be a religious belief. If she prays to, or sacrifices to, or makes a pilgrimage to the birthplace of or marks her body in recognition of her submission to a superhuman being, then on this account these would be religious practices. The required marker of religion here is that the phenomena in question refer to some kind of spiritual being or beings.

Which of these two kinds of definition is better? As I suggested above, answering this question turns on one's purposes. My own purpose as a philosopher of religions is to reflect critically on religious beliefs and practices *across cultures*. Many argue that the best definition for the study of religions across cultures, philosophical or not, needs to be a functional one. This is because functional definitions are not burdened with the idea that, to qualify as a religion, cultural phenomena must include a belief in God or some other common reality—an idea that is said to be implausible, if not covertly imperialistic. Functionalist definitions are more flexible and they permit one to study religions in whatever forms they take from one culture to another, and they permit one to recognize the emergence of new forms of religion. For these reasons, many think that the future of philosophy of religion as a multicultural phenomenon needs a functional definition of religion so as not to assume that all religions understand their focal objects in the same way. A functional definition would let philosophy of religion proceed with an openness to religious diversity and without limitations on or presuppositions about the nature of the religious reality.

On the other hand, there are also serious critiques of functionalist approaches. The primary objection is that without the recognition of some religious object that might distinguish religion from other forms of culture, the functionalist approaches are so inclusive and so open-ended that the term "religion" loses its analytic value. With functionalist approaches, it is said, any social practice, no matter how secular—including sports, politics, business, music, and so on—can be considered religious. In comparison, substantive definitions let us sort religion from nonreligion, and one religion from another, in a more straightforward fashion: only when one's beliefs, practices, and institutions involve God or some other spiritual being is one participating in a religion.

The proponents of these two strategies continue to seek to fine-tune their approaches, and debates about how best to define religion today are sprawling. In my judgment, there is something of a stalemate here. However, I think that the argument between functional and substantive definitions overlooks a third option.

Consider this. Many of the beliefs, practices, institutions, and communities that are called religious actually satisfy both kinds of definition. The beliefs, practices, institutions, and communities of Islam, to take just one example, have served the sociological function of uniting a community, the psychological function of making helplessness tolerable, and the existential function of providing an answer to the meaning of life, and so Islam can meet those functionalist definitions of religion. Likewise, Islam involves one's submission to a spiritual being and so it can also meet that substantive definition of religion. For this reason, the beliefs, practices, institutions, and communities of Islam can qualify as religious under both sets of criteria. The same can be said of Jainism and Scientology and Yoruba religion and most of the cultural phenomena that are widely considered religious. This observation points to what we might visualize as a significant area of overlap in the extension of the two definitions, an area in which one can find cultural phenomena that are religious according to either strategy.

The two strategies differ, to be sure. They differ, in the first place, because each provides a different perspective on cultural phenomena, foregrounding certain features as definitive of religion rather than others. But in order to overcome the stalemate between them, it is important to see that some theorists of religion have focused on what the two strategies foreground to the extent that the theorists become purists, so to speak, in either a functionalist sense or a substantive sense. A purist about the functional approach to religion would be one who says: a religion is whatever functions in someone's life in a religious way *even if it does not include anything that is substantively religious.* Given that approach, nationalism, Marxism, and secular humanism can be counted as religions. Let's call this approach "pure functionalism." Similarly, a purist about the substantive approach to religion would say: a religion is whatever involves a religious reality *even if it does not function in a religious way.* For example, this kind of purist would classify a person who believes that God exists as a religious person, even if he does not go to church, has not read the Bible, and does not gain comfort from the belief. On this purist view, the belief that God exists, even if it does not inform one's other beliefs and actions, it is nevertheless a religious belief. And if a practice involves spiritual beings, it is a religious practice, even if the practice is not very important to the person and he is just going through the motions. Thus "pure substantivism." The relation between the two strategies can be represented with a Venn diagram:

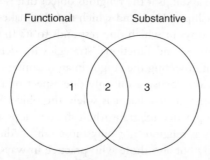

In this diagram, there are three regions: *Region 1* includes phenomena that are religious purely in terms of their function and not in terms of their content; *Region 3* includes phenomena that are religious purely in terms of their content and not in terms of their function; and the middle *Region 2* includes the phenomena that are both. Much of the heat in the debates about how best to define religion has been generated between the purists who endorse *Region 1* or *Region 3*. In other words, much of the debate has been "monothetic," in the sense that those who seek to develop a definition of religion have assumed that religion should be identified solely in terms of the substance of what is believed *or* the function of what is practiced. In *Region 2*, however, are those cultural phenomena that meet both criteria: to be put into that region, the phenomena have to be both functionally and substantively religious. They have to involve both an ontological and a pragmatic commitment. The criteria that define *Region 2* are therefore double. Together they articulate what might be called a mixed definition that identifies two features that are necessary for something to be recognized as a religion.

The possibility of *Region 2* and the coherence of a mixed definition are unsurprising, it seems to me, given the history of the word "religion." As described in the previous chapter, "religion" was not originally used as a generic concept. It was not used as what philosophers call a token of which there were many types. It was not used to categorize the variety of paths in different cultures but was used rather, among early Christians, for example, to identify proper practice. For Augustine, *religion* meant "worship of God." The phrase "worship of God," refers to what, according to the mixed definition I am recommending, would be (i) a religious object to which (ii) one responds in a religious way. Modern theorists of religion have then taken the form of this Augustinian understanding of the concept and pulled it apart. In effect, they have asked: is it the religious object that is most important to the idea of the worship of God, and which thereby makes the practice religious? Or is it the ways in which one responds to it? In this way, one can see that the substantive and functional strategies for defining religion are each the product of dissecting the Augustinian meaning of the term in one or the other direction, focusing on only one aspect of a concept that had had two. If a theorist judges that it is solely the object of worship that is essential to make a practice religious, then she develops a substantive definition that includes as religious not only those who dedicate themselves to God wholeheartedly but also those who practice in ways that are not central to the person's life, not most important, and so on, but are pointless or trivial, as long as they include that object. This produces a pure substantive definition. On the other hand, if a theorist judges that it is solely the depth with which that object is valued, the importance or ultimacy of one's concern, then one develops a functionalist definition that counts as religious not only practices connected to God or Gods but also those that do not involve a superhuman reality at all, as long as they are pursued or held with sufficient enthusiasm or value. This produces a pure functionalist definition.

My proposal is that the most useful definition of religion for the academic study of religions will be one that refuses to pull apart the earlier, two-aspect, Augustinian understanding. The categories of substance and function are not, like left and right, the two extremes or poles of a single issue. They identify rather the two required aspects of that earlier prototypical use of the term. One aspect concerns *why* a belief is held and a practice done, the functional or pragmatic aspect of religion. The other aspect concerns *what* the beliefs and practices are about, the substantive or ontological aspect of religion. If one does not insist on a pure functionalist or a pure substantive definition, then one can see that the two can overlap, in the sense that a belief or a practice or an institution can be both functionally religious (providing certain kinds of benefits) and also substantively religious (concerning certain kinds of realities). The best definition for the future of philosophy of religion, in my view, is therefore a mixed one.

To take this approach is to recognize that the concept of religion is a concept with a particular Western or European or Christian history. It is to see the definition of religion as having been stretched and enlarged from an earlier use, and it is to treat Christianity as a prototypical example of religion. Of course, this is not to accept Augustine's understanding of religion wholesale. On the contrary, I argue that the functionalist or pragmatic approaches capture an important aspect of religion, though Augustine's concept of "worship" is too narrow to be useful for cross-cultural or comparative study. And the substantive or ontological approaches capture the other important aspect, though Augustine's concept of God is similarly too narrow. Both aspects require stretching.

If one judges that a mixed or "dithetic"[1] definition of religion deserves greater attention, then how best to understand each of the two required aspects? The next two sections seek to answer that question.

ii. Making Promises: The Functional or Pragmatic Aspect of Religion

Functionalist or pragmatic approaches to religion focus on what people get out of participating in a religion, the benefit or consequences of religious belief, practice, and belonging. When I argue that the best definition of religion will be, in part, a functional or pragmatic one, I mean that one should begin by seeing religions as composed of actions that people do— religious people worship, they live according to a divine law, they fast, they circumcise, they cultivate virtues, they go on pilgrimages, they meditate, and so on—and, in the eyes of practitioners, such actions accomplish something. Religious people believe that religious actions help them. Religion solves problems. But which problems are the ones that define religious actions? What is the best way to understand the pragmatic aspect of religions?

Most of the traditional answers to this question have come from social scientists. For example, some functionalists sort religious beliefs, practices, and communities from nonreligious ones in terms of their *psychological*

121

functions: on this approach, religious beliefs and practices are those that help one manage one's cognitive and emotional energies, that integrate one's identity, and that alleviate fear and renew one with courage. Other functionalists sort the religious from the nonreligious in terms of their *social* functions: on this approach, religious beliefs and practices are those that serve to generate bonding sentiments, that legitimate authority, and that create communal identity. In these functionalist definitions, however, the focus is typically on benefits of religious practice that are unconscious or latent. Religious practitioners themselves seldom practice because they consciously or explicitly seek to manage libidinal drives or legitimate authority. And though one can redescribe and *explain* religious actions in terms that the practitioners don't know, one should not *identify* an action in terms that the practitioners themselves would not recognize.[2] Rather, we should identify actions in terms of the conscious or manifest goals of the practitioners. It is to mark this point that I call this a pragmatic definition.[3]

When one includes the manifest aims of religious practitioners, one gets a very broad range of religious goals. Religious communities claim that participating in their practices offers a means to receive a variety of kinds of blessings and to ward off a variety of kinds of misfortune, either in this world or another. Thus, the rituals, prayers, talismans, and spiritual disciplines of religions are said to ensure propriety, healthy children, moral clarity, longevity, liberation, wealth, victory in war, salvation, peace of mind, and innumerable other benefits. For the sake of organization, one might sort the disparate benefits promised by religions into three domains: the body, social relations, and nature.[4] In the domain of the body, one finds religious practices designed to stave off death, to cure disease, to bring fertility, or to curse the welfare of one's enemies. In the domain of social relations, one finds religious practices designed to initiate children to adulthood, to marry, to elevate rulers, and to excommunicate. In the domain of nature, one finds religious practices designed to bring rain, to predict weather, and to ward off droughts, plagues, and other natural disasters. And finally, some religious communities promise that participation leads to overcoming all problems and they promise some form of existence without suffering or weakness or lack of any kind.

When one includes manifest goals of religious practice like these, one makes practitioners' purposes central to what one identifies as religion. This is therefore a humanistic definition of religion, in the sense that it does not exclude human agency or conscious aims. One might also be tempted to call it a therapeutic model of religions, because here one sees religions as typically composed of embodied social practices that seek to heal one's life as a whole but also to cure and protect the body, the community, and the natural world. On such a model, different religions offer different diagnoses of what ails people and then offer different regimens for remedies in either this world or another. Or if the therapeutic register is too positive and fails to capture the destructive purposes of religion, then one might more neutrally call this a promissory model of religions, because here one sees religions as composed of embodied social practices that promise benefits. Either way, to locate religion in terms of its pragmatic function is to define religion as offering to its members a normative path: religion is composed of practices that teach people how to act wisely, properly, or best. Religion is therefore here defined not simply as a set of beliefs about religious realities but also as a set of practices that promise right living. Many in the study of religions have spent a great deal of energy distinguishing between religious practices that teach one how to act properly in ethical senses (what to do if one's ox gores one's neighbor or how to cultivate filial piety), in ceremonial senses (what to do to honor the dead or to marry two people), and in magical senses (what to do to curse an enemy or to protect one's crops). But I do not separate these purposes; I am content to stop with the general point that religion, by definition, consists in normative social practices that promise to solve problems for people.

Although most functionalists are social scientists, defining religion in terms of its pragmatic function has also appealed to some philosophers of religion, and especially to those interested in making philosophy of religion cross-cultural. The function of religion here is the distinctive one of providing an answer to the question of how one should live in general. Given this function, religion is that which gives one's life orientation and meaning and thereby directs our wills and our appetites. Here are three examples. The classic example is that of Paul Tillich, who writes that "[r]eligion, in the largest and most basic sense of the word, is ultimate concern." William Christian offers a definition that is cousin to Tillich's: "religion is interest in what is regarded as most important in the universe[, as] ... that which matters most in the universe." And Paul Griffiths defines religion as "a form of life that seems to those who inhabit it to be comprehensive, incapable of abandonment, and of central importance." Griffiths unpacks this definition, saying that to call a form of life "comprehensive" is to say that it provides a prescriptive frame for all other forms of life to which one belongs, and that

123

to call it "central" is to say that addresses the questions of paramount importance to the ordering of one's life. On such an account of the pragmatic function of religion, what makes something religious is that it provides the standard that guides the rest of one's values.

Philosophers of religion are sometimes guilty of seeing a religion merely as a set of beliefs, but to define religion functionally as these three philosophers do is to include much more. For Paul Tillich, following Heidegger's analysis of "care," to see religion as an existential "concern" is to see religion as an aspect of culture that involves the participation of the whole of the person. The religious function draws on the moral, cognitive, and aesthetic dimensions of the human personality. For William Christian, to see religion as a form of "interest" carries with it all the rich affective and conative dimensions that are implied in evaluative feeling, a feeling that is for Christian, here following Alfred North Whitehead, the basic way in which a subject relates to the world. And to see religion as a "form of life" for Paul Griffiths, picking up Wittgensteinian language, is to focus on the idea that a religion is a certain way of acting in the world and to highlight its inescapably social aspect. To define religion functionally in these Heideggerian, Whiteheadian, and Wittgensteinian ways is to belie the criticism that philosophy treats religion as merely propositions, that philosophy truncates religion to doctrines and makes it over in its own image as philosophy, or that philosophy assumes that religion is ahistorical or merely private. Like other functional definitions, these philosophical approaches focus on religions as patterns of desires, as emotional and volitional commitments, as investments in styles of living. Religion here involves people who develop projects with others over time, thereby creating individual and group identities. These philosophers therefore define religion not in terms of propositions, let alone in terms of reified systems of propositions, but rather in terms of attachment, of devotion and passion, of trust and hope.

These philosophical definitions share the functional or pragmatic focus of the promissory model. This is because, like the social scientists who define religious practices in terms of their psychological, social, and therapeutic functions, these philosophers define religious practices in terms of solving a human problem. It is distinctive problem: to define religion as providing an orientation for life, a center of value, a source of meaning, a comprehensive *telos*, or an image of personal or social perfection is to say that religions solve what might be called a meta-problem, namely: *how to rank* the relative values of the health of the body, one's social relationships, and the natural world. Religions often teach that certain pursuits should be subordinated to higher pursuits. One religious community might teach that family life is a good but sometimes family must be abandoned. Another might teach that the pleasures of food, sex, or a comfortable life are good but that there are conditions when they should be refused. If we call a community's teaching about how to rank the relative value of different goals its axiology, then these three functional definitions might be called axiological definitions of religion. Axiological definitions capture the fact that religions typically function to legislate comprehensive, all-inclusive paths, highest values, or ultimate norms. On these definitions, then, practices are religious when they provide people with a comprehensive evaluative standard that tells one how to live.

Should we add the axiological functions of religion to the promissory model? That is, should we say that religions are those forms of life that function to address both (a) the problems of body, society, and nature, and (b) the meta-problem of how to rank one's purposes? One can combine these, because both reflect functionalist approaches and so both treat religions as pragmatic, problem-solving enterprises. Both agree that religion teaches a normative order. Nevertheless, I believe that we should recognize the axiological function as a *typical* feature of religions without treating it as a *necessary* part of the definition. Though some religious communities have connected their therapeutic practices to that which matters most in the universe or to a prescriptive frame for all other forms of life, not all have, and one can recognize religious practices without it. If we treat the axiological function as a typical but not definitive feature of religions, then we end up with a definition of religion that treats religion as a social practice that aims at solving problems—including problems that arise from the body, society, and nature—and typically (but not necessarily or essentially) the meta-problems that arise when one seeks to rank one's ends.

This is, in my judgment, the right way to begin one's definition of religion: religions address a heterogeneous and open-ended variety of functions. This definition does not specify "the" religious function—or even the religious functions, in the plural. And this is good: the future of philosophy of religion—as well as the study of religions in general—are best served by a definition that has an *a posteriori* approach to the study of what religious communities care about. Such a definition is very inclusive but it is not vacuous, I judge, because it makes the point that religious beliefs, practices, institutions, and communities always offer a normative path. What is thereby ruled out are accounts of religion as a set of propositions that are not practical or functional. Such a definition excludes, for example, the idea that religion is simply a set of beliefs independent of the roles they play in the life of a community. In other words, what is ruled out is the content of *Region 3*.

But although I think that the right way to begin to define religion is to treat it as teaching a variety of normative practices, this cannot suffice as a definition of religion. It cannot suffice because *all* of culture is composed of normative practices. A culture simply *is* a normative order. To define religion as teaching beneficial ways to act is not yet to distinguish religion from other aspects of culture like medicine or sports or politics or art. Though it is valuable to frame religion as functional or pragmatic and not as, say, simply a product of theoretical speculation, it is not enough: one still must specify *which* normative practices are the religious ones.

The three philosophers quoted above recognized this specification problem. They dealt with it by saying that that religions are composed not of every practice, belief, or institution that is based on norms or values, but only those that are based on one's ultimate, most important, or comprehensive norms or values. They define religion in terms of what I called the axiological function. It is because they solve the problem in this way that all three of them are what I called "purely functional" in the sense that they do not require a religion to include any reference to God or Gods or another other religious object. In fact, they explicitly reject the boundaries on what counts as a religion that would follow from defining religion in substantive terms: Tillich developed his definition precisely to include nationalism as a demonic religion; Griffiths says that a sport may be one's religion. It is because they solve the specification problem in this way that these philosophers usually give little attention to any religious promises other than the general one of giving orientation to life.

My solution to this specification problem is to accept a functional definition of religion but to move away from pure functional definitions like Tillich's and to take the other (Augustinian or "mixed") option that specifies that religions are those normative practices that also refer to a religious reality. In other words, I move from *Region 1* to *Region 2*. My primary reason for rejecting pure functionalism is that pure functionalists dilute the analytic value of the term to the point that they make empirical study of religion difficult. But another reason for combining the functionalist with the substantive approaches is to highlight a feature of religions that is of special interest to philosophers of religion, namely, that religious communities understand their practices and the values they teach as in accord with the nature of things. To this ontological issue I now turn.

iii. Keeping Promises: The Substantive or Ontological Aspect of Religion

I am now ready to complete my argument that we should define religion dithetically not only as a form of culture that seeks functional and pragmatic benefits, but also one that refers to a certain distinctive reality or aspect of reality. My insistence that to be religious a practice, belief, or institution must make a certain kind of ontological claim may seem wrong-headed—and perhaps especially so to those who study religions across cultures. Those who agree with the functionalist and problem-solving approach described above may want to stop there and avoid opening the door to the nonscientific and contested questions of ontology. I therefore want to begin with an anecdote to make the connection between normative practices and ontology—between the religious marriage of facts and values—seem as commonsensical as I can.

When I was a kid, I used to play a ball game in the streets near my house. The players faced in toward each other, and so when a car came up the street behind those down the way, we'd warn them: "Get out of the street—cars coming." The first half of this shout is a recommendation for action. The second half is a description of something perceived that is intended to justify the recommendation. What I want to point out is how usual, how quotidian, is this linked pair of recommended action and ontological justification. In fact, to base one's recommendations on some alleged fact about the way things are in the world is so taken for granted that most likely we kids never said the entire sentence quoted above; we'd just holler, "Car!" and the meaning would be clear. Given our shared practice, the ontological claim by itself was enough to imply—or even constitute—the recommendation.

One can label this view that proper behavior should be based on something that exists: normative realism. How strange it would be to imagine one of us kids saying, "You should get out of the street" without the threat of a car, unless it was a joke. Analogously, it is not usual to make recommendations in other forms of practice without an explicit or implicit reference to a reality that is supposed to justify that action. That one should drink orange juice if one has a cold is said to be based on certain properties of the juice. That one should vote for so-and-so is said to be the right thing to do if one wants lower taxes. (The alleged realities may turn out to be specious, of course: that one should go to Tibet if one wants to see Shangri-La or that one should be more open to romance this month if one is a Sagittarius also involve claims about the way the world works, claims that may not hold up to scrutiny. But even recommendations for action based on specious claims illustrate how recommendations for action are usually linked to the way things are said to be.) People ordinarily understand their values as realistic. They hold that their values and ways of life are not arbitrary or groundless inventions, but rather based on the way things are.

My proposal is that religious values and ways of life are the same: religious communities make recommendations for how one should act in order to solve problems in one's life, with the understanding that those recommendations accord with the nature of things. The therapies that the religions offer are alleged to work because they are based on truths about what is real. To give three passing but well-known examples, laying on of hands is said to be effective because of the power of the Holy Spirit. The straight path of Islam that is marked out by Shariah law is justified by reference to the revealed word of the Creator and Judge of the world. And the monastic path of cultivating nonattachment in Buddhism is authorized by reference to the Buddha's insight that everything that exists is empty, impermanent, and without self and therefore attachment reflects false views. In both cases, the recommended practice is understood to be realistic. If we see religions as making promises, then the desire among religious communities to "go ontological" is not the product of metaphysical wonder or disconnected fantasy but rather a discursively expected implication of making a promise. Religions make ontological claims because such claims answer the question: what makes the promise true?

Granted, one might participate in a practice and not know why it works. In fact, one might participate in a practice and not even wonder why it works. Practitioners typically develop an explicit justification only when a practice fails or is challenged. Justifying one's practices is then a second order form of discourse and reflection. But as I described in the previous chapter, people have beliefs insofar as they take something as true, and they take something as true as soon as they act in any purposive way. Therefore, even in cases in which a religious community has not developed an explicit ontological account that justifies its practices, identifying practices by their ontology is still appropriate. This is so because agents have a prereflective understanding of the world in which they operate. It is precisely this prereflective engagement with the world that one seeks to make reflective when one's practices fail or are challenged. We might be able to find a religion that had not developed an explicit ontological justification for a given practice,

128

but we will not find one that does not have even a prereflective understanding of the world, an understanding of the world that makes that practice intelligible. For this reason, we can define religion as normative practices that at least implicitly make ontological claims in terms of which the practical norms are authorized. Moreover, a context of a pluralism of such paths has characterized almost all human history, at least since the emergence of cities roughly 5,000 years ago. As a consequence, inter-religious challenge and change over time are so usual that to find a religious practice that has not been pushed to reflect on its own practices and to develop explicit ontological claims to justify them will be rare. We might even say that teaching about the nature of things is one of the defining functions of religion, a cognitive function. Given my interest as a philosopher in the cognitive aspects of religious practice, I therefore include normative realism in my definition of religion.

On this definition of religion, then, the practical and the ontological aspects of religion are interdependent. Here, making truth claims is intrinsic to religion and one cannot identify religious practices without them. I distinguish between religious practices and the understanding of the world that gives them sense, as promises made and promises kept, but religion as it is lived is not on my understanding dichotomous, any more than is the shout "Car!"

iv. The Growing Variety of Religious Realities

I hope that I have said enough to explain why I think that religious communities do not merely make recommendations about activities that one should pursue but also that those recommendations reflect a commitment to a religious reality. But the question now is whether we *can* identify a certain distinctive reality or aspect of reality that can be used to distinguish religious from nonreligious practices, beliefs, and institutions. To distinguish religions by the kind of reality to which they refer is to develop a substantive definition. But is there a substantive definition that is broad enough to include everything that we want to study but not so broad that it returns us to the all-inclusive definitions above? Can one specify a kind of reality that defines religion?

This question is the linchpin of substantive definitions. The most popular substantive definition operating in the study of religions today is some version of Edward Tylor's definition of religion as belief in spiritual beings.

129

But it is not the only option. It is important to see that substantive definitions of religion have a history, a history of stretching and adapting the word "religion" for use in emerging circumstances and purposes. I distinguish four stages.

One sees the first stage in the history of substantive definition of "religion" among those Christians, the inheritors of Augustine's use of the word, who held, unsurprisingly, that the reality that defines religion is the reality of the Christian God. They employed the concept *religion* to refer to what they themselves did. It follows straightforwardly from this use of "religion" that those who did not know of this reality thereby lacked religion. One sees this identification of religion and Christianity in Christopher Columbus, for instance, when he wrote that the native Americans seemed to lack all knowledge of religion—even idolatry. This definition of religion still operated centuries later: writing in 1858, James Gardner states that the Xhosa in southern Africa lacks religion since "it seems that those of them who are still in their heathen state have no idea (1) of a Supreme Intelligent Ruler of the universe; (2) of the sabbath; (3) of a day of judgment; (4) of the guilt and pollution of sin; (5) of a Savior to deliver them from the wrath to come." This account of the Christian beliefs that makes something a religion is a substantive definition of religion, and given my claim that definitions of religion are strategies judged by their purposes and not by the world, I cannot say that it is incoherent definition. But it is useless for the cross-cultural study of religions.

The second stage in the development of a substantive definition of religion deliberately seeks to stretch the explicitly Christian understanding of God to create a concept that can include both Christian and at least some nonChristian phenomena. In this sense, the second stage is really the first that provides a definition of religion for cross-cultural or comparative accounts of religion. With this move, "religion" becomes a genus. This shift constitutes, as Wittgenstein would say, a change in the grammar of the concept. As an example of this process of stretching and abstraction, take the work of Edward Herbert.

To develop a concept of religions in the plural, Herbert distinguishes between what he calls the "natural"—that is, the generic—elements of religion from the idiosyncratic elements. According to Herbert, all religions do not worship the Christian God, of course, but they do all worship some notion of a supreme deity.[5] Call this a theistic definition of religion. It is clear that Herbert's idea of a supreme deity is adapted taken from the Calvinist Christianity he preferred. And Herbert no doubt promotes this least common denominator theism, this precursor of deism, in order to avoid the divisiveness that had led in the preceding century to so much violence among Christians. But to reach his theological goal of rejecting an exclusivist understanding of salvation, Herbert stretches the concept of religion, and so I want to consider his proposal not as a theological position, but as an attempt to develop a more inclusive understanding of what defines a belief as substantively religious. Herbert excises from the earlier understanding of the concept the idea of original sin and therefore he also excises the idea of a savior. He also fails to include not just the Gospels, or even some scriptures or other, but the need for any revelation at all. Since any savior or revelation would be present in one or some religions but not all, they cannot be part of the definition of religions in general.

The novelty of Herbert's theistic definition of religion has been noted before. But it is also worth noting that as Herbert stretches the privileged concept of religion to fit nonChristian materials (so to speak, using "our" word to apply to "them"), he performs a parallel move of deploying negative concepts previously used to disparage nonChristian religions to apply to Christianity. Thus Herbert takes the term "imposture"—until then used to refer to the teachings of false prophets, above all Muhammad—and uses it to apply to the "priestcraft" that Herbert says can be found in all religions, including Christianity. Given Herbert's definition, then, "religion" no longer refers only to Christianity and its heresies but rather to a variety of healthy and harmful ways that people have understood and related themselves to a supreme being.

How inclusive is this more inclusive substantive definition? What fit Herbert's theistic definition most easily will be other monotheistic religions: Herbert knows best the Protestant and Catholic churches, Judaism, Islam, and Zoroastrianism. Herbert knows about pagan polytheistic traditions as well, of course, but to make them fit his substantive definition he argues that multiple Gods or revered natural phenomena (such as the sun or stars) are actually representations of the supreme God. Despite this procrustean tactic, one can see that a theistic definition represents a conceptual shift that creates *religion* as a new taxon and makes the cross-cultural or comparative study of religions conceptually possible. This interpretation of Herbert's contribution gives us a much more radical interpretation of by Friedrich Max Müller's famous quote: "He who knows one, knows none." This slogan meant for Müller that one does not really know one religion until one compares it to others. But it can also point to the conceptual point that religions cannot be conceived *qua* religion until there are more than one. This definition does

131

not entail that all religions are equal. But it does entail that multiple paths are equally religions.

Given Herbert's generic Supreme Being, one can now see that Edward Tylor's animism is actually a third attempt at a substantive definition of religion. Like Herbert, Tylor sought to develop a more inclusive concept that would gather the cultural phenomena included in earlier substantive definitions, plus more. Also like Herbert, Tylor sees himself as working in the tradition of defining "natural religion."[6] But as Tylor explicitly notes, he excises even more elements from previous definitions in order to abstract from the data a thinner and therefore even more inclusive approach: "By requiring in this definition the belief in a supreme deity or of judgment after death [as Herbert had still required], the adoration of idols or the practice of sacrifice, or other partially-diffused doctrines or rites, no doubt many tribes may be excluded from the category of religious. But such narrow definition has the fault of identifying religion rather with particular developments than with the deeper motive which underlies them." Tylor consequently ends up with his animist definition of religion as simply "belief in Spiritual Beings." This definition then treats as religions not only the practices, beliefs, and institutions of the monotheistic traditions but also those concerning nature spirits, departed souls, and spiritual hierarchies. For the purposes of a cross-cultural philosophy of religions, Tylor's definition of the distinctive reality of religious phenomena lets us include polytheistic traditions without assuming that they are covertly or implicitly monotheistic. It is therefore better than its predecessors not because polytheistic religions "really are" religions and his definition reflects the discovery of that truth. Rather, it is better for those who want a broader genus that lets us include both monotheistic and polytheistic practices as religions.

If one looks on Tylor's animistic definition of religion not as "the" substantive definition but rather as an attempt—in fact, the third attempt—at a substantive strategy for defining religion, then we can now ask whether this strategy is one that that we want for our purposes. Herbert's strategy let people gather Christianity together with other monotheisms and thereby let one speak of religions in the plural. Tylor's strategy let one gather all of those monotheisms together with other beliefs in spiritual beings to that we could speak of monotheistic religions as kin to polytheistic religions (as Tylor confessed was part of his goal in treating the study of culture as a reformer's science). This puts us at the point at which one can develop an even broader understanding of the substantive or ontological aspect of religion. I recommend, namely, a definition of religion that treats as religious not only those who believe in the Trinity (with Augustine), not only those who believe in God (with Herbert), and not only those who believe in superhuman beings (with Tylor)—but also those who believe in religious realities that are not theistic. This understanding of religious realities is intended to include those other substantive approaches, plus more, and such a definition therefore enables the student of religions to recognize that, just as there can be many kinds of religious functions, there can be many kinds of religious realities.

The question whether there might be nontheistic religions has been an undercurrent in the debates about how to define religions for about a century. In fact, as soon as Tylor proposed that religion was defined by a focus on spiritual beings, his definition was critiqued as inappropriately excluding nonpersonlike religious forces such as the *mana* of Melanesia and the *wakan* of the Dakota. The two best known twentieth-century definitions of religion that include nontheistic conceptions as the substance of religion are probably those of William James, who defines religion in terms of any "unseen order," and Clifford Geertz, who defines religion in terms of any "general order of existence." And today more and more scholars are stretching definitions of religion which had referred to "agencies" or "beings" to refer more generally to both person-like and nonperson-like "powers" or "forces." Thus we find substantive definitions that refer to "a level of reality beyond the observable world known to science" or an "order of reality beyond or behind the apparent, given order." This is the fourth stage of substantive definitions of religion.

The primary and as yet unmet challenge to developing a substantive definition of religion that includes nontheistic realities as religious, however, is whether an idea like "unseen order" or "general order of existence" can be given analytic bite. "Order" and "level of reality" are pretty vague terms. How does one conceive of such religious realities as distinct from nonreligious ones? A view I consider a dead end is to try to identify religious realities with another world. The attempt to distinguish religious from nonreligious with the language of a world "beyond," "behind," "transcendent," or "supernatural," has had, in my judgment, a pernicious effect on the study of religions. These terms impose on all religions a cosmic dualism that is found in only some of them. And it is misleading in the extreme to say that religious people invest themselves in another world. Religious communities invest themselves in sacred lands, in certain human beings who are holy, and in those holy peoples' remains, and in temples, clothes, dances, gestures, sacrifices, temples, flags, drinks, and so on. Religion is no less "worldly"

133

than other dimensions of human culture. The study of religion needs to be rematerialized. Assuming dualism is not the way to ground a more inclusive substantive definition.

Here is my alternative. Without buying into any particular account of empiricism, one can distinguish between those realities that are available to our senses and those that are not.[7] The set of empirical realities includes everything that can be seen, tasted, smelled, touched, and heard, and also what can be perceived in these ways with technological help. Thus the empirical world includes this mountain range, that group of people, and the heat of the fire, and also other much larger or smaller realities like the horsehead nebula or water molecules. In the set of nonempirical realities, I place moral principles, aesthetic judgments, and mathematical rules. People claim to experience nonempirical realities like these when they feel the presence of values, including a sense of self-worth, a trust that life is good, the idea of being unforgiven, deserving, lovable, execrable, or ugly, and the moral requirement that one act in one way rather than another.

Now, to say that religions always teach normative paths, as I have been recommending, is to say that religious communities always teach behavior based on and beliefs about nonempirical values. Thus when a religious community regards an action as a divine command or it regards a person as a holy person, for example, it sees in that action or that person a sanctity, righteousness, or piety that is not apparent to the senses. But nonempirical judgments are equally found among nonreligious people. Political communities, for instance, hold up as models those actions and people that they consider patriotic, aristocratic, noble, or otherwise worth following or emulating, and so political communities equally regard some actions and people as imbued with nonempirical values. In both the religious and the political cases, people, places, and actions are seen as embodying propriety or goodness—and this is what it means to say that culture is a moral order. All forms of culture involve nonempirical judgments. All forms of culture are evaluative and will seek to speak through symbols and metaphors to describe invisible orders of significance and value. As a consequence, one cannot say that the difference between what is and is not religion is that religions speak of nonempirical realities. The difference, rather, is this: if we ask whether the existence of those nonempirical realities—the norms of goodness, beauty, and justice and so on—depends on the human and other beings of the empirical world, religious communities are those that answer: no. Religious communities, on this account, are those that see nonempirical realities as existing

134

independent of empirical sources. Nonreligious communities, by contrast, are those that see the existence of their values as contingent on empirical sources—typically, either the particular social practices of human history or by practical reason as such. Religious communities are those that adopt values that they do not believe depend on human or other empirical forms of agency. I will call those nonempirical aspects of reality whose existence allegedly does not depend on empirical sources: superempirical. Thus religions are composed of those social practices authorized by reference to a superempirical reality, that is, a reference to the character of the Gods, the will of the Supreme Being, the metaphysical nature of things, or the like. In short, I define religion as forms of life predicated upon the reality of the superempirical.

This proposal for a more inclusive understanding of the substantive aspect of religion is intended to include everything in the previous versions. Augustine's Christian definition, Herbert's broader theistic definition, and Tylor's even broader animistic definition all sought to define religion in terms of a reality or realities that are superempirical. Those substantive approaches are therefore not replaced by but rather nested in this one.

v. **What this Definition Excludes**

This section has been rather abstract; let me be more concrete. If one agrees that this mixed definition of religion is the most useful, then one treats as religious those practices, beliefs, and institutions that recommend normative paths based on superempirical realities. How does this definition of religion sort the possible data of religious studies?

The approach I recommend classifies as religious some traditions, practices, and beliefs that were excluded by earlier substantive definitions. The most contested case in the modern study of religion is Buddhism, the so-called "litmus test" for a definition of religion.[8] But the concerns about Buddhism (especially Theravada Buddhism) arise because to classify Buddhism as a religion would be to admit an atheistic religion. Melford Spiro, defending a Tylorean definition of religion, argues that Buddhism can be treated as a religion because in practice it has absorbed belief in pre-Buddhist superhuman beings: "even if Theravada Buddhism were absolutely atheistic, it cannot be denied that Theravada Buddhists adhere to another belief system which is theistic to its core." Given the definition I propose, however, Buddhism could be counted as a religion not because Buddhists do not exclude relations with superhuman beings but because religion does not require them. Buddhism is a religion to the extent that its promise of liberation is based on the superempirical character of reality. Buddhists speak of selflessness, impermanence, and emptiness as the three marks of existence, truths about the character of reality which are not conditional and which one must realize to make progress on the Buddhist path. For Spiro, if Theravada Buddhists did eschew bodhisattvas, nats, and other superhuman beings, then the eightfold path would be best understood as nonreligious. But on my account, even if one sets aside the belief in superhuman beings, if Theravada Buddhists see their path as authorized by the nature of things, then they practice a religion.

Such a definition gives us a tool with which we might recognize other nontheistic traditions as religious. Here are five examples. If Confucianism, for example, is solely a state ideology or a form of virtue ethics, drawn from the teachings of sage kings, and not based on an invisible moral order, then it would not be a religion. However, if the kings were sage precisely because they were able to perceive a Dao that was not a product of human practices but rather a set of principles to which human families and institutions themselves ought to bend, then it would. Similarly, the Stoics sought to discipline human passions to put one's life in harmony with Logos, the universal reason inherent in all things. On this definition, their pantheism could be treated as religious and not solely as philosophical. For the Mimāmsā school of Hindu philosophy, the authority of ritual obligations and prerogatives is based on the Vedas alone, understood as authorless and eternal and so as a superempirical reality. Mimamsakas are not less religious because the dharma they teach is atheistic. And there is debate about whether Daoism teaches a Way that is a metaphysical reality or simply a balanced style of living. Insofar as Daoists teach the former, their promises are on my account religious. Lastly, on this definition, Alcoholics Anonymous, despite the deliberate vagueness of the Power it refers to, could also be classified as a religion.

This inclusiveness points to an important feature of the definition I recommend. I argued above that the word "religion" began as a Christian term of art. If the two notions of promissory functions and superempirical realities are coherent, however, they let us define religion in such a way that Christianity is still prototypical, but it is not more prototypical than, say, Buddhism or Stoicism. The concept of God is not more superempirical than that of karma or Logos. Moreover, since a religion on this definition is a set of practices and not simply a matter of superempirical beliefs, this definition avoids the criticisms of those considered in the previous chapter who argue that the term "religion" is inescapably colonialist or imperialist because it privileges interiority, faith, or beliefs.

My argument that the best definition of religion will include the possibility of nontheistic religions is not because "we now know" that Buddhism, Daoism, and so on really are religions. Given my view that a definition of religion is a strategy, I hold that scholars of religion cannot argue like that. My view is that *if* a philosopher of religion is interested in studying practices that refer to superempirical realities (whether theistic, polytheistic or non-theistic), *then* she should define religion in the way that I am recommending and say that religions can come in this form. My view is that a concept stretched in this direction to include nontheistic superempirical beliefs and practices is productive for the cross-cultural comparisons that we want to make today.

My own sense, however, is that the primary value of the definition I am recommending is not that it lets us include more. My sense is that the functional definitions of religion being used in the field—especially Tillich's and other axiological definitions that treats "religion" as that which provides orientation for life—are so capacious that they already let us include too much. In my judgment, the most important criterion for a definition of religion today is not that it recognizes a variety of religions but rather that it gives us a workable sense of where that variety begins and ends. What we want is *a bounded variety*. So let me return to my title: what is not religion?

On the definition that I am proposing, there are two sets of cultural phenomena that have been considered religious on other approaches but would not be considered religious here. On the one hand, there are those cultural phenomena in *Region 3* that refer to a super-empirical reality and are therefore substantively religious, but include no reference to a religious practice: call them "mere belief." Mere belief in Plato's ideas, Hegel's absolute idealism, and Nussbaum's Natural Law may be superempirical, but until they lead to rituals, ceremonies, or other practices, they would not count as religious. (By contrast, those like Aquinas or Locke who see Natural Law as a creation of the God they worship would be religious philosophers.) Religion is not identical to metaphysics. On this definition, a religion is not a private mental state and so a belief that God or some other superempirical reality exists, independent of its relevance to conduct, would not count as religious.

On the other hand, excluded by this definition are those *Region 1* cultural phenomena that are functionally religious but which include no reference to a superempirical reality. This position is much more popular in religious studies, so let me discuss two illustrative examples.

Samuel Snyder uses the language of religious experience to understand those anglers who speak about their wet hours of fly-fishing as meditative times, of rivers as sacred places, and of fishing as providing a sense of connection to nature and motivating them to environmental conservation, and he suggests that fly-fishing can therefore be considered a religion. On my approach, whether this is a religion turns, we might say, on the nature of the water. If fly-fishing is a way of enjoying a river or a day or the fish—tangible, visible, empirical realities—then on this account, it would not yet be a religion. Even if fly-fishing is tapping into an experience of nonempirical values such as individualism or family or participating in a tradition that has been handed down for generations, on this account it would not yet be a religion. Snyder suggests that in a traditional fly-fishing pole and the handmade lures, the sport has ritual implements; in the complicated steps involved in learning how to cast, it has ritual training; and in the physical movement to often remote and nonindustrialized mountains and rivers, it offers a form of pilgrimage. But these processes of ritualizing are not enough to make a practice a religion. Fly-fishing also leads some of its practitioners to treasure the natural world and to embrace an environmental ethic. But a moral path is not necessarily religious. However, if fly-fishing becomes a way for a person to get closer to the Creator or if a person actually comes to revere Nature-as-a-whole, à la Spinoza, as that which orients the authentic life (two possibilities that Snyder considers) or if the river is itself a divine being (another possibility that one finds in the world), then on this definition the actions could be considered religious. The key is that the rituals and the ethics of the activity need to connect the practitioners to a superempirical reality.

A second example comes from Ira Chernus, who suggests that for some neoconservative politicians the War on Terror is a religious act. Chernus quotes neoconservatives who argue that the war is far more than a geopolitical struggle; they connect that armed struggle with nonempirical values, saying things like, "It is crucial to all human beings at all times that they encounter a world that possesses transcendent meaning, a world in which human experience makes sense."[9] How would my approach deal with an example like this? There is no doubt that war can provide people with a sense of purpose and meaning: a nice example is the protagonist of the movie *The Hurt Locker* and Chris Hedges wrote a best-seller entitled *War is a Force that Gives us Meaning.* But if the War on Terror gives a soldier a sense of purpose—simply meeting that function does not make it a religion. If the war brings a nation together, meeting that function also does not make it a religion. However, if one holds that justice itself is not merely the product of the American way of life, American interests, and the U.S. Constitution, but is rather a transcendent aspect of the cosmos, then the war can be read as religious. Or if one feels that this war is just according to the Biblically inspired criteria of a just war and that therefore in taking up arms against terrorists one seeks to do God's will, then the war can be read as religious. And many of the neoconservatives whom Chernus quotes believe precisely this. Wars are religious when they are based on reference to a superempirical reality.

The mixed pragmatic-ontological definition of religion is able to exclude putative examples of religion like these because it rejects the purely functional approach to religions. Limiting the scope of what is labeled "religion" in this way has two important consequences for the study of religions around the world. First, it facilitates the study of secularization. If one defines religion in axiological terms as a commitment to whatever functions as one's ultimate concern, then religion is made universal by definition. Given that approach, it follows that though the mode of religiosity might change, no individual and no culture can become less religious, let alone nonreligious, and the hypotheses of secularization are disproven without empirical work. Second, using a limited definition of religion like mine makes it possible to speak of multiple religious identities. Again, if one defines religion functionally as an ultimate concern, then it is problematic if not incoherent to say that a person has multiple concerns that are all ultimate. An axiological definition of religion implies that a person can fully participate in only one religion. By contrast, this bounded definition does not let one see every individual or every culture as religious. As a result, questions such as "Does the spread of modern forms of life entail the decrease in religious belief and practice?" and "To how many religious communities does a person belong?' are open questions on this definition of religion.

The nonempirical/superempirical distinction is central to what this definition excludes. The nation, for example, is a nonempirical reality, an imaginary community that cannot be seen with the eyes. Given the definition of religion at play here, reverence for the nation would not be counted as religious when the nation is seen as solely a product of human blood, sweat, and genius. But when the nation is seen as the embodiment of values that exist independent of human activities—such as the will of God—then one

139

can speak of religious nationalisms. Similarly, Adam Smith's "invisible hand" of capitalism is not superempirical since its existence depends on the human practices of the market. Analogous cases can be made for Marxism, for fans of sports teams, for the love of money, or for secular humanism: if the proletariat, the team, the lucre, or humanity itself is seen solely as the product of human activity, then devotion to them would not be counted as religions. Formally speaking, what is not religion are the contents of *Region 1* and *Region 3* in the Venn diagram. A slogan for my proposal, then, might be that on this account what is not religion is: mere practice or mere belief. One must have both.

As I said at the outset, religion is not a natural kind and so the test of any definition of "religion" is its usefulness. It follows that definitions of religion are not neutral but rather serve some purpose or another. What then is the usefulness of this definition? Why pick out this set of practices as a distinct social taxon? The definition of religion I have proposed gives scholars a principled way to include nontheistic traditions as religious without also thereby including all forms of communal meaning-making. Though scholars are not limited to the colloquial use of terms, what this definition treats as religion and what it excludes tracks the colloquial use nicely. Moreover, it names this set of human activities as distinct in order to make them subject to two broad kinds of inquiry. The first kind comes from those philosophers and others interested in normative questions about the character of reality, what people can know of it and how, and whether this knowledge does or should influence proper behavior. This definition picks out the practices predicated on the idea that superempirical realities exist, that one can know them, and that one ought to live in accord with them, so that these practices can be the object of metaphysical, epistemological, and ethical debate. The second kind of inquiry comes from those historians and others interested in explanatory questions about the ways in which social identity and a social order are formed and legitimated. This definition picks out those forms of social management that are said to be authorized by a reality that has no empirical source, so that these practices can be the object of anthropological, psychological, and political inquiry. This definition does not separate religion from politics or culture. Nor does it suggest that religion is unique in its function of providing meaning for life, that it is universal, or that it is intrinsically irrational or violent. But it does permit both normative and explanatory kinds of inquiry makes possible a pursuit of the study of religions that is multidisciplinary and polymethodical.

Bibliographic Essay

In this chapter, I argue that that functionalist definitions of religion tend to be far too inclusive and that substantive definitions need to find a way to include nontheistic religious realities. In their place, I propose a mixed or "dithetic" definition of religion. Because the promiscuity of what I will call "pure functional" definitions is central to my case, it may be worth providing a sense of the frustration of those who oppose them. In an extremely influential paper written half a century ago, Melford Spiro complains that with "[pure] functional definitions of religion ... it is virtually impossible to set any substantive boundary to religion and, thus, to distinguish it from other sociocultural phenomena. Social solidarity, anxiety reduction, confidence in unpredictable situations, and the like, are functions which may be served by any or all cultural phenomena—Communism and Catholicism, monotheism and monogamy, images and imperialism—and unless religion is defined substantively, it would be impossible to delineate its boundaries" (1966: 89–90). More recently, Timothy Fitzgerald complains that, given a pure functional definition of religion, "one finds in the published work of scholars working within religion departments the term 'religion' being used to refer to such diverse institutions as totems ... Christmas cakes, nature, the value of hierarchy, vegetarianism, witchcraft, veneration of the Emperor, the Rights of man, supernatural technology possession, amulets, charms, the tea ceremony, ethics, ritual in general, The Imperial Rescript of Education, the motor show, salvation, Marxism, Maoism, Freudianism, marriage, gift exchange, and so on. There is not much within culture that has cannot be included as 'religion'" (1997: 92–3; cf. 105). Martin Riesebrodt continues, saying that pure functional definitions dilute the concept of religion "to the point of futility, considering barbecues with guitar music, soccer games, shopping in supermarkets, or art exhibitions to be religious phenomena. Everything becomes 'somehow' or 'implicitly' religious. Others criticize the concept of religion as an invention of Western modernity that should not be applied to premodern or non-Western societies. In their opinion, Hinduism, Buddhism, and Confucianism are Western inventions that cannot be termed religions without perpetuating colonialist thinking. When soccer games are seen as religious phenomena and the recitation of Buddhist sutras is not, something has obviously gone wrong" (2010: xi; cf. 73).

Peter Berger's statement that definitions of religion can only be evaluated in terms of their utility, not their reference, is from Berger (1967: 175). For a nice discussion of this point, see Martin (2010: Ch. 1). In agreeing with Berger, I am disagreeing with, for example, Emile Durkheim when he says that "[i]t is not our preconceptions, passions, or habits that must be consulted for the elements of the definition we need; definition is to be sought from reality itself" (1995: 22). As Spiro (1966) puts it, a definition of religion is properly a "nominal" definition and not a "real" definition. For examples of how scholars' findings about religion turn on their definitions of what religion is, see Donovan 2003.

The idea that the concept of *religion* operates prototypically has been developed and defended by anthropologist Benson Saler (1993, 2008). I don't discuss polythetic definitions of religion in the chapter, but I would argue that they tend to be, like pure functionalist definitions, too inclusive. For defenses of polythetic definitions, see Alston (1967); Edwards (1972); and Southwold (1978). Among those who despair of coming up with a single definition for religion given the fragmentation of the field of religious studies is J. Milton Yinger, who writes: "In dealing with a subject so complex and concerned with a range of data so broad as religion, a topic approached for many different purposes, one must give up the idea that there is *one* definition that *is* 'correct' and satisfactory for all" (1957: 6). Gary Lease argues similarly (2000: esp. 287–8).

In the chapter, I recommend a mixed definition of religion that combines functional and substantive elements. Another philosopher of religion who explicitly recommends a mixed definition is Keith Yandell, who defines a religion as "a conceptual system that provides an interpretation of the world and the place of human beings in it, bases an account of how life should be lived given that interpretation, and expresses this interpretation and lifestyle in a set of rituals, institutions and practices" (1999: 16). For a project in comparative philosophy of religions that adopts a substantive understanding of religion that includes nontheistic conceptions of ultimate realities, see Neville (2001c). Augustine's discussion of religion as "worship of God"— or, more fully, that "true religion means the worship of the one true God, that is, the Trinity, Father, Son, and Holy Spirit"—is found in his *Of True Religion* (Augustine 1953). Given the lack of clarity about the meaning of the word religion today, it is worth noting that in his *Retractions* Augustine notes that he himself was dealing with multiple etymologies for the term (Augustine 1953: 221).

The organization of religious practices into promises having to do with three domains—the body, social relations, and nature—I borrow from Riesebrodt (2010: 90). The quotes for the three definitions of religion in the chapter that I label "axiological" come from Paul Tillich (1959: 7–8); William Christian (1941: 412–13); and Paul Griffiths (2001: 7, 9, 11); respectively. I do not want to give the impression that a Tillichian or axiological definition of religion only appeals to philosophers: the definition has been widely influential and many sociologists and anthropologist have also adopted versions of it, including Robert Bellah (1957); Lessa and Vogt (1958); and Yinger (1970). Though Tillich offers what J. Z. Smith (2010: 1150) calls a "caring-deeply" definition of religion, Tillich also speaks of an ontological element—namely, the absence or presence of the unconditioned, infinite, or truly ultimate reality—that lets him distinguish between idolatrous and nonidolatrous religions (e.g., Tillich 1957: 95–8). For Tillich's account of how the religious function draws on the moral, cognitive, and aesthetic dimensions of the human personality, see Tillich (1957). Similarly, William Christian defines religion in a purely functional way, and is explicit about that choice, but he also recognizes the fact that religious people tend to ascribe reality to their ideal values, which is the fact that leads to my mixed definition (1941: 413). For a nice discussion of the difference between a worldview merely as a set of beliefs and more richly as a set of things one cares about—or, as he likes to say, "gives a damn about"—see French (1997: Ch. 1). For a seminal argument that religions pursue disparate ends, see Mark Heim (1995).

My project is indebted to Christian Smith's (2003) argument that culture is always a moral order. For a critical discussion that connects Smith's moral account of human nature to evolutionary theory, see David Sloan Wilson (2004). Although I am a critical realist and Alasdair MacIntyre, as far as I know, is not, my argument that religious practices assume a reference to the nature of things finds support in MacIntyre's well-known account of traditional moral enquiry. MacIntyre argues that the separation of moral recommendations from a vision of the way things are reflects a particularly modern form of alienation: "The variety of words translatable as 'ought' in ancient and medieval languages never have a sense which allows them a mandatory force independently of the reasons given for uttering the statements which are expressed by means of them" (1990: 193).

In this chapter, I argue that substantive definitions of religion have evolved through four stages. The first is the identification of the substance of religion with the Christian God. Columbus's claim that the indigenous people of America lacked religion can be found in his diaries (see Stroumsa 2010: 14). James Gardner's claim that the Xhosa have no religion can be found in (Chidester 1996: 85). The second stage moves from the

Christian form of a substantive definition of religion to the generic form of "a Supreme Being." This move is rejected by John Milbank who argues that "religion is not a genus" (see Milbank 1990: esp. 176–81). Roger Johnson (1994) makes an important point that for Herbert the "common notions" provide ideal norms for what a religion must include, as a definition should, but they cannot and do not constitute a religion themselves. For this reason, according to Johnson, Herbert does not develop—or even mention—the idea of a natural religion, an idea developed later by his epigones. For Herbert, any actual religion would always have to, so to speak, combine nature and culture by instantiating or clothing the abstract common notions with the particularities of their social and historical context. For a much richer account of the emergence of the comparative study of religion as a project of the Enlightenment, and an argument that this emergence should be dated to the seventeenth century, see Stroumsa (2010); Johnson concurs 1994. Both Preus (1987: esp. ix–xii and 206) and Stroumsa Ch. 1 call Herbert's revised definition of religion a "paradigm shift." For perhaps the best analyses of how the Enlightenment concept of natural religion puts Christianity into comparable history, see Byrne (1989) and Harrison (1990). I owe the observation that Herbert takes the term "imposture" and stretches it to apply to Christianity to Stroumsa (2010: 34 and Ch. 6). Friedrich Max Müller's famous statement "He who knows one [religion], knows none" is quoted in Sharpe (1986: 36).

The third stage in the history of substantive definitions of religion expands from belief in a Supreme Being to belief in any kind of spiritual beings. For important defenses of Edward Tylor's definition of religion, see Goody (1962); Spiro (1966); Horton (1993: esp. Ch. 1—2); and Guthrie (1993). J. Z. Smith notes that Tylor's definition was the organizing taxon in the *HarperCollins Dictionary of Religions* for which he served as editor (2004: 165). The literature on Tyler includes considerable debate about what makes a being "spiritual." Some prefer to speak of "supernatural beings," Spiro recommends "superhuman beings" (1966: 96), and some cognitive scientists use "non-obvious" or "counter-intuitive beings."

The fourth and final stage in the evolution of substantive definitions expands from spiritual beings to include nonperson-like religious realities. The best known examples of definitions of religion that include nontheistic religions are those of the psychologist and philosopher William James and the anthropologist Clifford Geertz. Recognizing the disparate varieties of religious experience, James sought to frame "religion in the broadest and most general terms possible," and he arrived at a dithetic or mixed formula

144

for religion as "the belief that there is an unseen order, and that our supreme good lies in harmoniously adjusting ourselves thereto" (1961: 59). James saw religions as competing recipes for how people might understand the relation of their own powers to the other forces that make up the world, and the "unseen order," the ontological substance of religion, was *whatever it is* that sustains moral purpose in the universe. On James's idea of a moral order, see Proudfoot (2000). For his nontheistic understanding of the ontological possibilities, I read James as drawing on Matthew Arnold, who had argued a generation earlier for a nontheistic reinterpretation of God as "the not ourselves which makes for righteousness" (1883 [1873]: 46). I read Arnold in turn as drawing on Emerson's *Essays*, and Emerson was James' godfather.

Geertz's famous multipart definition of religion is often treated as a functional definition, but it is actually a mixed one since, like James's, it includes as its ontological element "conceptions of a general order of existence" (1973: 90). In Geertz's eyes, religion does have pragmatic functions, namely, to understand the natural world, how to suffer, and how to be good. Thus the pragmatic aspect of religion for Geertz is to provide and sustain a meaningful framework for interpreting the world—especially in the face of the challenges of baffling, anomalous experiences, of suffering, and of moral struggles (1973: esp. 100–6). But the solutions to these problems that are on this definition religious solutions are only those that ground a meaningful life in a vision of "the very nature of reality" or of "the way things in their sheer actuality are" (1973: 128, 127). Unlike the instincts of nonhuman animals, Geertz argues, the symbols of human culture seek simultaneously to guide action and to offer an ontological account of the way the world is, an account that makes the recommended action realistic. As Geertz puts the ontological point, religious people are realists: "though in theory we might think that a people could construct a wholly autonomous value system independent of any metaphysical referent, an ethics without an otology, we do not in fact seem to have found such a people" (1973: 127). For critiques of Geertz's definition of religion, see Asad (1993: Ch. 1) and Frankenberry and Penner (1999b); for a defense, see Schilbrack (2005). The other examples of "Stage 4" substantive definitions that refer, like James and Geertz, to "a level of reality beyond the observable world known to science" or an "order of reality beyond or behind the apparent, given order" came from David Martin (1978: 12) and Byrne (1999: 385), respectively.

Jack Goody, a Tylorean, says that "the main difficulty" of substantive approaches is how to distinguish between religious and nonreligious realities (1961: 145). My proposal to use the term "superempirical" is meant to address this problem. I borrow the term "superempirical" from Christian Smith, who offers this definition: "religions are set of beliefs, symbols, and practices about the reality of superempirical orders that make claims to organize and guide human life" (2003: 98). By "metaphysical," I follow Charles Hartshorne's definition of metaphysics as: nonrestrictive existential claims (see Hartshorne 1983: esp. Ch. 2, 8). My definition of religion is therefore similar to what Peter Byrne (1998) has proposed as "the moral definition of 'religion'" in that he and I agree on the important points that functionalist and substantive aspects of religion have a "necessary interdependence" (Byrne 1999: 387) and that a definition of religion today needs to include nontheistic conceptions. My proposal differs from his, however, in that it recommends (i) a broader understanding of the functions which religions seek to provide in addition to theodicy, and (ii) with the concept of the superempirical, greater specificity about what it means to identify a nontheistic but still religious "order of reality beyond or behind the apparent, given order" (1999: 385).

The maximalist overlap of religion and politics is on my account unsurprising, and so I want to signal clearly my disagreement with those like Daniel Philpott who define religion in terms of superempirical *rather than* political or other worldly concerns: "religions are not first and foremost concerned with or defined by what political orders do or look like, that is, their principles of legitimacy, structure, policies, or pursuits. Rather, they are communities of belief and practices oriented around claims about the ultimate grounds of existence" (Philpott 2009: 192).

It is worth noting that to limit the range of religion in the way I am recommending has two important consequences for the study of religions around the world. First, it makes possible the study of secularization. If one defines religion in pure functional terms as a commitment to whatever functions in a certain way (for example, as one's ultimate concern), then religion is made universal by definition. Given a Tillichian or axiological definition, it follows that though one's mode of religiosity might change, no individual and no culture can become less religious, let alone nonreligious, and the hypotheses of secularization are disproven without empirical work. Second, using a limited definition of religion like mine makes it possible to speak of multiple religious identities. Again, if one defines religion functionally as an ultimate concern then it is problematic if not incoherent to say that a person has multiple concerns that are all ultimate. An axiological definition of religion implies that a person can fully participate in only one religion. Griffiths is explicit about this (2001: 13). By contrast, on my definition of religion, questions such as "Does the spread of modern forms of life entail the decrease in religious belief and practice?" and "To how many religious communities does a person belong?' are open questions.

That the study of religion needs to be rematerialized is persuasively argued by Vásquez (2011). For the discussion of fly-fishing as religious, see Snyder (2007) (and Maclean 1976). For contemporary treatments of nature itself as a religious reality, see Crosby (2002) and Hogue (2010). For the discussion of the War on Terror as religious, see Chernus (2008, 2006) and see also Hedges (2002).

In the chapter, I note that my proposed definition tracks the colloquial use of the term well. I hope that my proposal thereby provides evidence against the Martin (2010: 17–9) who suggests that because "religion" is a social construction, no monothetic definition can make sense of the colloquial use of the term. Mine is also a multidisciplinary and polymethodical approach to the study of religions and for an argument against polymethodism, see Martin and Wiebe (2012).

Endnotes

1. Since my mixed definition has two elements, I would like to be able to call it a "dithetic" definition of religion. But since it proposes that there is *only one set* of necessary and sufficient elements that classifies a social practice as religion, mine is properly speaking a monothetic definition of religion.
2. I owe this point to Proudfoot (1985).
3. The good achieved in religious practices in some cases may be achieved simply by participating in the practice; the benefit of participating is often intrinsic to and not external to the practice. In other words, "pragmatic" here does not necessarily mean instrumental.
4. I owe this way of sorting religious functions, as well as my use of the idea of religious "promises" in my section titles, to Riesebrodt (2010).
5. More specifically, Herbert proposes that the generic elements of religion, what he calls the five "Common Notions," include both pragmatic and ontological elements: a religion will teach (1) that there is a supreme Deity; (2) that this Deity ought to be worshipped; (3) that combining one's piety with virtue is the most important aspect of religious practice; (4) that people should repent of their wrong-doings; (5) that there is reward and punishment for one's actions, both in this life and after it. See Herbert (1705).
6. Tylor (1970: 11). The other two quotes in this paragraph from Tylor are both from Tylor (1970: 8).

7. Religious worldviews vary so greatly that a fascinating project would be to compare how religious communities themselves conceptualize the multiple kinds or levels of reality: the visible and the invisible, Heaven and Earth, the conditioned and the unconditioned, the realm of people and animals and the realm of spirits, and so on. Though I suspect that the distinction I make between what is or is not available to the senses would be common, I don't assume that it is the only or the best place to begin to generalize about religious realities as such.

8. For the claim that Buddhism is the "litmus test" for a definition of religion, see Bryan Turner (2011: xxiii; cf. Southwold).

9. This quote comes from Chernus (2008: 848).

Chapter 6

Are Religions Out of Touch
With Reality?

i. Religious Metaphysics in a Postmetaphysical Age

As I argued in the previous chapter, I judge that the best way to define religion is by categorizing beliefs, practices, experiences, and institutions as religious when they are justified by reference to a superempirical reality. On this definition, a religious community presents its way of life as the means to align people with something out of the ordinary. Their practices, claims the community, are the ones willed by God. Or they are the ones in accord with the Way of things. Or they are the ones that realize the emptiness of all phenomena. The realities to which different religious communities aim to connect are of various kinds and they include not only God, the Way, and Emptiness but also ancestors, the mandate of Heaven, angels, the demiurge, nats, Nirvana, loa, Goddesses, kami, and others. This raises the important point that, despite their differences, a religious community is typically realist: it promises not simply that its path is the right path but also that its path is accurately based on some truth about the way things are. Religious communities claim that their practices put people in touch with reality.

The realism of religious communities ties what they offer to realities that are alleged to be not the physical product of the nuclear furnaces of the stars, nor the biological products of evolution, nor the social products of human ingenuity. Even if one does not agree that the attempts to connect

Philosophy and the Study of Religions: A Manifesto, First Edition. Kevin Schilbrack.
© 2014 Kevin Schilbrack. Published 2014 by John Wiley & Sons, Ltd.

one's values, life, and community to superempirical realities are the best way to *define* religion, I hope that my readers will agree that such attempts are common. I suspect that most would agree to include in the category of the superempirical what Jews call YHWH, the creator who works in history to reconcile with his stiff-necked people. I suspect that most would agree to include in this category what Daoists call the Dao, the invisible force that flows through all the changes of the seasons. Also included would be what Muslims call Allah, the merciful judge of the world; what Stoics call the Logos, the natural order that permeates all things and with which we can put ourselves in harmony; what Advaita Hindus call Brahman, the ocean of being and blissful consciousness in which we are swimming right now without knowing it; what Christians call the Triune God that created the world, became human, and dwells in people; and what Mahayana Buddhists call Dharmakaya, the body of the Buddha that is found wherever someone finds truth. As I said: extraordinary realities.

The realities to which religious communities refer—these principles and spirits and Gods and cosmic orders—are diverse, but in this chapter I want to focus on what I take to be the most problematic kind. Some superempirical realities are said to exist not here and there, but always and everywhere. They are said to be the source of or an aspect of or the condition for the possibility of every reality other than itself. I want a word for this subset of superempirical realities, the realities that are said to be somehow implicated in everything that exists or reality in general. If we follow Aristotle and name the attempt to speak of reality in general as "metaphysics," then we can call religious discourse about such realities "religious metaphysics." To be explicit, then, I am using the term "religious metaphysics" not to refer to religious claims about another world, its inhabitants, or the after-life, but solely in its classical sense to refer to claims about realities that are alleged to exist under all actual conditions.

How one answers the question of the cognitive status of religious metaphysical claims has enormous repercussions for how one studies religion.[1] For most scholars of religion, their answers to this question can remain implicit, but it is the part of the task of philosophy of religion, I judge, to ask and answer this question explicitly. And the question of religious metaphysics is especially complicated because even if most scholars of religion would agree that religious communities ground their ways of life on views that are metaphysical, many would also hold that the idea that such views are problematic, if not hopeless. Many twentieth-century philosophers would agree. As a form of inquiry, metaphysics is widely seen as discredited, and the assumption that any human beings can get at the nature of reality in general is considered arrogant or confused or worse. Almost all of the most influential philosophers of the last century repudiate metaphysics. Though there are exceptions, thee opponents of metaphysics include all or almost all of the positivists, phenomenologists, existentialists, pragmatists, deconstructionists, and critical theorists. And this includes all or almost all of those who see themselves as drawing on Martin Heidegger, Ludwig Wittgenstein, John Dewey, or Jacques Derrida. As Jürgen Habermas puts it, we now live in a "post-metaphysical" age.[2] In this philosophical context, then, insofar as religious communities speak about the nature of things, they proffer teachings that are no longer credible.

The study of religious metaphysics in a postmetaphysical age faces a dilemma. If (a) religious ways of life are typically based on metaphysical realities but (b) metaphysics is unsalvageable, then it appears that the study of religion is the attempt to make sense out of nonsense. Several scholars have therefore sought to challenge (a). They have sought to reinterpret religious practices by arguing that religious discourse that appears to describe the character of reality in general is actually about something else entirely. Apparently metaphysical claims are really expressions of the practitioner's commitment to live a certain way or to understand certain values as ultimate or to see oneself under a certain frame of reference—but religious discourse is not actually, as a realist interpreters would have it, about some extraordinary aspect of the world. I want to argue for a different position. In this chapter, I judge that religious discourse often does make or imply metaphysical claims, but I offer an interpretation of metaphysics that present metaphysics as a legitimate form of human inquiry. In other words, I accept (a) and I challenge (b).

Here is how the rest of this chapter proceeds. In the next section, I consider the several arguments against metaphysics and I argue that, despite their variety, they share a common picture of human experience of the world that imagines a gap between knowing subjects and known objects. This dualistic notion of an epistemic gap, I suggest, is the primary source of modern and postmodern opposition to metaphysics. If one can think with another picture of human experience—that is, if one can develop a plausible account of our experience of the world without a gap, an account of experience as unmediated or direct—then metaphysics as a legitimate form of intellectual inquiry would be possible. In the section after that (i.e., section iii), I suggest three philosophical allies who contribute to that alternative account. In the section after that, I make explicit the connection between the notion of unmediated or direct experience of the world and metaphysical inquiry. And then in the fifth and final section, I return to the question of how to interpret metaphysical claims that are religious and I argue that if metaphysics is intelligible as a cognitive form of inquiry, then religious metaphysics is as well.

ii. Antimetaphysics Today

If one takes a look at the range of approaches in contemporary philosophy of religion, whether Anglophone or Continental, antimetaphysical positions abound. As I noted above, "metaphysical" has largely become a pejorative term. Of course, this is not to say that that all of those who oppose metaphysics are referring to the same beast. On the contrary, contemporary definitions of and arguments against metaphysics are so sprawling and discordant, I would argue, that one could not coherently agree with all of them. However, I will propose that anti-metaphysical thinkers generally share and rely on a certain picture of experience. Moreover, it is a picture that is evitable and some philosophers today work without it. I will therefore argue that to the extent that antimetaphysical arguments assume this picture of experience, they do not provide an obstacle for those who want to pursue metaphysics without it.

Let me begin by putting on the table a working definition of metaphysics that is intended to be theory-thin and relatively uncontroversial. So: if one understands metaphysics as a form of inquiry into the character of things not insofar as they are the particular things that they are, but rather insofar as they are anything at all, then one understands metaphysics (in this classical, Aristotelian way) as the study of reality-as-such or being *qua* being.[3] A metaphysical inquiry on this understanding is an investigation into the character that all things have in common. It is a study of what, if anything, is the case always and everywhere or under all actual conditions. The scope of a metaphysical inquiry then is by definition wider and more inclusive than that of any other form of inquiry. Metaphysical claims allege to name truths about the world that hold not only locally but always and everywhere.

Why do so many contemporary philosophers oppose the idea of metaphysical inquiry? At the beginning of Kevin Hector's helpful recent book, *Theology without Metaphysics*, Hector offers a diagnosis of the problem and says that there are two features of metaphysical inquiry that contemporary philosophers find objectionable: "Once these features have been made explicit, it is easy to see why one would want to avoid metaphysics, since it seems alienating, violent and idolatrous;" Hector calls the two features "essentialism" and "correspondentism."[4] Each of these two labels stands for a compact summary of multiple arguments about what is problematic about metaphysical ways of thinking, speaking, and writing, and so it is worth looking at each one closely.

The first problematic feature is that metaphysics, according to its critics, seeks to describe reality "at a remove from" or "apart from" ordinary experience. The antimetaphysicians hold that there is a kind of gap or division or rift between the human subject and the world. On the near side of the gap is "the phenomenal realm," the world as it is given in human experience, the realm of appearances. On the far side of this gap is the world independent of the way it seems to me or to us, independent of our practical interests, our language, and our particular perspectives. According to these critics, metaphysics is the incessant but hopeless attempt to describe the far side of the gap; it is the attempt to describe reality as it is "in itself." It is Immanuel Kant who famously argues against this "essentialist" aspect of metaphysical discourse by introducing the distinction between phenomena and noumena, a distinction that seeks to identify the limit of what human beings can know. And this is to say that this particular antimetaphysical argument is part of the subjective turn that emerged in modern philosophy and has come to pervade most philosophical work since Kant.[5] I will therefore call the argument that metaphysics involves a hopeless attempt to describe reality free from the categories of experience "the modernist critique of metaphysics," and it seems to me that some version of the modernist critique informs most of the antimetaphysical positions in contemporary Anglophone philosophy.

The second problematic feature of metaphysics (as Hector notes) also depends upon the picture of a gap or division or rift between human subjectivity and the world. But here the critics of metaphysics object that metaphysics identifies reality not with what lies *outside* human concepts and outside the phenomenal realm, but rather within what one has grasped. According to this criticism, metaphysics is a form of discourse that takes it for granted that language is adequate to reality. It takes as real precisely the linguistic products of human practical interests and assumes that the world cannot be otherwise. In Hector's words, "Metaphysics thus seems to limit an object's particularity to that which fits within one's pre-established ideas about it, which explains why [metaphysical discourse] is commonly criticized as 'totalizing,' 'calculating,' and 'instrumentalizing.'"[6] This criticism of metaphysics can be traced primarily to Heidegger's argument that the metaphysical tradition "forgets" Being. This is to say that this particular antimetaphysical argument is part of the linguistic turn that has characterized contemporary philosophy and it has come to pervade most of the philosophical work in Europe since Heidegger.[7] I will call this argument the postmodernist critique of metaphysics, and it seems to me that some version of the postmodernist critique informs most of the antimetaphysical positions in contemporary continental philosophy.

Although the modernist and postmodernist critiques proceed from profoundly different accounts of what it is that metaphysical inquiries try to do, they agree that the very idea of a metaphysical inquiry is problematic. Moreover, once those interested in metaphysical inquiries into the character of reality in general come to see how these two criticisms complement each other, they may have a sense of "damned if I do, damned if I don't." If they understand reality as such as something that lies beyond our experiences and our language—so to speak, on the far side of the gap between the subject and the world—then their inquiry is subject to the modernist critique. And if they understand reality as such as something fully within our experiences and language—so to speak, on the near side of the gap—then they are subject to the postmodernist critique.

The contemporary opposition to metaphysics comes in a variety of versions. Hector's account of the two central criticisms is valuable for my purposes, however, because he shows that both the Kantian, modernist critique and the Heideggerian, postmodernist critique assume a gap, a division, a rift, or (to use Jean-Luc Marion's word) a distance, between mind and world.[8] Put in other words, the critiques of metaphysics at work in philosophy today largely share a picture of experience in which any access the subject has to the world must be bridged, navigated, or "mediated." To the extent that their arguments presuppose this dualism, they assume that subjects do not have direct or unmediated awareness of things. This observation about antimetaphysical arguments today raises the possibility that if one were to develop an account of the mind in which direct experience of the nature of things were available, then it would not be subject to these critiques. This is the idea I want to explore in the rest of this chapter.

Let's call this idea the idea of *unmediated experience*. I want to argue that the idea of unmediated experience has the potential to rehabilitate metaphysics as a legitimate form of inquiry and so, before turning to that idea fully in the next section of this chapter, I would like at least briefly to put the proposal in historical context. Toward that end, here is a breakneck, one-paragraph history of western philosophy.

Classical western thinkers presented the subject matter of philosophy as reasoned inquiry into all of the things of the world. It is understandable, therefore, that Aristotle lectured not only on aesthetics, ethics, and logic but also on stars, animal reproduction, and constitutions. For Aristotle and other classical thinkers, philosophers studied reality in all of its variety, and metaphysics was simply the study of things-in-general. By contrast, the thinkers whom we now label as "modern" philosophers are those who made the subjective turn in the sense that they held that the central object of philosophy is not the things of the world themselves but rather our experience of those things. With this idea, epistemology displaces metaphysics as the central work of philosophy. There are, of course, many ways to reflect on the relation between the person and her experiences. But one way is to see experience as that which mediates the world to the person. Here, to use a visual metaphor, one conceives of experience as a kind of a window onto the world, as a kind of lens, as that which gives the human mind access to the external world. Descartes, for instance, argued that what one knows best is the ideas in one's own mind and not the things in the external world that they are meant to represent, and Kant argued that the categories of understanding make experience possible even as they make metaphysics in the classical or Aristotelian sense impossible. For these modern philosophers, the crucial insight is that we do not know the world directly but only through the mediation of our experiences. Knowledge of the things apart from experience (i.e., metaphysical knowledge, according to Kant) is unavailable. The thinkers whom we now label as "postmodern" philosophers are those who make the linguistic turn in the sense that they see the subject's experience as itself inevitably shaped by the concepts found in the socially and historically emergent languages of one's discursive community. For postmodern philosophers, then, epistemology is itself displaced as the central task of philosophy and is supplanted by reflection on language. One can therefore draw this comparison: whereas modern philosophers after Kant tend to argue that subjects do not have direct access to things in themselves, because all knowledge of the world is mediated by the filters of experience, postmodern philosophers tend to argue that we do not even have direct access to experience because all knowledge of experience is mediated by the filters of language. A typical statement of this view is that claim that "[e]lements of what we call 'language' ... penetrate so deeply into what we call 'reality' that the very project of representing ourselves as being 'mappers' of something 'language-independent' is fatally compromised from the very start."[9] This brand of "postmodern" thought has been called "most modern" thought insofar as it does not divert from but rather repeats the modern idea that the world must be mediated to us. By continuing the modern view of knowledge as mediation, postmodern thought makes metaphysics—that is, knowledge of the things of the world as such—if even coherent at all, now doubly unavailable.

From the perspective of this book, neither the subjective turn in modern philosophy nor the linguistic turn in postmodern philosophy is wrong-headed. The problem, rather, is the way in which this history of thinking about experience has entrenched the dualistic assumption that there is a gap, rift, or distance between person and world that must be bridged by one's concepts. The idea of unmediated experience therefore proposes that experience should not be understood as the internal processing of symbols "in the head" which, when arranged properly, connect a person's ideas to the external world. Experience should be understood instead as the direct or immediate interaction of an organism with its environment. On such an approach, there is no gap between mind and world that has to be jumped, for persons are not seen as separated or divorced from reality in the first place. I turn now to exploring this idea.

iii.   Constructive Postmodernism and Unmediated Experience

If the account given in the previous section is right, then most opposition to metaphysics today is based on the view that there is a gap between people and the world that must be conceptually mediated and that, according to either a modernist or a postmodernist argument, this gap makes metaphysical claims about reality in general seem dubious. The opposition to metaphysics arises, in other words, when it is assumed that human experience of the world is trapped within our concepts. This leads to the question: What would it be like to think of human experience, agency, and cognition without that gap? What would it mean to see human perception as directly "in touch with" reality?

I would like to suggest that focusing on this question is not a sneaky way to rehabilitate metaphysics but is rather the best way to understand all of the major movements of twentieth-century philosophy. That is, all the contemporary philosophical attempts to conceive of human subjectivity as embodied, embedded, and social can be profitably read as attempts to answer this question. This is how I read Martin Heidegger's and

158

Maurice Merleau-Ponty's and the existentialists' accounts of being in the world, Charles Peirce's and John Dewey's and the pragmatists' rejection of doubts unrelated to real life problems, and Ludwig Wittgenstein's and John Austin's and ordinary language philosophers' relocation of the sources of meaning to the norms of social forms of life.[10] One can call these movements "postmodern" in the sense that they are—and they all explicitly saw themselves as—repudiating Cartesian mind–body dualism and the quest for foundationalist certainty. But these postmodern movements are not solely negative, criticizing the modernist turn to the subject. They also provide the tools with which one might develop a positive account of subjectivity, and so they properly represent a *constructive* postmodernism. I understand my defense of metaphysics as part of that project.

Within this overarching goal of contributing to a constructive postmodernism, and to underline that the rehabilitation of metaphysics that I am proposing is not beyond the pale, I want to focus on three contemporary philosophical positions that I consider allies in developing an account of experience as not imprisoned by language but in direct touch with reality.

The first ally in my aim to develop an account of unmediated experience is the philosopher of language, Donald Davidson. In his essay "On the Very Idea of Conceptual Scheme," Davidson famously argues for the incoherence of what he calls scheme–content dualism. He describes scheme–content dualism as a dogma of empiricism, but it is also found in many other philosophies whenever they divide experience into two parts, a conceptual scheme provided by one's mind or one's language and the preconceptual content provided by the world. Davidson notes that philosophers have tried to explain the relationship between one's conceptual scheme to the unconceptualized content either by saying that one's scheme "organizes" the content or that the scheme "fits" it. But Davidson argues that neither of these two ways of individuating, giving form to, or schematizing the otherwise uninterpreted, formless content of our experience works. A conceptual scheme cannot "organize" experience because to organize something implies that the something is plural. We can only organize distinct objects. As Davidson says, "[s]omeone who sets out to organize a closet organizes the things in it."[11] But *distinct* objects are already structured entities. They are not formless we-know-not-whats, waiting to be given form by our concepts. Whether we speak of objects like knives and forks or cabbages and kingdoms, or we speak of events like losing a button or stubbing a toe, as soon as the world falls under a description—or as Davidson likes to say, as soon as part of the world is "individuated"—it can no longer play the role of unconceptualized content. A parallel problem arises for the metaphor that one's conceptual scheme fits or maps the facts of the world. The problem is how one can locate or identify any facts without already using one's conceptual scheme. As Davidson says, "One can locate individual objects, if the sentence happens to name or describe them, but even such location makes sense relative only to a frame of reference, and so presumably the frame of reference must be included in whatever it is [that a sentence is said to fit]."[12] Once again, to make the scheme–content model coherent requires one to meet an impossible need to refer successfully to the things of the world but without using the concepts that would give sense to that reference. Since it is impossible to identify what it is that gets organized or gets fitted, except in the already-interpreted terms of the conceptual scheme, the very idea of a conceptual scheme founders on the problem of identifying something without interpreting it. It founders, in other words, because it tries to appeal to an idea of a "raw" or noumenal world that is otherwise uninterpreted or preconceptual or theory-neutral.

Davidson is explicit that when one rejects the dualistic idea that a conceptual scheme filters our awareness of the world, one is led to see experience of the world as unmediated: "In giving up the dualism of scheme and world, we do not give up the world, but re-establish unmediated touch with the familiar objects whose antics make our sentences and opinions true or false."[13] And Davidson is equally explicit that re-establishing unmediated touch with the world provides for the possibility of truth in metaphysics. Davidson's argument against conceptual schemes thus provides a valuable tool for a constructive postmodernism that links a postempiricist account of experience to, in Davidson's words, "studying the most general aspects of reality."

A second philosophical ally in my aim to develop an account of unmediated experience can be found in the critical realist movement initiated by Roy Bhaskar. Critical realism began as an argument that the practice of experiments in the natural sciences necessarily implies a world independent of the experiment, but it has since also made the case for a similar realism in history and the social sciences as well. What I borrow from critical realism is in fact its central idea: the distinction between what Bhaskar calls the "transitive" and the "intransitive" aspects of knowledge. The transitive aspect refers to the fact that knowledge is a product of human inquirers. Human knowledge is therefore theory-laden, historically contingent, and socially situated. The intransitive aspect refers to the fact that what knowledge is *about* is not a product of those human inquirers. That about which one theorizes, the reality one describes, must exist independent of the claims made about it. Thus the transitive aspects of any of the inquiry are, but the intransitive aspects are not, the products of the inquirers. And inquiry can be defined as "a social activity whose aim is the production of the knowledge of the kinds and ways of acting of independently existing and active things."[14] Making this transitive/intransitive distinction lets one recognize both that (i) inquiry is a social activity and that therefore the knowledge produced is dependent on and relative to the conceptual tools, institutional contexts, and social history of the inquirers and also that (ii) inquiry is of structures and mechanisms that do not depend on that knowledge.

Bhaskar argues for this distinction with a transcendental argument. He argues, in other words, that the practice of inquiry isn't possible unless that about which one inquires is independent of one's knowledge of it. The independence of the world from one's inquiry is a condition for the possibility of one's inquiry. To confuse the transitive and the intransitive aspects of knowledge—that is, to collapse reality into human experience or language, to identify ontology with epistemology—is to commit what Bhaskar names "the epistemic fallacy." He points to this fallacy in the empiricism of David Hume, who denies that one can speak of causal structures and mechanisms at work in the natural world since such structures and mechanisms cannot be perceived. Bhaskar also identifies the epistemic fallacy in the positivists, Hume's intellectual descendents, who used a verification principle to argue that if a claim about reality could not be verified by sense experience, then it could not be cognitively meaningful. Unsurprisingly, both Hume and the positivists reject the legitimacy of metaphysical claims, religious or not. And the epistemic fallacy is also committed by postmodern philosophers when they argue that there is no more to reality than what can be found in human language.

Although not all critical realists have used Bhaskar's critical realism to argue explicitly for direct or unmediated perception, Margaret Archer is one who does. As she says, "the gatekeepers [of modern and postmodern philosophy] ... confine us to mediated experiences alone," but if we are to do justice to the impact of the world that gives rise to human persons, then we need to "allow for the possibility of unmediated experiences which are not *necessarily reducible* to [our conceptual categories]." Citing the work of Maurice Merleau-Ponty, she argues that this idea of unmediated experience is crucial to the role that critical realism gives to the embodied interaction with the world that she calls "the primacy of practice."[15]

161

A third, very different ally for developing an account of unmediated experience comes from the still-developing discipline of embodied cognitive science. When it first emerged as an interdisciplinary study of human mental life, cognitive science took the computer as a model for the mind and understood cognition as an internal process of creating, storing, and using symbolic representations of the world. Thinking was understood as an interior activity, in abstraction from bodily perception ("input") and behavior ("output"). But *embodied* cognitive science argues that bodily sensing and acting do not merely supply unconceptualized data to the mind but at least sometimes play a causal or constitutive role in thinking. This model of cognition can therefore serve as an ally to the epistemological position defended here.

The important idea is that embodied cognitive science understands the interaction between an organism and its environment as "tightly coupled" in the sense that thinking crosses the boundaries between the brain, the body, and the environment. Often drawing on philosophers of engaged bodily experience like Maurice Merleau-Ponty (for whom the primary mode of knowledge is unreflective being-in-the-world) or on James Gibson's notion of ecological perception (in which what agents directly perceive are action possibilities in their environment), embodied cognitive science describes cognition as a dynamic sensorimotor activity. To return to my theme, those who hold a computational model of cognition may object to the idea of "unmediated experience." They may assume that cognition simply *is* the combination of sensory input on the one hand with mental concepts on the other, so that, by definition, thoughtful action requires mediation by the inner representations. But insofar as embodied cognitive science is persuasive, it provides a model of thought in which the organism's experience of its environment does not require a gap between unprocessed world and inner processor. On such a model, one does not first see, for example, a stump and then judge that one might sit on it, but rather first sees (already conceptualized and evaluated) a place to sit.

On this point, Anthony Chemero makes a useful distinction between two forms of embodied cognitive science.[16] The first, which he calls "situated embodied cognitive science," seeks to *minimize* the role of inner representations and to recognize ways in which agents use the world as its own best model, from which they extract information on a "just-in-time" basis or onto which they offload some of the steps of thinking. The second, which Chemero calls "radical embodied cognitive science," seeks to *eliminate* inner representations altogether. Both forms of embodied cognitive science agree, however, that the mind is, first and foremost, a tool for guiding one's actions and not for gathering action-neutral information. And both forms therefore seek to develop a model of cognition that undermines the assumption that empirical research into how thinking mind works requires a dualism of mind and world.

In closing this section, let me draw these three threads together to give a better picture of the resources I see for developing a constructive postmodernism that can enable the philosophical study of religious metaphysics. The primary opposition to metaphysics today, I judge, is the assumption that knowledge of the world is conceptually mediated, that our knowledge of the world is trapped in varied concepts that are by definition local, and that metaphysical claims about the world in general are therefore nonstarters.

These three allies come from different branches of philosophy and they do not speak in the same idiom. Nevertheless, I judge that all three are responses to a common problem, namely, a concern that a strict dualism of mind and world makes an understanding of either mind or world incoherent. And I would argue that all three come to realist conclusions that are, if not the same, at least mutually supportive. Davidson's arguments against the very idea of a conceptual scheme support Bhaskar's opposition to what Bhaskar calls the epistemic fallacy. The embodied cognitive scientists' case that intelligent behavior requires few or no mental gymnastics supports Davidson's account of subjectivity that re-establishes unmediated touch with the familiar objects of the world. And I suggest that both Davidson and the embodied cognitive scientists would agree with the critical realist distinction between the transitive and intransitive aspects of knowledge. All three allies therefore help us to draw a picture of the human subject not as a homunculus, hidden in one's skull, watching an inner theater of representations of the external world, but rather as a social creature in unmediated contact with a shared world.

iv. Unmediated Experience and Metaphysics

The previous section of this chapter presented three philosophical allies for the development of an account of experience as unmediated. To the extent that those positions are persuasive, philosophers today ought to shift to a picture of direct experience tightly coupled to a stratified environment. Nevertheless, one might insist that accepting the idea that subjects of experience have unmediated contact with their present local surroundings is still a very different thing from the view that they can have knowledge of reality

163

in general. It may seem that it is clearly possible to accept the constructive postmodern picture of immediate experience and yet still reject metaphysics. In fact, I judge that exactly this is the position that Kevin Hector takes in his *Theology without Metaphysics*, and so I want to return to his careful account. In the end, however, I judge that Hector is another ally not only to the constructive postmodernism I am here developing but also – despite the title of his book – to the rehabilitation of metaphysics I recommend.

Hector describes his project as a kind of therapy that helps us avoid metaphysics. His primary concern is that when theology has sought to ground the norms of the Christian community, it has become entangled with metaphysics and has to that extent become unpersuasive. According to Hector, recall, the double problem with metaphysics is that it either tries to describe the way things are independent of their appearances ("essentialism") or it reduces reality to what corresponds to one's own concepts ("correspondentism"). Both versions of metaphysics presuppose that concepts come "between" one and an unconceptualized world, that concepts "mediate" the world to the subject. Hector agrees with my account of the implicit dualism in a great deal of contemporary philosophy; he agrees, that is, that philosophers today largely assume that if judgments about the world are conceptually informed, then they must also be conceptually mediated. As he puts it, "concepts are thought to stand like a veil between one and objects ... such that one's language and thoughts could never be in touch with—or genuinely about—objects themselves." But Hector argues that one can avoid this dualism by seeing that conceptually informed judgments about the world are typically not applied to an unconceptualized reality but are rather already implicit in the dispositions that one learns simply by participating in the practices of one's community. In other words, it may seem from a reflective perspective that when a person makes a judgment, one applies a concept to something that is not conceptualized. But Hector holds that in the usual case one's judgments are immediate, noninferential responses to one's environment rather than the product of explicit deliberation. Although taking-as-true is something that one will have learned in a particular social context, such judgments usually become part of a pre-reflective and nondeliberative attunement to one's circumstances. "In the overwhelming majority of cases, then, there is no interval between beliefs and what they are about ... [and so] one need not construct a theory that explains how such an interval might be bridged." In short, then, Hector argues against the "claim that concepts should be thought to mediate objects to us in such a way that we have no access to objects themselves" and for the claim that, properly understood, "it no longer makes sense to think of [our concepts] as go-betweens ... [since] concepts are applied non-inferentially, and so immediately, in everyday perception."[17]

Like Wittgenstein, Hector presents his approach as philosophical therapy. It avoids the gap between reflective thought and the world, and so it offers a way not to bridge that gap but rather to dissolve it. In this way, he presents his approach as a way to understand human experience as immediate contact with the world and so it does not generate the problems that seemed to call for metaphysical solutions. From my perspective, however, to overcome the gap between person and world and to operate with a picture in which persons are always already in touch with the world makes metaphysics in the sense at work in this book not only possible but commonsensical. That is, insofar as we see persons as agents in touch with their environments, we will expect them to develop hypotheses both about particular parts of the world and also, when they find it helpful, the whole. Hector therefore offers a promising approach for philosophy of religion in two ways. First, he shows that two problematic ways in which philosophy can be "metaphysical"—that is, either its essentialist attempt to transcend one's conceptual framework to get at the things in themselves or its correspondentist attempt to rest content with one's conceptual framework and to treat its deliverances as the final word about what is—both presuppose a dualistic picture of knowledge. And, second, he provides a postmodern approach that circumvents those features. But this is to offer not a path without metaphysics but rather theology without "essentialist–correspondentist metaphysics."[18] Metaphysics in the sense defended in this chapter—the Aristotelian sense of inquiry into the nature of reality in general—is not overcome but rather enabled by seeing that human knowledge is already unreflectively in touch with reality. Hector grants that his book can be understood as defending a revisionist metaphysics—and that is how I do understand his view, and mine.[19]

I am proposing that metaphysics as a form of cognitive inquiry is relegitimized when one drops the assumption that all experience of the world is mediated by concepts. But I want to be clear about this central point: I am not claiming that metaphysics requires the idea that some experiences are free of concepts. On the contrary, whenever anyone consciously or unconsciously judges that an X is Y, one requires concepts. This defense of the possibility of metaphysics therefore does not require an appeal to experiences that are pure, transcendent, raw, noumenal, or otherwise independent of the particularity of the experiencer. But this defense does lead us to recognize that the ubiquitous claim that the concepts in our experience or language "mediate" the world to us is really a metaphor, that it is a strange metaphor, and that we should do without it. We should do without it because the metaphor of mediation creates a wedge in our knowledge of the world, dividing knowledge of "things as they appear" from that of "things in themselves." It puts realism perpetually on the defensive and makes the reasonable interest in how things as a whole hang together into a yearning for the impossible. The metaphor of mediation also generates the problem that has dominated philosophy in both its modernist and postmodern forms: the problem of skepticism that asks how one can know whether *any* of one's ideas successfully cross the gap between knower and known. Given unmediated experience, however, there is no "gap" and no "other side." To accept this idea therefore involves a shift of metaphor: perception is not mediated, but it is still *perspectival*, in the sense that I experience the world from my location and with my capacities and interests, and others experience the world from theirs. But neither I nor they are insulated from the world by a window or filter or a grid formed by the categories of experience. Similarly, language is a human creation developed to sort the things of the world into the categories we find useful, just as a silverware sorter helps us divide teaspoons from tablespoons. But the claim that language intercedes "between" me and the world is a metaphor, and a pernicious one.

Let me illustrate this central idea with a quick example from the study of religion. Imagine that a religious community judges that a certain person is a holy person. Whether one unreflectively experiences that person in saintly terms or one reflectively puts that person into that privileged category, the community's judgment makes a distinction between types of people. The concept of the "holy" sorts people into tradition-specific categories. Now, if a philosopher understands the role of concepts like *holy person* as a form of mediation, then the philosopher will say that the concept "filters" the experience of the person for those who adopt it. The concept "provides access to" the person for those who use it. But this mediating, filtering, or access-providing metaphor is problematic to the extent that it drives a wedge between (i) the person as conceptualized and as she appears to believers and (ii) the person as unconceptualized and "in herself." Whether one identifies reality (i) with the unconceptualized (Hector's "essentialism") or (ii) with the conceptualized (Hector's "correspondentism"), I suggest that one has introduced a dualism that cannot be coherently bridged. To avoid this dualism, it is better to see concepts as the pragmatists see them, namely, as tools for picking out and characterizing that aspect of the world on which one finds it useful to focus. When concepts are seen as go-betweens, then one only has access to that which concepts reveal and the world is well lost. But when concepts are seen as tools, one can ask: what does the concept pick out and foreground? What does the concept occlude and leave in the background? In short, then, the idea of unmediated experiences does not depend on a claim that experiences can be unconceptual but instead on an argument that it is confused to think that concepts come "between" the subject and the world. The proposal of this chapter is that the concept-employing subject is always already in the world, submerged or (to use the vocabulary of embodied cognitive scientists) "tightly coupled" as an organism in its environment, and having and needing no "go between" or bridge to reach the world.

v. The Rehabilitation of Religious Metaphysics

I want now to return to what I called the central philosophical problem for the future of philosophy of religion, namely, the question whether metaphysical claims made by different religious communities might be the objects of reasoned debate. I want to defend the possibility that religious metaphysical claims can be cognitive and that therefore such debates are possible.

I hope that it is clear that on the constructive postmodern defense of metaphysics sought here, there is (and can be) no appeal to noumena. By seeing experience as embodied, embedded, and social, this account seeks to avoid the dualism between the conceptualized world, and in that way to pursue an understanding of metaphysics that is not guilty of essentialism or correspondentism. Metaphysics on this account does not require a view from nowhere or a God's eye view. The only components of this account are people investigating their environments. Sometimes they will be interested in and become aware of some particular part of their environment, some particular something that they make the focus of their attention. They may point it out to others and use words to identify this particular something. Sometimes, however, they will be interested in realities that are more inclusive and more general, things that one cannot just look at or hold in one's hands but require more abstraction and imagination. As an example of this distinction between something relatively particular and something more inclusive and general, contrast a single classroom, whose boundaries one might indicate with relatively little controversy, and a university as a whole, which includes the classroom but whose boundaries are fuzzier. Or contrast one person and the human race. Or a single banana and the category of "fruit."

I take it that distinctions between relatively concrete particular some-things and relatively general and inclusive somethings form a spectrum. What is its upper limit? One can imagine ever more inclusive realities: even more abstract and more inclusive than the university, for example, one can imagine "education." And then: "culture." Then: "all of human history." Then: "everything that has happened since the Big Bang." In some sit-uations, people will be interested in and want to think and speak about their environment so expansively that they mean to include, strictly, *every-thing*. Such all-inclusive discourse is not so unusual. For example, one can hear even nonphilosopher say things like, "everything is made of atoms" or "everything changes." When we get to statements of this all-inclusive scope, this level of nonrestricted generality, then we are speaking about metaphys-ical claims.

Some of the critics of metaphysics might want to draw the line at this idea of "everything." They may agree with me that the idea of noumenal things outside of all experience should be dropped and they may support my idea of embodied, social located, and world-submerged awareness. But they still don't want to accept the legitimacy of metaphysical claims because, they point out, there is no way for someone to experience "everything," the whole of reality, all of space and time, and therefore there is no way to experience whether something is always and everywhere true. This point is correct, but it is no obstacle to metaphysics. There is no way for me to experience all of a university, let alone of all of education, let alone all of human history or everything that happened since the Big Bang. Human beings are finite parts of the universe and we are not omniscient. But the limitations on human experience, as real as they are, do not keep us from meaningfully being interested in and talking about the whole of things—and they certainly do not keep the whole of things from existing!

Let me suggest an analogy. I know a swimming hole in the Ozark Moun-tains. The locals call it Rockhole, and it is a beautiful natural pool fed by rainwater and springs, about half the size of a football field. Now, imagine a sweltering hot day in the summer and imagine that you go to Rockhole for a dip. You and your friend walk over the gravel and put your feet in the water and it turns out the water is surprisingly cold, almost frigid. At this point, you are only in the water up to your ankles. If you say to your friend, "I bet that the water in this swimming hole is this cold all over," then this is a prediction of what your experience will be if you keep going into the water and if you swim around to the other side or you swim down to the bottom. This is a hypothesis about the whole of the pool. It is a speculative hypothesis. But speculative hypotheses like this are coherent and they make perfect sense. If your friend answers, "To speculate about the *whole* of something makes no sense. There is no way of knowing whether the pool is cold *everywhere*," it is not likely that you would say, "Thank goodness you were here to show the illusion I was under." It is more likely that you would think of your friend: you sound like someone who has only had a little philosophy. I judge that the objection to metaphysics on the grounds of that one cannot experience everything is similarly unpersuasive.

I hope that it is clear that I am not claiming that thinking and talking about the whole of reality is possible because we have some special mental faculty or that we can transcend our finitude. I am only claiming that the claims that we think and that we make about the whole of reality can be cognitive ones. They are continuous with the generalizing and abstracting and imagining that we do when we think and talk about the more inclusive aspects of our lives. But if I am right that generalizing about the whole of things is a coherent and everyday way of thinking, then it is not true that we live in a postmetaphysical age. In fact, if I am right about this, then we will never be in a postmetaphysical age or and we will never "overcome" metaphysics—any more than human thinking will overcome generalizing or abstracting or imagining.

In closing, let me focus on *religious* metaphysics. The example of the swimming hole is intended to illustrate an everyday way in which one legitimately takes a small experience and generalizes it to the whole, thereby creating a hypothesis that, one hopes, can guide a wide range of experiences. And one can do the same for hypotheses that are so wide that they are intended to guide *all* of one's experiences, or even so wide that they are intended to guide all of *everyone's* experiences. I suggest that religious metaphysical claims about YHWH, the Dao, Allah, the Logos, Brahman, the Tri-une God, or Dharmakaya can be understood as speculative hypotheses of this type. That is, religious communities, like people in other contexts, take experiences that they have had and they extrapolate them to create a model of the whole of reality and then treat that model as something that is true always and everywhere. Thus we find examples like the community of people who escaped from slavery in Egypt. Some of them took that experience as a sign that they were watched over and protected. They then took that story of their liberation and creation as a people and connected it to other stories—of their victories, of their kings, of their prophets, of

169

their losses, and so on—and extrapolated the idea of their liberator to the point that they came to embrace and teach the view that there is a Lord of history, of all nations, from the beginning to the end of time. Other religious communities focus on experiences that are very different. For example, we find some communities who see a pattern or a rhythm in the warmth that begins to increase at the winter solstice and grows until the peak of summer when the warmth then again decreases and the leaves begin to fall and winter returns. And they extrapolate this cyclical pattern of warmth and cold, and of light and dark, into rhythm that governs their health and their relationships and their sense of beauty. And they hold that this way of things is present always and everywhere. Apart from it, they say, there is nothing.

In both of these examples, some members of a community take an insight that they find in a particular experience, an insight that gives them a sense of purpose or order or guidance, and they put it forward as a claim about all of reality. There really is, they say, a creator of the world before whom all nations should bend their knees. There really is, they say, a force that runs through the myriad things and with which governors of states should put their states in order.

On this approach, religious practices informed by metaphysical claims may presumably turn out to be ungrounded projections of human fantasy, out of touch with reality. In fact, all religious practices may be. I am not arguing that the metaphysical claims that religious communities make are true. In fact, I think that they often contradict each other and most of them—and perhaps even all of them—are false. Moreover, one can always ask about the political uses to which religious metaphysical claims have been put: there is a clear ideological value in arguing that female submission, slavery, the caste system, or the imperial authorities are not a contingent product of social forces but rather part of the inevitable metaphysical nature of things. To defend the cognitive legitimacy of metaphysical claims is compatible with a hermeneutics of suspicion toward them.

Nevertheless, on this approach, we do not know that religious teachings are false just because the claims they make about the world are metaphysical. Given an account of experience as immediate contact with the world, claims about the nature of things are intelligible and one cannot reject metaphysical claims just because they seek to describe the character of reality as such. And therefore the desire found among some religious people for principles and truths that are so inclusive that they are always and everywhere true is not a hopeless or arrogant desire. If religious accounts of the character of reality are false, it is because those accounts of the world get things wrong. It is not because they are not in touch with reality.

Bibliographic Essay

In this chapter, I argue, first, that given the definition of religion as forms of life predicated upon the reality of the superempirical, religious communities hold that they are in touch with something real. Sometimes this reality will be metaphysical, but I argue, second, that, despite widespread opposition, metaphysics is a legitimate form of intellectual inquiry and so the study of religion need not become "postmetaphysical" (Habermas 1994).

The philosophical interest in metaphysics, long languishing in the shadow of empiricism, seems today to be making a comeback. The definition of metaphysics that I defend—that is, the study of the character of reality as such—is meant to be, as I say in the chapter, "theory-thin" and to permit different ways of approaching such a study and different answers to the question about the character of reality. It is informed primarily by Aristotle's definition of metaphysics as the study of being *qua* being and by Charles Hartshorne's account of metaphysics as the study of nonrestrictive existential claims (see Aristotle 1984: esp. bk. 4; Hartshorne 1983: esp. Ch. 2 and Ch. 8). I describe my project as one of constructive postmodernism, a phrase I borrow from David Ray Griffin who distinguishes between, on the one hand, a "deconstructive or eliminative postmodernism" that seeks to overcome the modern worldview with an anti-worldview that eliminates concepts such as self, purpose, meaning, or truth as correspondence and, on the other hand, a "constructive or revisionary postmodernism" that seeks to overcome the modern worldview through a revision of those concepts. See the introduction to each volume in the book series "Constructive Postmodern Thought" (e.g., Griffin 1988). The best survey of and response to postmetaphysical positions in theology I know is that of William Meyer (2010).

I found Kevin Hector's antimetaphysical book, *Theology without Metaphysics* (2011) especially helpful both as a sketch of why contemporary philosophers oppose metaphysics, and as a pragmatist ally for those who seek to develop a postCartesian account of the subject. I propose the idea of unmediated experience and I argue that one can find support for this idea not only in Hector but also in Donald Davidson, Roy Bhaskar's critical realism, and embodied cognitive science. Davidson's critique of the dualism of

171

conceptual schemes can be found in Davidson (1984: Ch. 13). The paragraph describing Davidson's project borrows from Schilbrack (2002), where a fuller treatment can be found on how Davidson supports metaphysics. For Davidson's argument that re-establishing unmediated touch with the world provides for the possibility of truth in metaphysics, see Davidson (1984: Ch. 14). The second ally is the critical realist movement. The classical statement of critical realism is Bhaskar (1975). For a clear introduction to the movement, see Bhaskar (1989) or Collier (1994); the best overview of the range of work in the movement is Bhaskar et al, eds. 1998. The third ally I describe is found in recent work in embodied cognitive science. Perhaps the best-known scholar defending the idea that the mind is, first and foremost, a tool for guiding one's actions and not for gathering action-neutral information, is Andy Clark (see esp. 1997). For Anthony Chemero's distinction between "situated embodied cognitive science," which is represented by Clark, and "radical embodied cognitive science" which Chemero himself defends, see Chemero (2009: esp. Ch. 2). Another good discussion of the two styles can be found in Wilson and Foglia (2011).

One last ally: I owe the metaphor of language as a silverware sorter to Craig Martin.

Endnotes

1. For an anthology that shows how different approaches to the study of religions reflect one's answers to the possible truth of religious belief, see Frankenberry and Penner, eds., 1999a.
2. See Habermas (1994); for a good analysis of Habermas's views of religious metaphysics, see Meyer (1995).
3. I prefer the phrase "reality as such" to "being *qua* being" since the latter suggests that all things are beings or substances. Being *qua* being is to that extent a proposed answer—in fact, it is Aristotle's answer—to the question about the nature of things and not simply the question that informs the inquiry.
4. See Hector (2011: 15). Here is Hector's definition of these two terms: essentialism, the first problematic feature of metaphysics, is "a picture according to which an object's ultimate reality is identified with a real, idea-like 'essence' that stands at a remove from ordinary experience, such that the latter may come to seem shadowy, second-rate, a realm of 'mere appearance,' etc. Because fundamental reality is thus thought to stand apart from experience, it might appear that human knowers are cut off from reality, since we are immediately in touch only with the phenomenal realm. This leads to a second feature of metaphysics,

namely, what I am calling correspondentism, according to which the distance between human persons and fundamental reality is supposed to be bridged by dint of our ideas and words hooking up with or corresponding to such reality" (2011: 14–5).

5. My own view is that Kant's distinction does not *challenge* the alleged metaphysical desire to describe noumenal reality but rather *invents* it. I don't agree that there is a gap between experience and reality-in-itself that Kant discovers and shows that we cannot overcome. I judge, instead, that the idea of noumena is incoherent and that, to avoid that fate, any coherent thoughts about reality must refer to the nonnoumenal world. The difference between nonmetaphysical and metaphysical claims, in my view, is that the former concern particular realities and metaphysical claims concern reality as such or reality in general. In other words, I grant that people distinguish between what is real and what is merely appearance in a variety of ways, and I expect that human knowers will never overcome such a distinction. But the distinction between appearance and reality need not lead to Kant's dualism between a phenomenal realm that appears in experience and a noumenal realm that can never be experienced but can only be thought.

6. See Hector (2011:11).

7. My own view is that Heidegger's phenomenological account of being-in-the-world drops the Kantian concept of a noumenal world—as one should—and he therefore helps us to leave behind the dualistic picture of a gap that must be bridged between the world of our experience and the "real" world. In this sense, it is Heidegger who provides a prolegomena to any future metaphysics.

8. The other central value of Hector's book is that it seeks to give an account of human agency and subjectivity without that gap. I return to this point below.

9. The quote is from Hilary Putnam (1990: 28).

10. Appropriately, these are the three movements identified by Richard Rorty in *Philosophy and the Mirror of Nature* that can serve as the paths to overcoming the spectator view of knowledge. From my perspective, Rorty is right to see postmodern philosophy as providing for a transition away from a Cartesian or representationalist view of knowledge, but (like Hector) he is wrong to think that an unmediated account of experience must also be antimetaphysical. To overcome the gap and to understand human cognition and agency without a conceptual "screen" that mediates the world to the subject rehabilitates metaphysical inquiry.

11. See Davidson (1984: 192).

12. See Davidson (1990: 303).

13. The quotes in the paragraph come from Davidson (1984: 198 and 201).

14. See Bhaskar (1975: 24).

15. The quotes in this paragraph can be found at Archer (2004: 67–8).

16. See Chemero (2009).

17. The three quotes in this paragraph from Hector come from pages 186, 213–4, and 186–7, respectively. Cf. 153–6.

18. Hector specifies that what he is opposing is "essentialist–correspondentist meta-physics" on p. 47 and that his book can be read as revisionist metaphysics on p. 3.

19. Whether or not I am right that Hector supports my view of metaphysics, he does support the idea of unmediated experience. He sees his pragmatic proposal as following Friedrich Schleiermacher's strategy of grounding norms in what Schleiermacher calls feeling (*Gefühl*), that is, an "immediate presence" charac-terized by the unity of a person and his or her physical and spiritual world, a presence which lacks any opposition between subject and object (2011: 77). Hector describes this feeling as a prereflective harmony or at-oneness between oneself and one's environing circumstances (2011: 77–8).

Chapter 7

The Academic Study of Religions: a Map With Bridges

i. Religious Studies as a Tripartite Field

In this final chapter, I want to take the proposal for philosophy of religion that I have presented in this book, defend its place in the academic study of religions generally, and show how the work of philosophy of religion does not operate in a silo but rather inherits from and can contribute to other approaches to the study of religions.

The key idea in this chapter is that much of the discipline of philosophy of religion is *normative*. It is normative in that it seeks not only to understand but also to evaluate the reasons that can be given for holding certain religious beliefs true and for acting in certain religious ways. Most philosophers of religion aim to ask and answer the question whether the reasons for religious beliefs and practices are good ones. When they consider religious reasons and find fault with them—finding them unjustified, unreasonable, unwarranted, confused, or flawed in some other way—they come to a normative conclusion. That is, they judge that those who hold these beliefs or do these practices should not, that they are wrong to do so. When philosophers of religion find religious reasons justified, reasonable, warranted, or the like, they again come to a normative conclusion and judge that those who hold those beliefs or do those practices are not wrong to do so. This normative or evaluative or judgmental aspect of philosophy of religion is typical of philosophy in general.

Philosophy and the Study of Religions: A Manifesto, First Edition. Kevin Schilbrack.
© 2014 Kevin Schilbrack. Published 2014 by John Wiley & Sons, Ltd.

In this book, I have proposed that philosophy of religion ought to expand beyond its traditional understanding of its task. I have argued that the discipline of philosophy of religion ought increasingly to grow to include critical reflection (i) on the teachings of all religions, (ii) on the ethical, political, and ritual aspects of practiced religious life, and (iii) on the philosophical aspects of the study of religions. Philosophers of religion are increasingly taking up that first task and I see this book as contributing to the emergence of a global philosophy of religion. Seeking to address that second, less appreciated desideratum, I argued that religious practices can be not merely mechanical or thoughtless activities but can also be cognitive inquiries in which practitioners explore their possibilities for living better, inquiries that usually focus both on their own character—their sensibilities, imagination, desires, and will—and on the world as a set of resources and opportunities for their action. Including the study of religious practices in this way should not, I argued, lead philosophers of religion to give up the concept of belief since beliefs are an ineliminable aspect of agency. Seeking to address the third desideratum, I argued that philosophers should include as part of their study of religion their own concepts, especially the sorting term "religion" itself. I argued that the indisputably historical and ideological character of all such sorting terms does not undermine the legitimacy of describing some patterns of behavior as religious, and I proposed that the most useful way to define religion is with a "mixed" (i.e., a combined functional and substantive) definition in terms of practices based on belief in superempirical realities. This focus on superempirical realities reflects my view that the discourse and practices of religious communities are overwhelmingly realist in the sense that they make or imply claims about the world. Some of these claims are metaphysical in that they purport to describe the character of reality as such, and I proposed that a constructive postmodern view that sees experience as in unmediated contact with one's environment provides a way to see such religious metaphysical claims as coherent. In short, then, I have argued that the future of philosophy of religion should be more inclusive, more focused on practice, and more self-reflexive, but I do not think that philosophy of religion should give up the traditional normative task of evaluating religious claims about the nature of reality.

The aim of this final chapter is to describe how the evaluative questions in philosophy of religion connect to the other questions pursued in the academic study of religions. This is a topic that philosophers of religion do not often write about, but it is also a pressing one, I judge, because some scholars of religion have proposed accounts of the field that exclude the evaluation of religious phenomena. That is, they argue that the academic study of religion should be understood in such a way that students of religion do not ask and answer the kinds of normative questions that have been central to philosophy of religion. And so my aim in this chapter is to provide a map of the academic study of religions that includes such normative questions and to defend their place as a coherent part of the field. The map I propose is therefore by no means uncontested: like the other chapters in this book, this chapter seeks to make a case for a particular way of seeing the field.

Now, if one wants to draw a map of religious studies that includes philosophy of religion, then the first thing that one should say is that the academic study of religions is not a single discipline. If a discipline is a form of inquiry identified by single method and/or a single goal, then one should see religious studies not as a single discipline but rather as a multidisciplinary field. It is a field united not by a common method or a common goal but rather by a common subject matter, investigated from multiple perspectives.

That the academic study of religions is a multidisciplinary field is an idea that is widely agreed on. But there is a thorny and long-running debate about which forms of inquiry do and do not belong in the field. And these disputes about the proper character of the academic study of religions are often exclusionary. Many argue as if the academic study of religious phenomena requires a single approach, as if religion is a ball and there is only one way to play with it.[1] For example, those who champion an interpretive approach often seek to exclude explanatory approaches on the grounds that the latter are "reductionist" and necessarily distort what they explain. Those who champion an explanatory approach in turn often seek to exclude interpretive approaches on the ground that they are "religionist" in the pejorative sense that they assume the truth and the *sui generis* character of religion. Both the interpreters and the explainers often seek to exclude evaluative approaches on the grounds that the academic study of religions has made a paradigm shift away from theology and therefore away from any approach that seeks to argue for or against a certain normative position about what is real or true or good. And, lastly, though those involved in evaluative approaches rarely exclude other approaches explicitly, often this is because they consider the methodological disputes concerning interpretation and explanation irrelevant to the asking and answering of evaluative questions, and this sort of benign neglect is exclusionary in its own way.

In this chapter, I present a nonexclusionary proposal. My proposal is that the academic study of religions should be seen as a field of inquiry that includes three distinguishable goals: *describing* religious phenomena, which

179

must be done in terms of the agents' understandings; *explaining* those phenomena in terms of their causes; and *evaluating* the reasons that are or can be given for them. The proposal I will make here is an irenic proposal that seeks to defend the coherence of methodological pluralism in religious studies. This proposal might seem problematic since the three goals I identify are often seen by their proponents as contradicting and excluding each other rather than complementing each other. I seek to avoid such conflicts by arguing that the three goals represent different stages, that each task has its own "moment" in the study of religion, and that practicing any one of them does not exclude any of the others from the field. Consequently, this chapter will note both what I take to be the contribution of each task to the overall goals of religious studies and also what each needs to concede in terms of the value of the other tasks. My goal is to be synthetic without being simplistic.

ii. Describing and Explaining Religious Phenomena

The first goal—and the one that must be included in any academic study of religions—is to *describe* religious beliefs, practices, experiences, and institutions accurately, which is to say, to identify them in a way that captures how they are understood by the practitioners themselves. Since religious phenomena are human phenomena, to describe a religious belief, practice, experience, or institution accurately requires reference to the agents' self-understanding. In other words, to describe what the agent holds, does, feels, or joins accurately, one must include what she understands herself to be holding, doing, feeling, or joining. A classic example that illustrates this relation comes from Gilbert Ryle, who argues that whether the closing of an eye is a wink or as a blink depends on the agent's intentions. In such cases, the agent's understanding of what she takes herself to be doing is constitutive of what she is in fact doing. The agent's view of what she is up to is essential to the identity of the action. This connection between agent's intentions and the identity of the action is ineliminable, rather than optional, and the same holds true for beliefs, experiences, and institutions.[2]

Given that this is so for such simple gestures, it is all the more true for the more complex social behavior that one finds in religion. Whether one should describe washing as "a baptism" or killing as "a sacrifice" or traveling as "a pilgrimage" turns on the views of the agents. That is, to describe an action accurately requires one to describe the significance of the action, a significance that will depend on the culture in which that action is engaged. This first task of the study of religions can therefore be labeled a phenomeno-logical task—or, more precisely, one of cultural phenomenology—in the sense that the goal is of describing beliefs, practices, experiences, and institu-tions as they appear to the historically shaped and culturally informed agents concerned.

It is also worth keeping in mind that even when scholars of religion seek to describe a religious phenomenon in a way that captures the views of the participants, they are usually re-describing, re-presenting, and so re-interpreting it to a new audience. Consequently, most of the descriptive efforts in religious studies involve translation and interpretation, and this work will inevitably misrepresent or distort what is being described to some degree. Scholars describe religious phenomena in a scholarly context and for scholarly purposes; they use their own conceptual vocabulary rather than solely the language of those described. Nevertheless, the aim of scholarly work at this first stage, the stage of description, is still to re-present the par-ticipants' understandings as well as one can. Thus, if a scholar identifies a practice as an example of "worship," for example, it may be that the partic-ipants in question do not use that English word. In this case, the scholar is implying that the concept of "worship" best translates the indigenous term or best interprets the actions performed. A scholar may also use descriptive terms that do not simply translate indigenous terms but which, she argues, best capture what the participants are up to. The development and constant revision of abstract categories for sorting complex phenomena is therefore a permanent part of the descriptive work in the study of religions. In fact, as I argued in Chapter 4, the word "religion" itself sometimes involves this kind of interpretive translation. In such cases, the scholar is implying that the sorting term accurately reflects what the practitioners are doing, believing, feeling, or joining. Thus nonindigenous terms can be used at this stage when the goal is to describe the phenomenon in a way that captures the inten-tions of the agents themselves. For this reason, this first task of the study of religions can be also labeled a hermeneutical task, insofar as it involves interpreting experiences, acts, beliefs, and social arrangements accurately in terms the agents may not use themselves.

What is excluded from this first phenomenological–hermeneutical stage of describing religious phenomena accurately are explanatory and evaluative terms that the agent would not accept. Consider this example: if someone in the ill–lit woods comes across a fallen tree trunk but believes that it is a bear, grows afraid, and shrinks back, one cannot identify his belief, his expe-rience, or his action in terms of a tree trunk. The task of describing religious phenomena accurately requires the scholar to temporarily set aside causes (such as "tree trunk") and evaluations of the action (such as "mistakes") that the participants would not recognize. At this stage, the study of religion leaves open the question whether the religious beliefs are caused by the factors the participants recognize, and it leaves open the question whether the religious beliefs are veridical or illusory, and so it proceeds according to what Ninian Smart calls methodological agnosticism. It is at the descriptive stage—but only at this stage—that the study of religious phenomena involves *epochē* or "bracketing."[3]

Now, some of the most heated arguments about the proper task of the academic study of religions have centered on precisely this, the claim that the religious practitioners' self-description should be treated as normative for how scholars identify religious phenomena. Some scholars have argued that the academic study of religion is (or should be) modeled on the sciences and so its goal is—solely—to explain religious phenomena. These scholars therefore seek to exclude phenomenological and hermeneutic approaches. A resolutely scientific view is defended, for example, by Donald Wiebe who argues that "[t]he insider approach in Religious Studies is not acceptable in the academy" and that bracketing explanations involves an inappropriate theological commitment. In this chapter, I am arguing that the academic study of religions properly operates with multiple methods, including those of phenomenology and hermeneutics, but Wiebe quips that this kind of polymethodism is "Polly Anna-ism," in that it lets back into the academy the methods that were originally excluded when religious studies was created as a field distinct from theology. I would respond, however, that if one sees bracketing and methodological agnosticism not as excluding explanation completely but as operating at only this, the first stage of description, then they should be acceptable to scholars of religion, including those who have a reductionist program. Even a critic of phenomenological approaches to religion like Robert Segal agrees that the social scientist cannot ignore the believers' self-understanding. As he says, "Any social scientist who did would have little left to explain."[4]

The second goal that I hold should be included in the academic study of religions is to *explain* religious phenomena. This goal involves offering an account that answers the questions of what causes religious communities to subscribe to their beliefs, what generates their experiences, why their practices are performed, and what functions their institutions have.[5]

Describing a belief, experience, practice, or institution accurately requires one to identify it in terms that participants would accept, but explaining it is not limited in that way. One might explain religious phenomena in terms of the conscious intentions of the agents: for example, one might explain the Crusades in terms of the crusaders' stated belief that God wanted them to liberate Jerusalem. But one can also explain the Crusades or other religious phenomena in terms of unconscious motivations, social functions, economic forces, or biological drives of which the practitioners are unaware. One's explanation for why people are drawn to religious beliefs, practices, experiences, and institutions may therefore draw on causes that are not known—or that, if known, would not be accepted—by the practitioners. My proposal, then, is that scholars of religions should not treat participant-informed description and causal explanation as rivals, only one of which can characterize the proper study of religion. They should instead treat them as two distinct stages in a process of the academic study of religion: the goal of description is to provide an accurate account of what participants understand themselves to be doing, and the goal of explaining is to provide a causal account. (And, to be sure, these two tasks can be done by one scholar if she has the skill to wear two hats.) The goal of describing religious phenomena accurately requires the student of religions to draw on the skills that one learns in the humanities, especially the skills involved in reading texts carefully, in translating languages, and in interpreting cultures. The goal of explaining religious phenomena requires the student of religions subsequently to use the products of those efforts as their data and to give an account that explains the origin and the function of those religious beliefs, experiences, practices, and institutions. Combined, the two tasks of describing and explaining constitute the social scientific approach to the study of religions.

I mentioned above that the work of those who seek to explain religious phenomena presupposes (and therefore cannot exclude) the work of those who seek to describe the data accurately. Before a religious phenomenon can be explained, it must be properly identified and described and this work requires the scholar to articulate the agents' understanding of what they take themselves to be doing, believing, or experiencing. Those who seek to explain religious phenomena therefore have to concede that phenomenology and hermeneutics cannot be excluded from the academic study of religions. I now want to argue that the reverse is also true: the explanatory question of why people are religious not only should not but also cannot be excluded from the academic study of religions.

Explaining religious phenomena cannot be excluded from the academic study of religions because even to interpret some particular discourse or practice *as religious* includes an embedded causal claim. That is, if something is

183

identified as religious precisely because the practitioners claim that it comes from a superempirical source, to identify it as religious already includes the practitioner's explanation of the phenomenon. They say, for example, that their book is holy because it is a product of revelation, that their practices are proper because God requires them, that their experiences are sacred because they provide access to a higher reality, or that their institutions are ordained because they reflect a cosmic order. The connection to something superempirical is precisely what is said to make the phenomena religious. In effect, then, those who seek to exclude social scientific explanation from the academic study of religion are arguing not that scholars should not seek to explain religious phenomena causally, but rather that the only permitted explanations are the religious ones. This is why those scholars are often accused of being crypto-theological.

Some have tried to exclude explanation by pointing out that using explanatory terms that the participants would not accept necessarily distorts one's understanding of religious phenomena. Explanations that treat religious phenomena as, at their causal root, psychological or social replace supernatural explanations with naturalistic ones, and some critics complain that such reductionism drains the phenomena of their religious significance and replaces them with nonreligious simulacra. These critics of explanatory approaches might grant that explanation is inevitable in the academic study of religion, but they argue that as a scholar *of religion*, one needs to attend to the explanations given by the participants themselves and not by those who discount the participants' account. They therefore hold that describing religious phenomena without judgment exhausts what scholars of religions should do, and that coming to understand religious phenomena with care is the only appropriate goal of the field.

But this argument is confused. On the two-stage account given here, the goals of description and explanation are not in competition. One first describes the religious beliefs and practices accurately, telling an explanatory story about them comes second, and each stage has its own integrity. The two goals are connected in that explanation requires description, but once a religious phenomenon is identified and described, causal questions can legitimately arise. What historical conditions made the belief, action, experience, or institution possible and attractive? What social or psychological functions does it serve? What motivates the participants? If one excludes such questions, then one is defining the academic study of religions as a field in which the participants' explanations are the only ones permitted and which cannot be critiqued. When scholars block social scientific (and philosophical)

184

inquiry in this way, they advocate implicitly proreligious constraints on the academic study of religions and thereby become "religionists" in the pejorative sense.

At this point in drawing my map of the academic study of religions, I have argued that description and explanation are two distinct stages, and that between them there is a particular kind of relationship—a kind of one-way "bridge"—because providing an explicit explanatory account presupposes an accurate description, but not vice versa. The descriptive account of religious phenomena is bedrock. One can describe religious beliefs, practices, experiences, and institutions as the practitioners understand them without yet raising the question whether those beliefs, practices, experiences, and institutions serve functions that the agents themselves do not know. However, the question of causes is at least implicit in the study of religion from the first and therefore scholars of religions can legitimately ask it explicitly and critically. Some social scientists argue that it is only when one goes beyond the descriptive stage and "crosses the bridge" to ask the critical explanatory questions that one begins a properly academic study of religion. But this view is not right, since the work of historians, linguists, ethnologists, translators, and anthropologists to re-present the data fairly is equally appropriate—indeed, crucial—for the academy. But it is true that to exclude the explanatory question—to block that bridge—is a protectionist tactic, inappropriate for the academic study of religion.

iii. Evaluating Religious Phenomena

The third goal that I hold should be included in the academic study of religions is to *evaluate* religious beliefs, experiences, practices, and institutions normatively, which is to say, to make an assessment of their value. Evaluative approaches to the study of religion pursue the questions whether religious beliefs are true, religious practices moral, religious experiences real, and religious institutions just.[6]

I distinguish evaluative goals from the descriptive and explanatory goals that have come before, and this is why I propose that the academic study of religions be imagined as a tripartite field. One might represent the relationships between the three kinds of inquiry as like the shape of the letter Y. At the base, there is the unavoidable task of description. Academic inquiries presuppose that one has understood beliefs, practices, experiences, or institutions accurately. But once one has identified and described them, one can then ask *why* the beliefs are held, the practices performed, the experiences occur, and the institutions created and maintained. "Why" questions are famously ambiguous in that one may be asking either for causes or for reasons. Weighing the causes leads to an explanation of the phenomenon and weighing the reasons leads to an evaluation of it. Pursuing those two lines of inquiry then produce the two "arms" of the Y.

There is a parallel between the two arms. Until one has identified and described the religious phenomena in question, one cannot explain them, and the task of evaluation presupposes and waits upon accurate description in the same way. However, once one has accurately described a religious phenomenon, one can legitimately raise the explanatory questions that lead to a causal explanation, and one can with equal legitimacy raise the evaluative questions that lead to a normative assessment. Combined, the two tasks of describing and evaluating then constitute the humanistic approach to the study of religions. Moreover, the task of evaluation, like that of explanation, is a form of critical inquiry, in the sense that it does not assume that the practitioners' perspective is correct. Thus, explanatory approaches take religious beliefs, practices, experiences, and institutions critically and seek causes for them, an approach that involves interrogating the causes given or implied in the practitioners' selfunderstanding and, when necessary, providing causal accounts that contradict the understanding of the practitioners. In a parallel fashion, evaluative approaches also take those religious phenomena critically and seek reasons that can be given for them, an approach that involves interrogating the reasons given or implied in the practitioners' self-understanding and, when necessary, providing other or rival reasons that contradict the understanding of the practitioners. Indeed, on this account, what distinguishes the academic study of religion from other forms of religious study is precisely that it is critical, that is, that it includes the two "arms" of the Y.

I want to develop further this parallel between the humanities and the social sciences as both critical forms of inquiry. I argued in the previous section that explanation is not only a legitimate but also an ineliminable aspect of the field. Explanations of religious phenomena are ineliminable in the academic study of religions because practitioners at least implicitly claim that their beliefs, practices, experiences, and institutions respond to or engage with something superempirical, and so simply giving an account of religious phenomena as the practitioners understand them will include a causal explanation of the phenomena. The field-defining question for academic students of religions, then, is whether the participants' causal claims should then be made explicit and reflected on critically using the tools of the social sciences.

Evaluations of religious phenomena are ineliminable in a parallel way. Evaluations are ineliminable because religious practitioners not only live in terms of their beliefs, practices, experiences, and institutions but also claim at least implicitly it is right and proper to do so. Typically, they hold that their form of life is right and proper because their beliefs are true, their practices moral, their experiences real, and their institutions just. (Pursuing these religious justifications takes us back to the discussion of normative realism in Chapter 6.) The field-defining question for academic students of religions, then, is whether these evaluative claims are to be made explicit and reflected on critically using the tools of the humanities. If evaluative approaches are not part of the academic study of religions, the result will not be that evaluations are not included in the field, but rather that the evaluations already present in religious phenomena will be presented uncritically.

Now, there is a fair amount of dispute among scholars about whether evaluative approaches ought to be included in the academic study of religions. As I mentioned above, there are some "describers" who hold that the academic study of religions should not include critical approaches that contradict the self-understanding of the religious practitioners, and there are some "explainers" who argue that the academic study of religions should not privilege the practitioners' perspective. I have argued that neither of these two exclusionary arguments is persuasive and that each side should concede the value and legitimacy of the other. Whether or not the describe-only camp and the explain-only camp can get along, however, both sides often agree with each other on this point: the academic study of religions should not include evaluative approaches. Their opposition to evaluative approaches is often termed as a rejection of "theology." Theology, they say, by definition makes evaluative judgments that some religious views are true and that others are false. Any evaluation of religions will reflect the perspective of just one religious point of view, and some describers argue that this is good reason to exclude such judgments from the academic study of religions. And evaluative judgments typically do not operate by public criteria, but rather by tradition-specific criteria, and some explainers argue that this is good reason to exclude them. Despite the disagreements between the describers and the explainers, many in both camps therefore agree that the academic study of religions is best practiced without raising the judgmental and controversial questions of whether religious teachings are true, moral, real, or just.

How should those interested in pursuing the goal of evaluating religious phenomena respond? A first response is irenic. This is simply to make

187

it clear that because the three approaches pursue separate goals, they can complement and need not interfere with each other. Evaluating the reasons why one might hold religious beliefs or engage in religious practices should not impede an accurate description of them. In fact, even those who evaluate some particular religious phenomena and conclude that the reasons given for them are not persuasive—those who conclude, for example, that the beliefs are false, the practices immoral, the experiences projections, or the institutions oppressive—can still describe them accurately and fairly. In fact, they *must* describe them accurately and fairly if their evaluations are going to have any merit. Similarly, the goals of evaluation are typically separate from those of explaining. For example, a social scientist might come to the conclusion that a religious belief is held because of social pressures or for psychological benefits, but this does not determine whether that belief is true or false. And conversely, an evaluator might judge that some religious community is justified in engaging in a given practice, but this does not explain the origin of the practice nor why the community accepts it. The error of thinking that the origin of some phenomenon determines its value is called the genetic fallacy. In most cases, then, the humanistic study of religions and the social scientific study of religions operate independently in that one can explain religious phenomena however they are evaluated and one can evaluate them however they are explained.

As an illustration of these differing relationships between the three goals of the field, imagine the study of a religious institution like a monastery. Scholars who seek to provide an accurate description of what the monastery is would seek to give an account of how the practitioners understand that institution, including the rules that govern it and the experiences of those who live by them. They might also wrestle with the fit of nonindigenous labels like "scholasticism" or "asceticism." This phenomenological–hermeneutic account would include not only the practices promulgated in the monastery but could also include (a) the participants' explanatory claim that the monastery was founded by a hero of their tradition and that its continued existence is explained by fealty to the founder's wishes, and (b) the participants' normative claim that the monastery is a school of virtue. The social scientific scholars who seek to explain the institution would take the insiders' account as their data, and they might conclude that the participants were right that the institution was in fact founded by their hero and that fealty to that founder is the primary cause of its endurance, or they might conclude that the institution's origin and continued existence are better explained by other forces. The humanistic scholars who seek to evaluate the institution would also take the insiders' account as their data, and they similarly might conclude that the participants were right that institution in fact is a school of virtue, or they might conclude that the ways in which the institution shapes the character of its participants are narrow, one-sided, or otherwise disordered. In this common-sense way, the humanistic assessment of virtues operates independently of the social scientific account of origins and functions, and vice versa.

This irenic response will not persuade all of those who want to exclude evaluative approaches from the academic study of religions. Even if the goals of the evaluative approaches to religion are logically distinct from the goals of describing religious phenomena accurately and explaining them causally, some of those who want to exclude evaluative approaches do not oppose them because they fear that evaluation impedes their own interpretive or explanatory work. Let me turn now to those scholars who may grant that the three goals are autonomous enough that the academic study of religions *could* be coherently understood as a field that includes describing, explaining, and evaluating, but they argue that it *shouldn't*. These opponents hold not merely that the interpretation and explanation of religious phenomena should be included and not impeded by religious views, but specifically that evaluative approaches are not appropriate. I therefore judge that those like me who are interested in pursuing normative questions about religions should address the concerns of those who hold that evaluative approaches simply do not belong in the academic study of religions.

iv. Do Evaluative Approaches Belong in the Academy?

Even if evaluative inquiries can be pursued without interfering with the other forms of inquiry in the field, some scholars nevertheless consider them inappropriate for the academy. Clearly, I am going to give a positive answer and make a case for the legitimacy of evaluative inquiries in the academic study of religions. But I want to underline that that the question of what distinguishes properly academic work from other ways in which people study religions is a valid and important one. Philosophers of religion rarely reflect on their institutional context, but I would suggest that one who seeks to be a member of the academy should be able to give an answer to why one's work belongs there. That is the aim of this section of the chapter.

189

What then are the arguments for excluding evaluative questions from the academic study of religions? I will consider two, which we might label an empiricist position and a critical position.

To put these two positions in context, I should begin with the view proposed by the philosophical movement of logical positivism. The logical positivists wanted to take seriously the achievements of the natural sciences and sought to draw from the sciences a criterion of what makes a statement a factual one. They proposed a criterion that to be factual—that is, to say something that could possibly be true or false—a claim had to be grounded either in empirical observations or logic. Scientific claims clearly met this standard. They were paradigmatic examples of discourse about the world. Scientific hypotheses could therefore turn out to be true or false, but claims that did not meet the positivist criterion could not. Such claims were not false but rather uninformative or, to use the positivists' term, "cognitively meaningless." The positivists therefore excluded from the category of the factual those forms of discourse whose claims could not be supported by either the senses or by logic: theology, ethics, metaphysics, aesthetics, and other discourse about values. It follows that if one defines religious claims so that they seek to refer to superempirical realities (the definition I prefer), then positivists would say that religious claims about God or Brahman or the Dao or Śūnyatā or Logos or karma or other superempirical realities are cognitively meaningless. Such claims might serve as slogans for one community or another, and one might insist that they are known to be true on the basis of some religious authority, but there is no way to debate them rationally. They can be the data for the academic study of religions, but there is no academically appropriate way to pursue an evaluative inquiry about whether they are true or false, real or not unreal, moral or immoral, and so on. The cognitive evaluation of such claims is already over.

The positivist movement eventually deteriorated, and there are few who describe themselves as positivists today. One of the central problems with the movement was that their criterion—that cognitively meaningful statements must be grounded either in sensory evidence or in logic—was itself grounded neither in sensory evidence nor or in logic. The positivists' criterion therefore failed to meet their own standard of what should be counted as cognitively meaningful. This suggests that their criterion was too narrow: the sciences do not exhaust the range of statements that can be true and so they do not exhaust the range that can be rationally debated. Despite the collapse of this particular philosophical movement, I began with the positivists because the assumption that the sciences are the paradigmatic example

190

of cognitive claims continues to influence much of the twentieth-century studies of religion. Their identification of cognitive status with empiricism and their rejection of metaphysics have been discredited in principle, but they continue to be presupposed by those theorists of religion who work with the assumption that superempirical claims cannot be rationally debated and so the evaluation of superempirical claims cannot be properly academic.

One way in which one might seek to make an empiricist argument for excluding evaluation is by specifying that the sciences do not provide the criterion for everything that is cognitively meaningful (as the positivists had claimed), but they do provide the criterion for what belongs in the academy. Donald Wiebe has championed such an argument. Wiebe says that the study of religion emerged as legitimate academic field only when it distinguished itself from the practice of religion. What characterizes the practice of religion but corrupts any academically legitimate study is the assumption that the teachings of one's own religion are valid, good, true, real, and so on. Wiebe makes the good point that the academic study of religions is threatened not only by those scholars who practice what he calls a "capital-c" confessional theology that seeks to promote the teachings of a particular religion but also by those putatively secular academics whose scholarship and teaching may not promote the teachings of a particular religion, but do promote the idea that religion "in general" is good, or at least that it is not to be criticized, an idea Wiebe calls "small-c" confessional theology. For Wiebe, the goal of the university is objective knowledge, and so the focus ought to be "'pure'—that is, areligious and apolitical—research."[7] The natural and social sciences are the only means to this kind of knowledge, and so the sciences are the only legitimate models for the study of religion.[8] He therefore proposes that the academic study of religions operate, like the rest of the academy generally, according to the widely accepted criteria of the sciences. Doing so entails that the academic study of religion would not include evaluative arguments that some religious claims are true or false, religious practices moral or immoral, religious experiences real or unreal, or religious institutions are just or unjust. It would also mean that this field would not see itself or offer itself as the means for students to discover the meaning of their lives, the proper formation of their character, or the ultimate truth about human existence. Wiebe is not arguing that no one should pursue such issues, but only that it is not appropriate for the academy, because to take sides on such subjects contradicts the distinction between teaching religion and teaching about religion on which the field is founded.

Now, those like Wiebe who seek to identify the academic study of religions with the social scientific approach are right that evaluating the reasons that can be given for religious beliefs, practices, experiences, and institutions is typically not a scientific enterprise. But they are wrong to say that such nonscientific projects are not appropriate for the academy. My response to the empiricist argument has two parts.

In the first place, I contend that one cannot separate social scientific inquiries from questions of evaluation because the social sciences themselves cannot be purged of evaluative commitments. To be sure, the social sciences do not take it as their explicit task to evaluate religious phenomena. But the social sciences are nevertheless value-laden both in that social scientists are people who bring to their work their own perspectives and interests, their own historical location and cultural assumptions, and also in that the very practices of interpreting and explaining human culture require scholars to make normative judgments about what is valuable, reasonable, and real (a point to which I return and develop in the next section). It is therefore unsurprising that, outside the academic study of religion, the rest of the university does *not* hold itself to scientific criteria: in departments of history, literature, political science, and on and on, discussions abound about what people should do, what makes sense, what is beautiful, and what is fair. I propose therefore that the criterion for what belongs in the academy is not whether one's inquiries are value-laden—they always will be—but whether those values are open to challenge and critique.

In the second place, I contend that though the evaluation of religious reasons is typically not a scientific enterprise, it can still operate by criteria that are intersubjective and rational, and that when evaluative debates do so, they are appropriate for the academy. Consider two quick examples. Say a class on religious ethics studies the vow to become a bodhisattva as described in Śāntideva's *Bodhicaryāvatāra* and then seeks to assess the ethics of such a vow by asking, for example, whether the maxim of such a decision could be universalized in the manner that Kant requires for any act to be moral. Or say that a class on religious thought studies the monistic metaphysics as described in Śaṅkara's commentary on the *Brahma Sutra* and seeks to assess such claims about the nature of things by asking, for example, whether Śaṅkara's arguments involve the logical inconsistencies that Charles Hartshorne says they do. My point is not that evaluative inquiries like these will definitely prove that some religious claim is illogical or some religious activity is immoral. My point is rather that evaluative inquiries can illuminate the implications and thus the intellectual costs of a given belief, practice, experience, or institution and that such analyses can be done according to public criteria. Such normative inquiries do not *assume* the truth or goodness of religious beliefs. Whether one calls them philosophy of religion or philosophical theology, as long as they follow publicly available criteria of rationality, they are as appropriate in the university as philosophy is.

In response to the empiricist argument, then, I draw the conclusion that, just as the positivists were not able to use empiricism as a criterion that separates the cognitively meaningful from the cognitively meaningless because what can be rationally debated is larger than the scientific, empiricism also fails to mark the kinds of study that are appropriate in the academy from those that are not: the academically appropriate is also larger than the scientific. Scholars of religions who prefer the clarity of empirical work can hold themselves to social scientific approaches and eschew evaluative ones. In other words, they can accept what I called the irenic position. But they have not given reasons why others in the academy cannot legitimately pursue evaluative questions.

A second argument for excluding evaluation from the academy is based on the idea that what distinguishes the academic study of religions from nonacademic approaches is that the former should be critical. Russell McCutcheon has championed such an argument. McCutcheon agrees with Wiebe that to belong in the academy, a study of religions has to distinguish itself from the practice of religion; in his terms, scholars of religion should be "critics" and not "caretakers." Like Wiebe, therefore, McCutcheon would exclude from the academy discourse that seeks to advance or repudiate first-order views, and many in the academy would understand this to be precisely the task of theology. However, McCutcheon agrees with the point I made above, that no academic work is pure of normative commitments. All scholarship is perspectival, politically implicated, and value-laden.

Unlike the empirical approach, therefore, the critical approach does not seek an allegedly value-neutral position but rather distinguishes between the kind of values expressed by religious communities and those proper to the academy. Religious communities allege that their way of life connects them to the real nature of things. According to religious practitioners, their beliefs, practices, experiences, and institutions are justified by reference to something that is not the product of human labors. The academy, by contrast, makes no pretension to pierce all mere appearances nor to transcend history. Given this contrast, therefore, the academic study of religions does not enter into the evaluative debates whether or not God really exists, whether or not Daoist internal alchemy really leads to immortality, nor whether or not submission to Allah really inculcates proper humility. The scholarly task is instead to redescribe religious phenomena from a human perspective and to explain the ways in which religions are, like other human institutions and practices, ideologically driven modes of social formation. Such an approach is thus critical in that the academic study of religions seeks to expose the rhetorical mechanisms by which social norms are constructed, to historicize what communities claim is eternal, and to demonstrate the contingency of what communities claim is necessary.

Given such a view of the field, the evaluative questions common in philosophy of religion are excluded. The critical approach does not justify this exclusion with a claim that superempirical realities do not exist or that they cannot be rationally debated, because to do so would be to take sides in evaluative debates at the same time that it held that such debates do not belong in the academy and so, like the positivist position, it would not be coherent. The critical approach seeks to exclude evaluation not on the presupposition of a materialist ontology or an empiricist epistemology, but rather (merely) on discursive rules: the exclusion is based, in other words, on a view of what kinds of discourse should be practiced where. Avoiding substantive philosophical positions, this division of labor does not say or imply that one cannot pursue the evaluative questions, but only that they don't belong in the academy.

How should those drawn to the tripartite model respond? A central point is that the tripartite model reflects a particular view of human activity, that is, a particular philosophical anthropology, which it seems the critical approach does not share. The evaluation of religious reason-giving found in the tripartite model reflects a view that human beings not only live their lives but also lead them, in the sense that human beings are purposive agents who can and sometimes do weigh reasons, decide between them, and act on them. On this view, human social activities, including religious practices, are potentially reasonable, and the academy should therefore include critical reflection on the reasons by which such activities might or might not be justified. The rejection of evaluation of religious reason-giving found in the critical approach seems to reflect a view that human beings are not agents in the above sense. Human beings *behave*, to be sure, and they act in interested ways, but these interests can be explained whether or not the individual or community in question is conscious of those interests or can provide any justifications for them. Hence, at least some critical theorists exclude the evaluation of reason-giving because such evaluation presupposes a liberal humanist view of the subject that the critical approach does not share.

194

If the choice between these two models for the field turns on a choice between these two views of human activity, however, then it seems to me that the tripartite model has decisive advantages. First, it is more inclusive. In its two "arms," the tripartite model includes both the view that human activity is purposive and potentially reasonable and the view that it is interested and caused. Unless these two views of human activity are incompatible, the tripartite model irenically includes the critical view, but not vice versa. Adopting the tripartite model therefore carries into the academy all the benefits of the critical approach. Second, as with the positivist approach, there is a question of coherence. The question turns on whether the critical approach offers an account of human practice that fails to include the practice of the critical approach itself. To see this problem, note that the tripartite model can offer its view of purposive and potentially reasonable human agency in the hope that the plausibility of that view will persuade scholars that the evaluation of reasons should be included in the academy. But it does not seem coherent for the critical model to offer its alternative view of human activity in the hope that the plausibility of that view will persuade scholars that the evaluation of reasons should not be included in the academy. In other words, it does not seem coherent to ask scholars in the academy to evaluate the reasons why the evaluation of reasons should not be included in the academy. It does not seem coherent for the critical view to defend itself with an argument that depends upon a view of human subjectivity which it rejects.[9]

Perhaps, however, the critical approach need not be defended in this way. As mentioned, perhaps the critical approach can eschew all substantive philosophical views and proffer itself solely as a discursive rule. Can one defend the critical approach then, more consistently, as simply a procedural division of labor that does not take sides on the questions whether people act on reasons, or whether reasons can be evaluated, but affirms only that this is not the job of the academy? Perhaps such a defense would not raise problems of coherence since McCutcheon has already admitted (unlike Wiebe) that scholarship is necessarily value-laden and so, though the scholar should not be a caretaker for religious values, she must be a caretaker for academic values.

Now, those like me who want to pursue evaluative questions in the academy think that the academy should operate under a different set of discursive rules, namely, rules that include the humanistic study of religion. I hold that the critical study of religions can legitimately take two forms: the explanatory and the evaluative. So, there is a disagreement here about the discursive rules concerning what does and what does not belong in the academy, and since this is a disagreement about how people should conduct themselves, it is a normative disagreement. That is, to hold that the rules for proper academic discourse imply that scholars should not evaluate religious phenomena is to hold certain norms for the academy. But then the question is: can this normative proposal be debated in the academy? Can reasons be given for accepting this rule and excluding the evaluating of reasons? And asking this question seems to create a dilemma for the defenders of the critical approach: if they answer it affirmatively, and give reasons for their own normative position, then they grant that the evaluation of reasons is not inappropriate for the academy. But this is precisely the position that they are opposing and the coherence problem returns. However, if they answer negatively, then they are recommending their own normative position without offering any publicly available reasons. If they do not give reasons in support of their own position, and claim simply that "this is the way things are in the academy," then their approach does not seem appropriate for the academy on their own terms. In fact, if the critical approach is not defended with reasons, then there seems to be no formal difference between that position and the naturalizing or mystifying discourse that is often excluded from the academy as "theology."

McCutcheon (unlike Wiebe) does not base his proposal on a distinction between secular and theological norms. But a defender of the critical approach might seek to avoid the above dilemma by arguing that there *is* a formal difference between evaluating the reasons for academic norms and evaluating the reasons for religious norms, so that arguing about what goes on in the academy is permitted in the academy but arguing about religious reasons would be excluded. Perhaps the discursive rule which I am defending—according to which evaluating religious reasons is permitted—can be rejected because to treat religious claims as open to evaluation according to public criteria is a covertly pro-religious or theological position, inappropriate for the secular academy. The problem with such a response, however, is that both of the two positions under debate can be seen as covertly pro-religious or theological. That is, both the view that religious reasons can be evaluated by public criteria and the view that they cannot are held by religious communities; neither view is less theological than the other. In this light, the critical approach resembles those theological views that reject natural theology, and the humanistic approach resembles those theological views that permit it. It is therefore not the case that one of the two approaches is covertly pro-religious or theological in a way that the other is not and, as a consequence, debates about the norms appropriate to the academy cannot be insulated from religious debates. The evaluation of religious norms is therefore inevitable in the academic study of religions.

I draw the conclusion that the academic study of religion should be distinguished from other ways of studying religion not by excluding evaluative approaches but rather by excluding claims that cannot be challenged. What is excluded is the unwillingness to offer reasons for one's claims. This approach is more completely critical.

The empiricist and the critical arguments against including normative evaluation both seek to distinguish the academic study of religion from the practice of defending or rejecting first order religious claims. By contrast, I judge that the practice of religion sometimes includes reflective, self-critical elements that are not inappropriate for the academy and so I do not use the term "theology" for what is excluded. Despite this disagreement, I agree with these arguments that the question of what belongs in the academy should be pursued and that it should be pursued especially by philosophers of religion whose discipline is often the door through which nonacademic work enters the academy. The classroom is not a pulpit, and it is a shame that philosophers of religion so rarely reflect on the boundary question for the academic study of religions raised by the evaluation of religious phenomena.[10]

v. Interdisciplinary Bridges

The aim of this chapter (and, ultimately, this book) is to identify points of connection and growth of scholarship with regard to the philosophical aspects of the academic study of religions. In comparison with the insular way that philosophy of religion is practiced today, I judge that there are three such points that are largely overlooked, namely: philosophical assumptions at work in the interpretation of religions, philosophical assumptions at work in the explanation of religions, and the relation between justification and explanation. Let me close the book by highlighting them.

To this point in the chapter, I have presented a tripartite model of the academic study of religions in order to illustrate how students of religions can see the field as consisting of three distinct goals. More specifically, the Y-shaped model illustrates, firstly, that the goals "bridge" to each other in such a way that explanation and evaluation both logically presuppose description (though not the reverse) and, secondly, that the two forms of critical inquiry operate independently of each other. This model of the field is therefore useful for showing how scholars can see the three goals as complementary and not exclusionary. Nevertheless, the actual practice of studying religious beliefs, practices, experiences, and institutions is more complicated than the presentation I have given so far, and I would like to trace out these three other connections—other "bridges"—that operate between the three forms of inquiry. Recognizing that these connections are already at work should inform future discussions about the place of normative questions in the academic study of religion generally.

Here is the first bridge. As I have underlined, explaining and evaluating religious beliefs, practices, experiences, and institutions wait on describing them accurately, and in this sense explanatory and evaluative inquiries come after and presuppose the data-gathering work of the nonevaluative phenomenological and hermeneutic steps in description. However, it is also true that descriptions of religious phenomena are always informed by the interpreter's answers to explanatory and evaluative questions. Here are some examples of how this occurs.

Explanatory questions inform the work of description in the following way. Say that one seeks to interpret a religious text. Precisely insofar as religious texts reflect the interests of those who write and read them, an interpretation of a text will reflect the interpreter's assumption or hypothesis about what the text is intended to accomplish. Take as an example the Biblical books, I and II Kings. One interpreter might describe this section of the Bible as a historical account, and another might describe it as imperial propaganda. Either interpretation will reflect the interpreter's assumption or hypothesis about how best to capture why the text was written and why it was canonized. In this way, either description of the religious text reflects the interpreter's decisions about the causal issue of how to explain the text in terms of the aims of its writers and readers. We therefore might put the relationship between description and explanation this way: when one seeks to describe a religious text accurately, an interpreter will not offer explanations of the text that its original audience would not recognize, but her interpretation will nevertheless be informed by her own answers about the interests and the motivations that created the text. In this way, explanation has an inevitable role in interpretation.

Evaluative questions inform the work of description in a similar way. Say that one seeks to interpret a religious practice. Precisely insofar as religious practices are seen as in accord with reality by those who do them, an interpretation of those practices has to include the interpreter's assumption or hypotheses about what must be true in the eyes of the participants to make the practice warranted. Take prayer as an example. One interpreter might describe prayer as a petition to a being who is believed to have the ability to help the petitioner, and another might describe it as the cultivation of an attitude of piety with no expectation of help. Either interpretation will reflect the interpreter's assumption or hypothesis about how best to capture the reasonability of the activity, which is to say, how the prayer makes sense given the worldview of those who pray. In this way, either description of the religious practice reflects the interpreter's decisions about the ontological questions about reality that will make the most sense of the participants' practice. We therefore might put the relationship between description and evaluation this way: when one seeks to describe a religious practice accurately, an interpreter will not offer evaluations of the practice that the participants would not recognize, but her interpretation will nevertheless be informed by her own answers to the normative questions in terms of which one can interpret prayer as a rational practice. In this way, evaluation has an inevitable role in interpretation.

If this account is right, then one cannot engage in the description of religious phenomena without one's interpretation already being informed by explanatory and normative assumptions. It follows that an accurate map of the academic study of religion therefore must be more complex and—more importantly for my purposes—that the possible contributions of philosophy of religion to the field are multiple. If this account is right, then the scholars who put religious phenomena into words do not merely perceive passively and describe what is before them but also presuppose answers to ontological questions about what is real, epistemological questions about what can be known, and axiological questions about what is good. In this way, there are inevitable normative aspects already present in the interpretation of religion, and the academic study of religion should include not only the philosophical evaluation of religious claims, but also the philosophical evaluation of the claims about religion held by scholars. As I argued in the first chapter, therefore, philosophers of religion should understand their task as including the philosophical study of the study of religions.

One might expect that the primary contribution of philosophical reflection on the interpretation of religions would concern the ontological issue of what is real. And I do think that this issue is often treated poorly by interpreters of religion when they use terms like "transcendental," "noumenal," "mystical," "metaphysical," or "supernatural," with little sense of what they themselves mean by them. A fuller discussion of the ontological issue of what can intelligibly be meant by the nature of a religious reality is something that would benefit the field as a whole. But it would be just as significant to give more attention to the epistemic presuppositions in the field. For example, philosophers of religion can ask questions like: does an interpretation of religion presuppose a view of what can and cannot be known such that religious phenomena cannot be criticized—for example, because the interpreter treats religion as "a response to mystery" or "a feeling of the sacred"? Or the reverse: does the interpretation presuppose a view of what can and cannot be known such that religious phenomena cannot be justified—for example, because the interpreter treats religion as authoritarian by definition? The ontological and epistemic norms presupposed in interpretations of religions are often closely tied to the scholar's axiological assumptions. Some assume that the practice of religion improves one's character and that the study of religion can help in this process, and others assume that the practice of religion is an opiate of the masses and that the secular academy can help in the process of liberation. In both cases, interpretations of religion are shaped by scholar's presuppositions of what the academic study of religions is good for. Raising such presuppositions explicitly and reflecting on them critically is work for which philosophers would be ideally suited.

For the most part, however, philosophers of religion have abdicated the philosophical questions involved in the interpretation of religions. When one looks at philosophy of religion textbooks, the ones published, say, 50 years ago reflect a sense that the information about religions available to western scholars was exploding and that philosophers of religion had a contribution to make to the questions involved in sorting this data. Philosophy of religion textbooks therefore often began with a section with a subtitle like "What is Religion?" which addressed the philosophical aspects of defining religion as a genus. But most of those published more recently—say, since the emergence of Reformed epistemology—do not wrestle with questions about how best to interpret religions but simply assume a theistic answer to this question. They withdraw from engagement with the basic questions in the field and simply begin their texts with a discussion of the attributes of God. Given this insularity, the fact that some scholars of religion now propose accounts of the field that do not include philosophy of religion is therefore unsurprising. First, therefore, I would like to see greater attention given to the philosophical assumptions in the interpretation of religions.

Philosophical assumptions also play a role in the explanation of religions. Since explanations of religious phenomena require describing the religious phenomena, they are always informed by the assumptions just discussed concerning what is or is not real, what can or cannot be known, and what activities are or are not worth pursuing. As a consequence, the explanation of religion involves normative assumptions whose assessment is not scientific but philosophical. However, explanatory approaches seek not only to describe but also to provide causal accounts of religious phenomena, and the activity of explaining carries its own normative commitments. Clearly, an explanation of religious phenomena must presuppose an answer to the normative issue of how best to understand what explanation is. This central issue requires social scientists to take sides in philosophical debates about what an agent is, whether groups exist in addition to the individuals who make them up, and whether human action differs from mere behavior. Such questions in turn draw on some view of what human intentionality is and have implications for what is meant by social practices. Ultimately, the explanatory work of the social sciences presupposes views, although often inchoate or even contradictory, about how best to understand the concepts of "tradition," "history," "culture," and "human nature." There simply is no way to practice the explanation of religion without having answered a host of normative questions that make that practice possible.

This claim that the anthropologists, historians, and psychologists of religion draw on philosophy is not news: Clifford Geertz is explicit about his use of Ricoeur's account of actions as texts, Talal Asad is explicit about his use of Foucault's account of power, and Thomas Csordas is explicit about his use of Merleau-Ponty's account of embodiment. In general, I suspect that most social scientists recognize that their work is shaped by their agreements or disagreements with philosophical positions such as Kant's account of the limits of knowledge, Popper's account of explanations, Marx's account of ideology, and innumerable other philosophical contributions to the scientific study of human life. But philosophers of religion rarely see these philosophical aspects of explanation as a topic to which they can contribute. This is a mistake, I judge, both because it leaves those presuppositions uncritiqued and also because it means that an opportunity is lost for showing the relevance of the normative tools of philosophy to the study of religion generally, and it thereby leaves some students of religion with the impression that the social scientific approaches simply *are* the study of religion and that raising philosophical questions is inappropriately normative. Second, therefore, I would like to see greater attention given to the philosophical assumptions in the explanation of religions.

To this point, I have been arguing for the value of philosophy and its explicit reflection on normative questions to the interpretative and explanatory approaches to the study of religion. One might picture these as bridges *from* philosophy *to* the social sciences. But the relationship is reciprocal, and the explanatory work of the social sciences has a largely unacknowledged relevance to philosophical questions. Let me clarify.

I argued above that the causes of, say, a religious belief did not determine whether the belief is true or not; the origins of a religious practice do not determine whether the practice is moral or not. One commits the genetic fallacy when one holds otherwise. In fact, the Y-shaped model that I proposed is meant to illustrate that the two "arms" of the academic study of religions—explanation and evaluation—can be pursued independently. Despite that independence, however, the explanation of religious phenomena can have an impact on their philosophical assessment. The genetic fallacy says rightly that the truth of a claim is independent of its causes. The statement that "It will rain here tomorrow" might be true even if one hears it from someone who has no evidence whatsoever about local weather patterns, or even if one finds it written on a random piece of paper. The truth of a claim is logically independent of its source. But the *justification* of a claim is not independent of its source. In fact, it is commonplace that we assess the reliability of witnesses, and when we judge that their testimony can be accounted for by causes other than the reality of that of which they speak, we doubt them. This kind of assessment is altogether proper. Therefore, when a religious community seeks to justify a religious belief with reference to the cause of the belief—when they say, for example, that the belief is true because they have experienced it, or that it is true because it has been passed down to us from eyewitnesses—they are attempting to justify their claims with reference to the causes of the belief and they open their justification to challenge from rival explanations. Social scientific explanations can then conflict with the explanations given by the religious community, and assessment of the warrant for the belief requires one to weigh their relative plausibility. This is one reason why, as Robert Segal notes, even though social sciences need not presuppose the falsity of the religious beliefs they study, in practice they invariably do.[11]

Some philosophers of religion have insulated their work from challenge from the social sciences by appealing to the genetic fallacy. But as we philosophers of religion shift our attention from questions of truth to include those of justification (and from the issues of perception that are central to an individualist epistemology to the issues of trustworthiness and credibility that are central to a social epistemology), I judge that we will come to see the assessment of religious claims as necessarily in conversation with the causal explanations provided by the social sciences. Third, therefore, I would like to see greater attention given to the contribution of the social sciences on the philosophical questions of justification.

On these three points, then—the unavoidable role of philosophy in the interpretation and the explanation of religious phenomena and the unavoidable role of the social sciences to the assessment of religious claims—I hope that the future of the academic study of religions is increasingly informed by the contributions of philosophy.

Bibliographic Essay

In this chapter, I argue that descriptions of religious behavior have to begin with the agents' intentions. I illustrate this point with a famous example of the difference between a wink and a blink. That example comes from Gilbert Ryle, who used it to illustrate the concept of what he called "thick description" (1971: Ch. 37), and both the example and that concept were championed by Clifford Geertz (1973: 6–7). The strongest philosophical defense of the position that to describe cultural phenomena accurately requires one to grasp the subject's selfunderstanding comes from Wayne Proudfoot, who writes: "The subject's self-ascription is normative for describing the experience. This is a kind of first-person privilege that has nothing to do with immediate intuitive access to mental states versus mediated inferential reasoning. It is strictly a matter of intentionality" (1985: 194). I contrast the map of the academic study of religions that I recommend to the view of religion found in the work of the logical positivists. A concise statement of logical positivism and its rejection of the cognitive meaningfulness of metaphysics and theology can be found in A. J. Ayer (1936). The best survey I know of Christian theological responses to this movement is Diamond and Litzenburg (1975). For an argument that logical positivism is widely presupposed by contemporary theorists of religion, see Frankenberry and Penner (1999).

A reductive account of religion is one that departs from the believer's view of the origin and function of his or her religiosity; a nonreductive account tries to capture that view (see Segal 1992). In this chapter, I include phenomenology as a legitimate nonreductive method for the first stage in the study of religions. For a defense of phenomenology that does not seek an ahistorical essence of religion behind its manifestations but seeks instead a historically informed and contextually sensitive understanding, see Blum (2012). The idea of "cultural phenomenology" I borrow from Thomas Csordas (1999, 2011). For a nice statement of the point that all cultural translation across cultures involves some measure of transformation and distortion, see McMahan (2008: 16–8). The argument that to identify a phenomenon as religious already includes the practitioner's explanation of the phenomenon I owe to Proudfoot (1985: 216).

I argue that the critical approach represented by Russell McCutcheon that excludes normative approaches from the academic study of religions faces a dilemma: it needs to either to justify its position in the academy by offering normative reasons that can be evaluated (though this would contradict its position) or it must reject that debate and present itself groundlessly as simply the way things are in the academy. For an argument that McCutcheon takes the latter "protectionist" tack and constantly defers any evaluation of his own normative commitments, see Roberts (2004). For an argument that the critical approach uncritically inherits the largely Protestant theological position that religious norms cannot be defended with public reasons, and an argument supporting my view that normativity is inevitable in the academic study of religions, see Lewis (2009, 2012). For Wiebe's critique of McCutcheon, see Wiebe (2004, 2005). I also argue that interpretive and explanatory approaches to the study of religions are practiced with normative presuppositions. A good illustration is Bruce Lincoln's statement that he considers "immoral any discourse or practice that systematically operates to benefit the already privileged members of society at the expense of others, and I reserve the same judgment for any society that tolerates or encourages such discourses and practices" (Lincoln 1991: 112; quoted with approval in Martin 2012: xiv).

In this chapter, I complain about philosophy of religion textbooks that ignore the question of how to understand religion and simply treat religion as theism. Abernathy and Langford (1962, 2nd edition, 1968); Ferre (1967); and Smart (1970) are examples of earlier textbooks that include the interpretive question about the nature of religion. More recent philosophy of religion textbooks that jump straight to theism include Wainwright and Rowe (1998, 3rd edition); Stump and Murray (1999); Davies (2000); Mann (2005); Evans and Manis (2009. 2nd edition); and Pojman and Rea (2008, 5th edition)—though not Peterson et al 2012. This list includes, I think, most of the most widely used textbooks in the field.

Endnotes

1. Often this is done by arguing about what a particular religious text or practice "means" or what it "really" means. I avoid the word *meaning* in this chapter because some scholars use it to refer to how the text or practice is understood by the practitioners themselves, others use it to refer to how the text or practice functions in its social content, and still others use it to refer to that to which the text or practice refers—in other words, "meaning" is ambiguous among what I consider the three tasks in the field.

2. Further philosophical support for this position comes from the Wittgenstein-inspired Peter Winch, who writes, "Two things may be called 'the same' or 'different' only with reference to a set of criteria which lay down what is to be regarded as a relevant difference. When the 'things' in question are purely physical the criteria appealed to will of course be those of the observer. But when one is dealing with intellectual (or, indeed, any kind of social) 'things', that is not so. For their *being* intellectual or social, as opposed to physical, in character depends entirely on their belonging in a certain way to a system of ideas or mode of living. It is only by reference to the criteria governing that system of ideas or mode of life that they have any existence as intellectual or social events. It follows that if the sociological investigator wants to regard them *as* social events (as, *ex hypothesi*, he must), he has to take seriously the criteria which are applied or distinguishing 'different' kinds of actions and identifying the 'same' kinds of actions within the way of life he is studying. It is not open to him arbitrarily to impose his own standards from without. Insofar as he does so, the events he is studying lose altogether their character as *social* events" (1958: 108; cf. Schilbrack 2009).

3. The example of the tree-trunk taken as a bear comes from Proudfoot (1985: 192–3). Ninian Smart presents the idea of methodological agnosticism in Smart (1972).

4. The three quotes in this paragraph from Wiebe are from Wiebe (1999: 7, 146, and 283–4; cf. Martin and Wiebe 2012: 620). The quote from Segal is from Segal (1992: 5).

5. Usually, that which the academic study of religions seeks to explain are religious beliefs, experiences, practices, and institutions, though it may also (as in the work of Max Weber) reverse the relationship and treat religious phenomena as that which explains the social or cultural phenomena.

6. To be sure, philosophy of religion is not limited to this goal of evaluation; philosophers of religion are also interested in the other two goals of the field. For instance, there are those like Wittgenstein who (at least on some readings) sees philosophy as having a descriptivist methodology in which one seeks to interpret but not to evaluate the grammar of religious claims. And there are other philosophers of religion like Nietzsche who (on at least some readings)

sees philosophy as having an explanatory methodology that treats truth as an illusion and seeks to explain religious commitments in terms of the will to power. Thus philosophers of religion do not all pursue evaluation, and one might practice philosophy of religion without ever raising such questions. But it is the place of the evaluative questions in the academic study of religion that is in question, I judge, and that is why it is the focus of this chapter.

7. See Wiebe (2005: 8).
8. See Wiebe (2000: 362–3; cf. 2010: 139).
9. I once had a conversation with Russell McCutcheon that touched on this very point. I was arguing for the role of reasons in human agency and, as I remember the conversation, Russell responded that human subjectivity was "just the echo of social forces." I tried to answer in a way that showed the problem: "Is that an idea that you are asking me to think about and then decide whether I agree?"
10. How my tripartite map of the field differs from others can be highlighted by comparing it to the discussion by the historian of religions Leigh Schmidt (2012). Schmidt writes that the academic study of religions has been constituted by a struggle between "sympathy" (that is, nonjudgmental understanding of religious practitioners) and "suspicion" (i.e., approaches that contradict the selfunderstanding of the practitioners). My map and Schmidt's discussion are allied in that he resists the exclusionary arguments of each of these two sides and holds that the field therefore has a "double inheritance." Nevertheless, our views differ in that he seems to see the attempts of each side to exclude the other as wrong-headed but nevertheless still possible (perhaps because he focuses on scholars' attitudes of sympathy and suspicion, as opposed to the tasks of description and explanation), whereas I consider the exclusion of either side impossible. And, more importantly, I propose that the field also include evaluative questions and as therefore tripartite rather than just double.
11. I suspect that the other reason why is that social scientists often fail to recognize a distinction between truth and justification. The reference is to Segal (1980: 404).

Works Cited

Abernathy, Thomas A. and Langford, George L. (eds). 1962. *Philosophy of Religion.* New York, NY: Macmillan.

Allen, Amy. 2000. "The Anti-Subjective Hypothesis: Michel Foucault and the Death of the Subject," *The Philosophical Forum* 31:2 (Summer): 113–29.

Alston, William P. 1967. "Religion." In Paul Edwards (ed.), *The Encyclopedia of Philosophy*, vol. 7. New York, NY: Macmillan Publishing Co.

Alston, William P. 1991. *Perceiving God: The Epistemology of Religious Experience.* Ithaca, NY: Cornell University Press.

Archer, Margaret S. 2004. "Models of Man: The Admission of Transcendence." In Margaret S. Archer, Andrew Collier, and Douglas V. Porpora (eds), *Transcendence: Critical Realism and God.* London, UK: Routledge.

Aristotle. 1984. "Metaphysics." In Jonathan Barnes (ed.), *The Complete Works of Aristotle.* Princeton, NJ: Princeton University Press.

Arnal, William E. 2000. "Definition." In Willi Braun and Russell McCutcheon (eds), *Guide to the Study of Religion.* London, UK: Continuum.

Arnal, William E. 2001. "The Segregation of Social Desire: 'Religion' and Disney World," *Journal of the American Academy of Religion* 69:1 (March): 1–19.

Arnold, Dan. 2005. *Buddhists, Brahmins, and Belief: Epistemology in South Asian Philosophy of Religion.* New York, NY: Columbia University Press.

Arnold, Matthew. 1873. *Literature and Dogma: An Essay Towards a Better Apprehension of the Bible.* London, UK: Smith, Elder, & Co.

Asad, Talal. 1983. "Anthropological Conceptions of Religion: Reflections on Geertz," *Man New Series* 18:2 (June): 237–59.

Asad, Talal. 1993. *Genealogies of Religion: Discipline and Reasons of Power in Christianity and Islam.* Baltimore, MD: The John Hopkins University Press.

Philosophy and the Study of Religions: A Manifesto, First Edition. Kevin Schilbrack.
© 2014 Kevin Schilbrack. Published 2014 by John Wiley & Sons, Ltd.

Asad, Talal. 2003. *Formations of the Secular: Christianity, Islam, Modernity*. Stanford, CA: Stanford University Press.

Asad, Talal. 2012. "Thinking about Religion, Belief, and Politics." In Robert A. Orsi (ed.), *The Cambridge Companion to Religious Studies*. Cambridge, UK: Cambridge University Press.

Augustine. 1953. *Early Writings*. Translated by John H. S. Burleigh. Philadelphia, PA: Westminster Press.

Ayer, Alfred J. 1936. *Language, Truth, and Logic*. Oxford, UK: Oxford University Press.

Baker, Lynne R. 1989. *Saving Belief: A Critique of Physicalism*. Princeton, NJ: Princeton University Press.

Baker, Lynne R. 1995. *Explaining Attitudes: A Practical Approach to the Mind*. Cambridge, UK: Cambridge University Press.

Baker, Lynne R. 2009. "Persons and the Extended-Mind Thesis," *Zygon* 44:3 (September): 642–58.

Balagangadhara, S. N. 1994. *'The Heathen in His Blindness ...': Asia, the West and the Dynamic of Religion*. Leiden, NL: Brill.

Behe, Michael. 1996. *Darwin's Black Box: The Biochemical Challenge to Evolution*. New York, NY: The Free Press.

Bell, Catherine. 2002. "The Chinese 'Believe' in Spirits: Belief and Believing in the Study of Religion." In Nancy K. Frankenberry (ed.), *Radical Interpretation in Religion*. Cambridge, UK: Cambridge University Press.

Bell, Catherine. 2008. "Belief: A Classificatory Lacuna and Disciplinary 'Problem'." In Willi Braun and Russell T. McCutcheon (eds), *Introducing Religion: Essays in Honor of Jonathan Z. Smith*. London, UK: Equinox.

Bellah, Robert. 1957. *Tokugawa Religion: The Values of Pre-Industrial Japan*. Glencoe, IL: Free Press.

Bellah, Robert. 1970. *Beyond Belief: Essays on Religion in a Post-Traditionalist World*. New York, NY: Harper & Row.

Berger, Peter. 1967. *The Sacred Canopy: Elements of a Sociological Theory of Religion*. New York, NY: Doubleday.

Bernstein, Richard J. 1988. *Beyond Objectivism and Relativism: Science, Hermeneutics and Praxis*. Philadelphia, PA: University of Pennsylvania Press.

Bhaskar, Roy. 1975. *A Realist Theory of Science*. York, UK: Leeds Books.

Bhaskar, Roy. 1989. *Reclaiming Reality*. London, UK: Verso.

Bhaskar, Roy; Archer, Margaret; Collier, Andrew; Lawson, Tony; and Norrie, Alan. (eds). 1998. *Critical Realism: Essential Readings*. London, UK: Routledge.

Bilimoria, Purushottama. 2009. "What is the 'Subaltern' of the Philosophy of Religion?" In Purushottama Bilimoria and Andrew B. Irvine (eds), *Postcolonial Philosophy of Religion*. Dordrecht, NL: Springer.

Bilimoria, Purushottama and Irvine, Andrew B. (eds). 2009. *Postcolonial Philosophy of Religion*. Dordrecht, NL: Springer.

Works Cited

Bivins, Jason C. 2012. "Ubiquity Scorned: Belief's Strange Survivals," *Method and Theory in the Study of Religion* 24:4–5 (January): 55–63.

Blond, Philip. (ed.). 1999. *Post-secular Philosophy: Between Philosophy and Theology.* London, UK: Routledge.

Blum, Jason N. 2012. "Retrieving Phenomenology of Religion as a Method for Religious Studies," *Journal of the American Academy of Religion* 80:4 (December): 1025–48.

Boghossian, Paul A. 2006. *Fear of Knowledge: Against Relativism and Constructivism.* Oxford, UK: Clarendon Press.

Bourdieu, Pierre. 1990. *The Logic of Practice.* Translated by Richard Nice. Stanford, CA: Stanford University Press.

Bush, Stephen S. 2012. "Are Religious Experiences Too Private to Study?," *Journal of Religion* 92:2 (April): 199–223.

Byrne, Peter. 1988. "Religion and the Religions." In Stewart R. Sutherland et al. (eds), *The World's Religions.* Boston, MA: G. K. Hall & Co.

Byrne, Peter. 1989. *Natural Religion and the Nature of Religion: The Legacy of Deism.* London, UK: Routledge.

Byrne, Peter. 1998. *The Moral Interpretation of Religion.* Edinburgh, UK: Edinburgh University Press.

Byrne, Peter. 1999. "The Definition of Religion: Squaring the Circle." In Jan G. Platvoet and Arie L. Molendijk (eds), *The Pragmatics of Defining Religion: Contexts, Concepts, and Contests.* Leiden, NL: Brill.

Cannon, Dale. 1995. *Six Ways of Being Religious.* Belmont, CA: Wadsworth.

Casanova, José. 1994. *Public Religions in the Modern World.* Chicago, IL: The University of Chicago Press.

Caputo, John. 2001. *On Religion.* London, UK: Routledge.

Chalmers, David J. 2004. "The Representational Character of Experience." In Brian Leiter (ed.), *The Future for Philosophy.* Oxford, UK: Clarendon Press.

Chemero, Anthony. 2009. *Radical Embodied Cognitive Science.* Cambridge, MA: The MIT Press.

Chernus, Ira. 2006. *Monsters to Destroy: The Neoconservative War on Terror and Sin.* Boulder, CO: Paradigm.

Chernus, Ira. 2008. "The War in Iraq and the Academic Study of Religion," *Journal of the American Academy of Religion* 76:4 (December): 844–73.

Chidester, David. 2000. "Material Terms for the Study of Religion," *Journal of the American Academy of Religion* 68:2 (June): 367–79.

Chidester, David. 1996. *Savage Systems: Colonialism and Comparative Religion in Southern Africa.* Charlottesville, VA: The University Press of Virginia.

Christian, William A. 1941. "A Definition of Religion," *The Review of Religion* 5:4 (May): 412–29.

Christian, William A. 1964. *Meaning and Truth in Religion.* Princeton, NJ: Princeton University Press.

Works Cited

Churchland, Paul M. 1981. "Eliminative Materialism and the Propositional Attitudes," *Journal of Philosophy* 78:2 (February): 67–90.

Churchland, Patricia S. 1986. *Neurophilosophy: Toward a Unified Science of the Mind-Brain.* Cambridge, MA: The MIT Press.

Clark, Andy. 1997. *Being There: Putting Brain Body and World Back Together Again.* Cambridge, MA: The MIT Press.

Clark, Andy. 2003. *Natural-born Cyborgs: Minds, Technologies, and the Future of Human Intelligence.* Oxford, UK: Oxford University Press.

Clark, Andy. 2008. *Supersizing the Mind: Embodiment, Action, and Cognitive Extension.* Oxford, UK: Oxford University Press.

Clark, Andy. 2010. "Memento's Revenge: The Extended Mind, Extended." In Richard Menary (ed.), *The Extended Mind.* Cambridge, MA: MIT Press.

Clark, Andy and Chalmers, David J. 1998. "The Extended Mind," *Analysis* 58:1 (January): 7–19.

Clark, Andy and Toribio, Josefa. 1994. "Doing without Representing?," *Synthese* 101:3 (December): 401–31.

Clarke, Peter B. and Byrne, Peter. 1993. *Religion Defined and Explained.* Hampshire, UK: Macmillan.

Clooney, Francis X. 2010. *Comparative Theology: Deep Learning Across Religious Borders.* Oxford, UK: Wiley-Blackwell.

Collier, Andrew. 1994. *Critical Realism: An Introduction to Roy Bhaskar's Philosophy.* London, UK: Verso.

Connerton, Paul. 1989. *How Societies Remember.* Cambridge, UK: Cambridge University Press.

Cottingham, John. 2005. *The Spiritual Dimension: Religion, Philosophy, and Human Value.* Cambridge, UK: Cambridge University Press.

Covington, Dennis. 1995. *Salvation on Sand Mountain: Snake-handling and Redemption in Southern Appalachia.* New York, NY: Penguin.

Crane, Tim. 2001. *Elements of Mind.* Oxford, UK: Oxford University Press.

Crosby, Donald. 2002. *A Religion of Nature.* Albany, NY: State University of New York Press.

Csordas, Thomas J. 1990. "Embodiment as a Paradigm for Anthropology," *Ethos* 18:1 (March): 5–47.

Csordas, Thomas J. 1993. "Somatic Modes of Attention," *Cultural Anthropology* 8:2 (May): 135–56.

Csordas, Thomas J. 1994. "Introduction: The Body as Representation and Being-in-the World." In Thomas J. Csordas (ed.), *Embodiment and Experience: The Existential Ground of Culture and Self.* Cambridge, UK: Cambridge University Press.

Csordas, Thomas J. 1999. "Embodiment and Cultural Phenomenology." In Gail Weiss and Honi Fern Haber (eds), *Perspectives on Embodiment: The Intersections of Nature and Culture.* New York, NY: Routledge.

Works Cited

Csordas, Thomas J. 2011. "Cultural Phenomenology. Embodiment: Agency, Sexual Difference, and Illness." In Frances E. Mascia-Lees (ed.), *A Companion to the Anthropology of the Body and Embodiment*. Malden, MA: Wiley-Blackwell.

Davidson, Donald. 1984. *Inquiries into Truth and Interpretation*. Oxford, UK: Clarendon Press.

Davidson, Donald. 1990. "The Structure and Content of Truth," *Journal of Philosophy* 87:6 (June): 279–328.

Davidson, Donald. 2001. *Subjective, Intersubjective, Objective*. Oxford, UK: Oxford University Press.

Davies, Brian. (ed.). 2000. *Philosophy of Religion: A Guide and Anthology*. Oxford, UK: Oxford University Press.

Day, Mathew. 2004a. "The Ins and Outs of Religious Cognition," *Method and Theory in the study of Religion* 16:3 (September): 241–55.

Day, Mathew. 2004b. "Religion, Off-Line Cognition and the Extended Mind," *Journal of Cognition and Culture* 4:1 (March): 101–21.

Day, Mathew. 2009. "Constructing Religion without *The Social*: Durkheim, Latour, and Extended Cognition," *Zygon* 44:3 (September): 719–37.

Dean, Thomas. (ed.). 1995. *Religious Pluralism and Truth: Essays on Cross-cultural Philosophy of Religion*. Albany, NY: State University of New York Press.

Dennett, Daniel C. 1987. *The Intentional Stance*. Cambridge, MA: The MIT Press.

Dennett, Daniel C. 1991. "Real Patterns," *The Journal of Philosophy* 88:1 (January): 27–51.

Dennet, Daniel C. 1996. *Kinds of Minds: Towards an Understanding of Consciousness*. New York, NY: Basic Books.

Derrida, Jacques. 1972. "Structure, Sign, and Play: Discussion." In Richard Macksey and Eugenio Donato (eds), *The Structuralist Controversy: The Languages of Criticism and the Sciences of Man*. Baltimore, MD: The Johns Hopkins University Press.

Derrida, Jacques. 1981. *Dissemination*. Translated by Barbara Johnson. Chicago, IL: University of Chicago Press.

Derrida, Jacques. 1991. "'Eating Well,' or the Calculation of the Subject: An Interview with Jacques Derrida," interview by Jean-Luc Nancy, trans. Peter Connor and Avital Ronnell. In Eduardo Cadava, Peter Connor, and Jean-Luc Nancy (eds), *Who Comes After the Subject?* New York, NY: Routledge.

Diamond, Malcolm L. and Litzenburg, Jr., Thomas V. 1975. *The Logic of God: Theology and Verification*. Indianapolis, IN: Bobbs-Merrill.

Donovan, James M. 2003. "Defining Religion." In Stephen D. Glazier and Charles A. Flowerday (eds), *Selected Readings in the Anthropology of Religion: Theoretical and Methodological Essays*. Westport, CT: Praeger.

Dubuisson, Daniel. 2003. *The Western Construction of Religion: Myths, Knowledge, and Ideology*. Baltimore, MD: The John Hopkins University Press.

Dubuisson, Daniel. 2006. "Response," *Religion* 36:3 (September): 119–78.

Works Cited

Durkheim, Emile. 1995. *The Elementary Forms of Religious Life*. Translated by Karen E. Fields. New York, NY: The Free Press.

Edwards, Rem B. 1972. *Reason and Religion*. New York, NY: Harcourt Brace Jovanovich.

Eliade, Mircea. 1959. *The Sacred and the Profane: The Nature of Religion*. Translated by Willard R. Trask. San Diego, CA: Harcourt.

Evans, Stephen C. and Manis, Zachary R. (eds). 2005. *Philosophy of Religion: Thinking about Faith*. 2nd edition. Downers Grove, IL: IVP Academic.

Evans-Pritchard, Edward E. 1956. *Nuer Religion*. Oxford, UK: Clarendon Press.

Fasching, Darrell; deChant, Dell; and Lantiqua, David M. 2011. *Comparative Religious Ethics: A Narrative Approach to Global Ethics*. 2nd edition. Oxford, UK: Wiley-Blackwell.

Ferré, Frederick. 1967. *Basic Modern Philosophy of Religion*. New York, NY: Charles Scribner's Sons.

Fitzgerald, Timothy. 1997. "A Critique of 'Religion' as a Cross-Cultural Category," *Method and Theory in the Study of Religion* 9:2: 91–110.

Fitzgerald, Timothy. 2000. *The Ideology of Religious Studies*. New York, NY: Oxford University Press.

Fitzgerald, Timothy. 2007a. "Introduction." In Timothy Fitzgerald (ed.), *Religion and the Secular: Historical and Colonial Formations*. London, UK: Equinox.

Fitzgerald, Timothy. 2007b. *Discourse on Civility and Barbarity*. New York, NY: Oxford University Press.

Foucault, Michel. 1980. *Power/Knowledge: Selected Interviews and Other Writings 1972–1977*. New York, NY: Pantheon.

Foucault, Michel. 1982. "Afterword." In Hubert L. Dreyfus and Paul Rabinow (eds), *Michel Foucault: Beyond Structuralism and Hermeneutics*. 2nd edition. Chicago, IL: The University of Chicago Press.

Frankenberry, Nancy and Penner, Hans. 1999a. "Geertz's Long-lasting Moods, Motivations, and Metaphysical Conceptions," *Journal of Religion* 79:4 (October): 617–40.

Frankenberry, Nancy and Penner, Hans. (eds). 1999b. *Language, Truth, and Religious Belief: Studies in Twentieth-Century Theory and Method in Religion*. Atlanta, GA: Scholars Press.

French, Peter A. 1997. *Cowboy Metaphysics: Ethics and Death in Westerns*. Lanham, MD: Rowman & Littlefield.

Frisina, Warren G. 2002. *The Unity of Knowledge and Action: Toward a Nonrepresentational Theory of Knowledge*. Albany, NY: State University of New York Press.

Furey, Constance M. 2012. "Body, Society, and Subjectivity in Religious Studies," *Journal of the American Academy of Religion* 80:1 (March): 7–33.

Gallagher, Shaun. 2013. "The Socially Extended Mind," *Cognitive Systems Research* 25–26 (December): 4–12.

Geertz, Clifford. 1973. *The Interpretation of Cultures*. New York, NY: Basic Books.

Works Cited

Godlove, Jr., Terry F. 1989. *Religion, Interpretation, and Diversity of Belief.* Cambridge, UK: Cambridge University Press.

Godlove, Jr., Terry F. 2002. "Saving Belief: On the New Materialism in Religious Studies." In Nancy K. Frankenberry (ed.), *Radical Interpretation in Religion.* Cambridge, UK: Cambridge University Press.

Goody, Jack. 1961. "Religion and Ritual: The Definitional Problem," *The British Journal of Sociology* 12:2 (June): 142–64.

Griffin, David R. 1988. "Introduction to SUNY Series in Constructive Postmodern Thought." In David Ray Griffin (ed.), *The Reenchantment of Science.* Albany, NY: SUNY Press.

Griffiths, Paul J. 2000. "The Very Idea of Religion," *First Things* 103 (May): 30–35.

Griffiths, Paul J. 2001. *Problems of Religious Diversity.* Malden, MA: Blackwell.

Gschwandtner, Christian M. 2013. *Postmodern Apologetics? Arguments for God in Contemporary Philosophy.* New York, NY: Fordham University Press.

Guthrie, Stewart E. 1993. *Faces in the Clouds: A New Theory of Religion.* New York, NY: Oxford University Press.

Habermas, Jürgen. 1994. *Postmetaphysical Thinking: Philosophical Essays.* Cambridge, MA: MIT Press.

Hacking, Ian. 1999. *The Social Construction of What?* Cambridge, MA: Harvard University Press.

Harding, Susan F. 2001. *The Book of Jerry Falwell: Fundamentalist Language and Politics.* Princeton, NJ: Princeton University Press.

Hark, Michel ter. 2001. "Wittgenstein and Dennett on Patterns." In Severin Schroeder (ed.), *Wittgenstein and Contemporary Philosophy of Mind.* Hampshire, UK: Palgrave.

Harre, Rom and Gillett, Grant. 1994. *The Discursive Mind.* Thousand Oaks, CA: Sage.

Harrison, Peter. 1990. *'Religion' and the Religions in the English Enlightenment.* Cambridge, UK: Cambridge University Press.

Hartshorne, Charles. 1983. *Creative Synthesis and Philosophical Method.* Lanham, MD: University Press of America.

Hector, Kevin. 2011. *Theology Without Metaphysics.* Cambridge, UK: Cambridge University Press.

Hedges, Chris. 2002. *War is a Force that Gives us Meaning.* New York, NY: PublicAffairs.

Heim, Mark S. 1995. *Salvations: Truth and Difference in Religion.* Maryknoll, NY: Orbis.

Henkel, Heiko. 2005. "'Between Belief and Unbelief Lies the Performance of the Salāt': Meaning and Efficacy of a Muslim Ritual," *Journal of the Royal Anthropological Institute* 11:3 (September): 487–507.

Herbert, Edward. 1705. *The Ancient Religion of the Gentiles.* London, UK: John Nutt.

Works Cited

Hogue, Michael S. 2010. *The Promise of Religious Naturalism*. Lanham, MD: Rowman & Littlefield.

Horton, Robin. 1993. *Patterns of Thought in Africa and the West: Essays on Magic, Religion and Science*. Cambridge, UK: Cambridge University Press.

Hutchins, Edwin. 1995a. *Cognition in the Wild*. Cambridge, MA: MIT Press.

Hutchins, Edwin. 1995b. "How a Cockpit Remember its Speeds," *Cognitive Science* 19:3 (July–September): 265–88.

Idinopulos, Thomas A. and Wilson, Brian C. (eds). 1998. *What is Religion? Origins, Definitions, and Explanations*. Leiden, NL: Brill.

James, William. 1956. *The Will to Believe, and Other Essays in Popular Philosophy*. New York, NY: Dover.

James, William. 1961. *The Varieties of Religious Experiences: A Study in Human Nature*. New York, NY: Macmillan.

Johnson, Mark. 1987. *The Body in the Mind: The Bodily Basis of Meaning, Imagination, and Reason*. Chicago, IL: The University of Chicago Press.

Johnson, Mark. 1999. "Embodied Rationality." In Gail Weiss and Honi Fern Haber (eds), *Perspectives on Embodiment: The Intersections of Nature and Culture*. New York, NY: Routledge.

Johnson, Mark. 2007. *The Meaning of the Body: Aesthetics of Human Understanding*. Chicago, IL: The University of Chicago Press.

Johnson, Roger A. 1994. "Natural Religion, Common Notions, and the Study of Religions: Lord Herbert of Cherbury (1583–1648)," *Religion* 24:3 (July): 213–24.

Kessler, Gary E. (ed.). 1998. *Philosophy of Religion: Toward a Global Perspective*. Belmont, CA: Wadsworth.

King, Richard. 1999. *Orientalism and Religion: Post-Colonial Theory, India and "The Mystic East*. New York, NY: Routledge.

King, Richard. 2009. "Philosophy of Religion as Border Control: Globalization and the Decolonization of the 'Love of Wisdom.'" In Purushottama Bilimoria and Andrew B. Irvine (eds), *Postcolonial Philosophy of Religion*. Dordrecht, NL: Springer.

Lakoff, George and Johnson, Mark. 1980. *Metaphors We Live By*. Chicago, IL: The University of Chicago Press.

Lakoff, George and Johnson, Mark. 1999. *Philosophy in the Flesh: The Embodied Mind and its Challenge to Western Thought*. New York, NY: Basic Books.

Lakoff, George and Turner, Mark. 1989. *More than Cool Reason: A Field Guide to Poetic Metaphor*. Chicago, IL: The University of Chicago Press.

Leach, Edmund. 1968. "Virgin Birth [Correspondence]," *Man New Series* 3:4 (December): 655–56.

Lease, Gary. 1994. "The History of 'Religious' Consciousness and the Diffusion of Culture: Strategies for Surviving Dissolution," *Historical Reflections/Réflexions Historiques* 20:3 (Winter): 453–79.

Works Cited

Lease, Gary. 2000. "The Definition of Religion: An Analytical or Hermeneutical Task?," *Method & Theory in the Study of Religion* 12:1/2 (March): 287–93.

Lessa, William A. and Vogt, Evon Z. 1958. "General Introduction." In William Lessa and Evon Z. Vogt (eds), *Reader in Comparative Religion: An Anthropological Approach*. Evanston, IL: Row, Peterson & Company.

Lewis, Clive S. 1952. *Mere Christianity*. New York, NY: Macmillan.

Lewis, Thomas A. 2009. "The Inevitability of Normativity in the Study of Religion: Theology in Religious Studies." In Darlene L. Bird and Simon G. Smith (eds), *Theology and Religious Studies in Higher Education: Global Perspectives*. London, UK: Continuum.

Lewis, Thomas A. 2012. "On the Role of Normativity in Religious Studies." In Robert A. Orsi (ed.), *Cambridge Companion to Religious Studies*. Cambridge, UK: Cambridge University Press.

Lincoln, Bruce. 1991. *Emerging from the Chrysalis: Studies in Rituals of Women's Initiation*. Chicago, IL: The University of Chicago Press.

Lincoln, Bruce. 2003. *Holy Terrors: Thinking about Religion after September 11*. Chicago, IL: The University of Chicago Press.

Lincoln, Bruce. 2005. "Responsa Miniscula," *Method and Theory in the Study of Religion* 17:1 (March): 59–67.

Livingston, James. 2005. *Anatomy of the Sacred*. 5th edition. Upper Saddle River, NJ: Pearson/Prentice Hall.

Lofton, Kathryn. 2012. "Introduction to the Yale Roundtable on Belief," *Method and Theory in the Study of Religion* 24:1 (January): 51–54.

Lopez, Jr., Donald S. 1998. "Belief." In Mark C. Taylor (ed.), *Critical Terms for Religious Studies*. Chicago, IL: The University of Chicago Press.

MacIntyre, Alasdair. 1990. *Three Rival Versions of Moral Enquiry: Encyclopedia, Genealogy, and Tradition*. Notre Dame, IN: University of Notre Dame Press.

Maclean, Norman. 1976. *A River Runs Through It*. Chicago, IL: The University of Chicago Press.

Mahmood, Saba. 2005. *Politics of Piety: The Islamic Revival and the Feminist Subject*. Princeton, NJ: Princeton University Press.

Mann, William E. (ed.). 2005. *The Blackwell Guide to the Philosophy of Religion*. Oxford, UK: Blackwell.

Martin, Craig. 2010. *Masking Hegemony: A Genealogy of Liberalism, Religion and the Public Sphere*. London, UK: Equinox.

Martin, Craig. 2012. *A Critical Introduction to the Study of Religion*. London, UK: Equinox.

Martin, David. 1978. *A General Theory of Secularization*. New York, NY: Harper.

Martin, Luther and Wiebe, Donald. 2012. "Religious Studies as a Scientific Discipline," *Journal of the American Academy of Religion* 80:3 (September): 587–97.

Works Cited

Masuzawa, Tomoko. 2005. *The Invention of World Religions: Or, How European Universalism Was Preserved in the Language of Pluralism*. Chicago, IL: The University of Chicago Press.

McCutcheon, Russell T. 1997. *Manufacturing Religion: The Discourse on Sui Generis Religion and the Politics of Nostalgia*. New York, NY: Oxford University Press.

McCutcheon, Russell T. 1998. "Redescribing 'Religion' as Social Formation." In Thomas A. Idinopulos and Brian C. Wilson (eds), *What is Religion? Origins, Definitions, and Explanations*. Leiden, NL: Brill.

McCutcheon, Russell T. 2001. *The Discipline of Religion: Structure, Meaning, Rhetoric*. London, UK: Routledge.

McCutcheon, Russell T. 2003. *Critics Not Caretakers: Redescribing the Public Study of Religion*. Albany, NY: State University of New York Press.

McCutcheon, Russell T. 2012. "I Have a Hunch," *Method and Theory in the Study of Religion* 24:1 (January): 81–92.

McMahan, David L. 2008. *The Making of Buddhist Modernism*. Oxford, UK: Oxford University Press.

Menary, Richard. (ed.). 2010. *The Extended Mind*. Cambridge, MA: MIT Press.

Merleau-Ponty, Maurice. 1962. *Phenomenology of Perception*. Translated by Colin Smith. London, UK: Routledge & Kegan Paul.

Meyer, William J. 1995. "Private Faith or Public Religion? An Assessment of Habermas's Changing View of Religion," *Journal of Religion* 75:3 (July): 371–91.

Meyer, William J. 2010. *Metaphysics and the Future of Theology*. Eugene, OR: Pickwick.

Michael, Michaelis and Healy, John P. 2012. "A Guru-Discipline Tradition: Can Religious Conversion be Non-cognitive?" In Morgan Luck (ed.), *Philosophical Explorations of New and Alternative Religious Movements*. Surrey, UK: Ashgate.

Milbank, John. 1990. "The End of Dialogue." In Gavin D'Costa (ed.), *Christian Uniqueness Reconsidered: The Myth of a Pluralistic Theology of Religions*. Maryknoll, NY: Orbis.

Myerhoff, Barbara G. 1976. *Peyote Hunt: The Sacred Journey of the Huichol Indians*. Ithaca, NY: Cornell University Press.

Neville, Robert C. (ed.). 2001a. *The Human Condition*. Albany, NY: State University of New York.

Neville, Robert C. (ed.). 2001b. *Religious Truth*. Albany, NY: State University of New York.

Neville, Robert C. (ed.). 2001c. *Ultimate Realities*. Albany, NY: State University of New York.

Neville, Robert C. 2002. *Religion in Late Modernity*. Albany, NY: State University of New York.

Nicholson, Hugh. 2011. *Comparative Theology and the Problem of Religious Rivalry*. Oxford, UK: Oxford University Press.

Nye, Mallory. 2008. *Religion: The Basics*. 2nd edition. London, UK: Routledge.

Works Cited

Orsi, Robert A. 1998. *Thank You, St. Jude: Women's Devotion to the Patron Saint of Hopeless Causes*. New Haven, CT: Yale University Press.

Pailin, David A. 1984. *Attitudes to Other Religions: Comparative Religion in Seventeenth and Eighteenth Century Britain*. Dover, NH: Manchester University Press.

Paley, William. 1819. *Natural Theology, or, Evidence of the Existence and the Attributes of the Deity, Collected from the Appearances of Nature*. Hallowell, ME: E. Goodale.

Penner, Hans H. 1989. *Impasse and Resolution: A Critique of the Study of Religion*. New York, NY: Peter Lang.

Peterson, Derek and Walhof, Darren. (eds.). 2002. *The Invention of Religion*. New Brunswick, NJ: Rutgers University Press.

Peterson, Michael; Hasker, William; Reichenbach, Bruce; and Basinger, David. (eds). 2009. *Philosophy of Religion: Selected Readings*. 4th edition. Oxford, UK: Oxford University Press.

Peterson, Michael; Hasker, William; Reichenbach, Bruce; and Basinger, David. 2012. *Reason and Religious Belief*. 5th edition. Oxford, UK: Oxford University Press.

Phillips, Dewi Z. 1965. *The Concept of Prayer*. London, UK: Routledge & Kegan Paul.

Phillips, Stephen H. (ed.). 1995. *Philosophy of Region: A Global Approach*. Fort Worth, TX: Harcourt Brace.

Philpott, Daniel. 2009. "Has the Study of Global Politics Found Religion?," *The Annual Review of Political Science* 12 (June): 183–202.

Pojman, Louis P. and Rea, Michael. (eds). 2008. *Philosophy of Religion: An Anthology*. 5th edition. Belmont, CA: Thomson Wadsworth.

Preus, Samuel J. 1987. *Explaining Religion: Criticism and Theory from Bodin to Freud*. New Haven, CT: Yale University Press.

Proudfoot, Wayne. 1985. *Religious Experience*. Berkeley, CA: University of California Press.

Proudfoot, Wayne. 2000. "William James on an Unseen Order," *Harvard Theological Review* 93:1 (January): 51–66.

Purushottama, Bilimoria and Irvine, Andrew B. (eds). 2009. *Postcolonial Philosophy of Religion*. Dordrecht, NL: Springer.

Putnam, Hilary. 1990. *Realism with a Human Face*. Cambridge, MA: Harvard University Press.

Putnam, Hilary. 2004. *Ethics Without Ontology*. Cambridge, MA: Harvard University Press.

Reisebrodt, Martin. 2010. *The Promise of Salvation: A Theory of Religion*. Translated by Steven Rendall. Chicago, IL: The University of Chicago Press.

Reynolds, Frank and Tracy, David. (eds). 1990. *Myth and Philosophy*. Albany, NY: State University of New York Press.

Reynolds, Frank and Tracy, David. (eds). 1992. *Discourse and Practice*. Albany, NY: State University of New York Press.

Reynolds, Frank and Tracy, David. (eds). 1994. *Religion and Practical Reason: New Essays in the Comparative Philosophy of Religions*. Albany, NY: State University of New York Press.

Roberts, Michelle Voss. 2010. *Dualities: A Theology of Religious Difference*. Philadelphia, PA: Westminster John Knox Press.

Roberts, Tyler. 2004. "Exposure and Explanation: On the New Protectionism in the Study of Religion," *Journal of the American Academy of Religion* 72:1 (March): 143–72.

Rorty, Richard. 1970. "In Defense of Eliminative Materialism," *Review of Metaphysics* 24:1 (September): 112–21.

Rorty, Richard. 1979. *Philosophy and the Mirror of Nature*. Princeton, NJ: Princeton University Press.

Rowe, William L. and Wainwright, William J. (eds). 1998. *Philosophy of Religion: Selected Readings*. 3rd edition. Oxford, UK: Oxford University Press.

Rowlands, Mark. 2006. *Body Language: Representation in Action*. Cambridge, MA: The MIT Press.

Rubenstein, Mary-Jane. 2012. "The Twilight of the Doxai: Or, How to Philosophize with a Whac-A-Mole™ Mallet," *Method and Theory in the Study of Religion* 24:1 (January): 64–70.

Ruel, Malcolm. 1982. "Christians as Believers." In John Davis (ed.), *Religious Organization and Religious Experience*. London, UK: Academic Press.

Ruel, Malcolm. 1997. *Belief, Ritual and the Securing of Life: Reflexive Essays on a Bantu Religion*. Leiden, NL: E. J. Brill.

Runzo, Joseph. 2001. *Global Philosophy of Religion: A Short Introduction*. Oxford, UK: Oneworld.

Ryle, Gilbert. 1949. *The Concept of Mind*. London, UK: Hutchinson.

Ryle, Gilbert. 1971. *Collected Papers: Vol. II: Collected Essays, 1929–1968*. London, UK: Hutchinson.

Saler, Benson. 1993. *Conceptualizing Religion: Immanent Anthropologists, Transcendent Natives, Unbounded Categories*. Leiden, NL: E. J. Brill.

Saler, Benson. 2001. "On What We May Believe about Beliefs." In Jensine Andresen (ed.), *Religion in Mind: Cognitive Perspectives on Belief, Ritual, and Experience*. Cambridge, UK: Cambridge University Press.

Saler, Benson. 2008. "Conceptualizing Religion: Some Recent Reflections," *Religion* 38:3 (September): 219–25.

Schilbrack, Kevin. 2003. "Religious Diversity and the Closed Mind," *Journal of Religion* 83:1 (January): 100–07.

Schilbrack, Kevin. 2004. "Ritual Metaphysics." In Kevin Schilbrack (ed.), *Thinking Through Rituals*. New York, NY: Routledge.

Schilbrack, Kevin. 2005. "Religion, Models of, and Reality: Are We Through With Geertz?," *Journal of the American Academy of Religion* 73:2 (June): 429–52.

Works Cited

Schilbrack, Kevin. 2009. "Rationality, Relativism, and Religion: The Case of Peter Winch," *Sophia* 48:4 (November): 399–413.

Schilbrack, Kevin. 2012. "The Social Construction of 'Religion' and its Limits: A Critical Reading of Timothy Fitzgerald," *Method and Theory in the Study of Religion* 24:2 (March): 97–117.

Schmidt, Leigh A. 2012. "On Sympathy, Suspicion, and Studying Religion: Historical Reflections on a Doubled Inheritance." In Robert A. Orsi (ed.), *The Cambridge Companion to Religious Studies*. Cambridge, UK: Cambridge University Press.

Schwitzgebel, Eric. 2002. "A Phenomenal, Dispositional Account of Belief," *Noûs* 36:2 (June): 249–75.

Searle, John R. 1995. *The Construction of Social Reality*. New York, NY: The Free Press.

Segal, Robert A. 1980. "The Social Sciences and the Truth of Religious Belief," *Journal of the American Academy of Religion* 48:3 (September): 403–13.

Segal, Robert A. 1989. *Religion and the Social Sciences: Essays on the Confrontation*. Atlanta, GA: Scholars Press.

Segal, Robert A. 1992. *Explaining and Interpreting Religion: Essays on the Issue*. Atlanta, GA: Peter Lang.

Segal, Robert, A. 2005. "Classification and Comparison in the Study of Religion: The Work of Jonathan Z. Smith," *Journal of the American Academy of Religion* 73:4 (December): 1175–88.

Sharpe, Eric J. 1986. *Comparative Religion: A History*. LaSalle, IL: Open Court.

Siderits, Mark. 2003. *Personal Identity and Buddhist Philosophy: Empty Persons*. Surrey, UK: Ashgate.

Slingerland, Edward. 2003. *Effortless Action: Wu-wei as Conceptual Metaphor and Spiritual Ideal*. New York, NY: Oxford University Press.

Slingerland, Edward. 2004. "Conceptual Metaphor Theory as Methodology for Comparative Religion," *Journal of the American Academy of Religion* 72:1 (March): 1–31.

Slingerland, Edward. 2008. *What Science Offers the Humanities: Integrating Body and Culture*. Cambridge, UK: Cambridge University Press.

Smart, Ninian. 1970. *The Philosophy of Religion*. New York, NY: Random House.

Smart, Ninian. 1995. *Worldviews: Crosscultural Explorations of Human Beliefs*. Englewood Cliffs, NJ: Prentice-Hall.

Smart, Ninian. 1996. *Dimensions of the Sacred: An Anatomy of the World's Beliefs*. Berkeley, CA: University of California Press.

Smith, Christian. 2003. *Moral, Believing Animals: Human Personhood and Culture*. Oxford, UK: Oxford University Press.

Smith, Jonathan Z. 1982. *Imagining Religion: From Babylon to Jonestown*. Chicago, IL: The University of Chicago Press.

Works Cited

Smith, Jonathan Z. 1988. "'Religion' and 'Religious Studies': No Difference at All," *Soundings* 71:2/3 (Summer/Fall): 231–44.

Smith, Jonathan Z. 1993. *Map is Not Territory: Studies in the History of Religions.* Chicago, IL: The University of Chicago Press.

Smith, Jonathan Z. 1998. "Religion, Religions, Religious." In Mark C. Taylor (ed.), *Critical Terms for Religious Studies.* Chicago, IL: The University of Chicago Press.

Smith, Jonathan Z. 2004. *Relating Religion: Essays in the Study of Religion.* Chicago, IL: The University of Chicago Press.

Smith, Jonathan Z. 2010. "Tillich['s] Remains ...," *Journal of the American Academy of Religion* 78:4 (December): 1139–70.

Smith, Wilfred C. 1962. *The Meaning and End of Religion.* Minneapolis, MN: Fortress.

Smith, Wilfred C. 1977. *Belief and History.* Charlottesville, VA: University Press of Virginia.

Smith, Wilfred C. 1980. "Belief: A Reply to a Response," *Numen* 27:2 (December): 247–55.

Snyder, Samuel. 2007. "New Streams of Religion: Fly-fishing as Lived, Religion of Nature," *Journal of the American Academy of Religion* 75:3 (December): 896–922.

Southwold, Martin. 1978. "Buddhism and the Definition of Religion," *Man New Series* 13:3 (September): 362–79.

Southwold, Martin. 1979. "Religious Belief," *Man New Series* 14:4 (December): 628–44.

Spiro, Melford. 1966. "Religion: Problems of Definition and Explanation." In Michael Banton (ed.), *Anthropological Approaches to the Study of Religion.* London, UK: Tavistock Publications.

Stalnaker, Aaron. 2006. *Overcoming Our Evil: Human Nature and Spiritual Exercises in Xunzi and Augustine.* Washington, DC: Georgetown University Press.

Stich, Stephen P. 1985. *From Folk Psychology to Cognitive Science: The Case against Belief.* Cambridge, MA: The MIT Press.

Stowers, Stanley. 2008. "The Ontology of Religion." In Willi Braun and Russell T. McCutcheon (eds), *Introducing Religion: Essays in Honor of Jonathan Z. Smith.* London, UK: Equinox.

Strenski, Ivan. 1998. "On 'Religion' and Its Despisers." In Thomas A. Idinopulos and Brian C. Wilson (eds), *What is Religion? Origins, Definitions, and Explanations.* Leiden, NL: Brill.

Stroumsa, Guy G. 2010. *A New Science: The Discovery of Religion in the Age of Reason.* Cambridge, MA: Harvard University Press.

Stump, Eleonore and Murray, Michael J. (eds). 1999. *Philosophy of Religion: The Big Questions.* Oxford, UK: Blackwell.

Taliaferro, Charles; Harrison, Victoria S.; and Goetz, Stewart. (eds). 2012. *The Routledge Companion to Theism.* London, UK: Routledge.

Works Cited

Taylor, Charles. 1989. *Sources of the Self: The Making of the Modern Identity.* Cambridge, MA: Harvard University Press.

Taylor, Mark C. (ed.). 1998. *Critical Terms for Religious Studies.* Chicago, IL: The University of Chicago Press.

Thatamanil, John. 2006. *The Immanent Divine: God, Creation, and the Human Predicament.* Minneapolis, MN: Fortress Press.

Tillich, Paul. 1957. *Dynamics of Faith.* New York, NY: Harper & Row.

Tillich, Paul. 1959. *Theology of Culture.* London, UK: Oxford University Press.

Tillich, Paul. 1969. *What is Religion?* New York, NY: Harper & Row.

Turner, Bryan S. 2011. *Religion and Modern Society: Citizenship, Secularisation and the State.* Cambridge, UK: Cambridge University Press.

Tylor, Edward B. 1970. *Religion in Primitive Culture.* Gloucester, MA: Peter Smith.

Vásquez, Manuel A. 2011. *More than Belief: A Materialist Theory of Religion.* Oxford, UK: Oxford University Press.

Wainwright, William J. (ed.). 1996. *God, Philosophy and Academic Culture: A Discussion between Scholars in the AAR and the APA.* Atlanta, GA: Scholars Press.

Wax, Murray L. 1984. "*Religion* as Universal: Tribulations of an Anthropological Enterprise," *Zygon* 19:1 (March): 5–20.

Webb, Mark O. 2009. "An Eliminativist Theory of Religion," *Sophia* 48:1 (February): 35–42.

Westphal, Merold. 2007. *Overcoming Ontotheology: Toward a Postmodern Christian Faith.* New York, NY: Fordham University Press.

Wiebe, Donald. 1979. "The Role of 'Belief' in the Study of Religion: A Response to W. C. Smith," *Numen* 26:2 (December): 234–49.

Wiebe, Donald. 1992. "On The Transformation of 'Belief' and the Domestication of 'Faith' in the Academic Study of Religion," *Method and Theory in the Study of Religion* 4:1–2 (December): 47–67.

Wiebe, Donald. 1999. *The Politics of Religious Studies.* New York, NY: St. Martin's Press.

Wiebe, Donald. 2004. "The Reinvention or Degradation of Religious Studies? Tales from Tuscaloosa Woods," *Reviews in Religion and Theology* 11:1 (February): 3–14.

Wiebe, Donald. 2005. "The Politics of Wishful Thinking? Disentangling the Role of the Scholar-Scientist from that of the Public Intellectual in the Modern Academic Study of Religion," *Temenos* 11:1 (February): 7–38.

Wildman, Wesley J. 2010. *Religious Philosophy as Multidisciplinary Comparative Inquiry.* Albany, NY: State University of New York Press.

Wilson, Brian C. 1998. "From the Lexical to the Polythetic: A Brief History of the Definition of Religion." In Thomas A. Idinopulos and Brian C. Wilson (eds), *What is Religion? Origins, Definitions, and Explanations.* Leiden, NL: Brill.

Wilson, David S. 2009. "Evolutionary Social Constructivism: Narrowing (But Not Yet Bridging) the Gap." In Jeffrey Schloss and Michael Murray (eds), *The Believing*

Works Cited

Primate: Scientific, Philosophical and Theological Reflections on the Origins of Religion. Oxford, UK: Oxford University Press.

Wilson, Robert A. and Foglia, Lucia. 2011. "Embodied Cognition." In Edward N. Zalta (ed.), *The Stanford Encyclopedia of Philosophy,* Fall 2011 edn, http://plato .stanford.edu/archives/fall2011/entries/embodied-cognition/ (accessed September 26, 2013).

Winch, Peter. 1958. *The Idea of a Social Science and its Relation to Philosophy.* London, UK: Routledge & Kegan Paul.

Wittgenstein, Ludwig. 1966. *Lectures and Conversations on Aesthetics, Psychology, and Religious Belief.* Compiled from Notes taken by Yorick Smithies, Rush Rhees, and James Taylor. Edited by Cyril Barrett. Berkeley, CA: University of California Press.

Wittgenstein, Ludwig. 1976. *Wittgenstein's Lectures on the Foundations of Mathematics: Cambridge, 1939.* From the Notes of R. G. Bosanquet, Norman Malcolm, Rush Rhees, and Yorick Smythies. Edited by Cora Diamond. Ithaca, NY: Cornell University Press.

Wu Ch'eng-en. 1943. *Monkey: Folk Novel of China.* Translated by Arthur Waley. New York, NY: Grove Press.

Wu Ch'eng-en. 2012. *The Journey to the West,* vols. 1–4, revised edition. Translated by Anthony Yu. Chicago, IL: University of Chicago Press.

Yandell, Keith. 1999. *Philosophy of Religion: A Contemporary Introduction.* New York, NY: Routledge.

Yearley, Lee. 1990. *Mencius and Aquinas: Theories of Virtue and Conceptions of Courage.* Albany, NY: State University of New York Press.

Yinger, John M. 1957. *Religion, Society, and the Individual.* New York, NY: Macmillan.

Yinger, John M. 1970. *The Scientific Study of Religion.* London, UK: Macmillan.

Index

Philosophy and the Study of Religions: A Manifesto, First Edition. Kevin Schilbrack.
© 2014 Kevin Schilbrack. Published 2014 by John Wiley & Sons, Ltd.

Index